PEOPLE, MARKETS, GOODS:
ECONOMIES AND SOCIETIES IN HISTORY

Volume 18

Quakers in the British Atlantic World, c. 1660–1800

PEOPLE, MARKETS, GOODS:
ECONOMIES AND SOCIETIES IN HISTORY

ISSN: 2051-7467

Series editors
Steve Hindle – The Huntington Library
Jane Humphries – University of Oxford
Willem M. Jongman – University of Groningen
Catherine Schenk – University of Glasgow
Jane Whittle – University of Exeter
Nuala Zahedieh – University of Edinburgh

The interactions of economy and society, people and goods, transactions and actions are at the root of most human behaviours. Economic and social historians are participants in the same conversation about how markets have developed historically and how they have been constituted by economic actors and agencies in various social, institutional and geographical contexts. New debates now underpin much research in economic and social, cultural, demographic, urban and political history. Their themes have enduring resonance – financial stability and instability, the costs of health and welfare, the implications of poverty and riches, flows of trade and the centrality of communications. This paperback series aims to attract historians interested in economics and economists with an interest in history by publishing high quality, cutting edge academic research in the broad field of economic and social history from the late medieval/early modern period to the present day. It encourages the interaction of qualitative and quantitative methods through both excellent monographs and collections offering path-breaking overviews of key research concerns. Taking as its benchmark international relevance and excellence it is open to scholars and subjects of any geographical areas from the case study to the multi-nation comparison.

PREVIOUSLY PUBLISHED TITLES IN THE SERIES ARE
LISTED AT THE BACK OF THIS VOLUME

Quakers in the British Atlantic World, c. 1660–1800

Esther Sahle

THE BOYDELL PRESS

© Esther Sahle 2021

All Rights Reserved. Except as permitted under current legislation no part of this work may be photocopied, stored in a retrieval system, published, performed in public, adapted, broadcast, transmitted, recorded or reproduced in any form or by any means, without the prior permission of the copyright owner

The right of Esther Sahle to be identified as the author of this work has been asserted in accordance with sections 77 and 78 of the Copyright, Designs and Patents Act 1988

First published 2021
The Boydell Press, Woodbridge
ISBN 978-1-78327-586-1

The Boydell Press is an imprint of Boydell & Brewer Ltd
PO Box 9, Woodbridge, Suffolk IP12 3DF, UK
and of Boydell & Brewer Inc.
668 Mt Hope Avenue, Rochester, NY 14620–2731, USA
website: www.boydellandbrewer.com

A catalogue record for this book is available
from the British Library

The publisher has no responsibility for the continued existence or accuracy of URLs for external or third-party internet websites referred to in this book, and does not guarantee that any content on such websites is, or will remain, accurate or appropriate

Contents

Illustrations	vi
A Note on Terms and Language	vii
Abbreviations	viii

1.	The Institutional Foundations of Pre-Modern Trade	1
2.	The Society of Friends	23
3.	The Quaker Communities of London and Philadelphia	31
4.	Quaker Business Ethics	55
5.	Quaker Discipline in Practice	76
6.	The Quaker Reformation	96
7.	London Friends and Honesty in Business	101
8.	Trade and Debt in Philadelphia	119
9.	Marital Endogamy	135
10.	War and Political Crisis	155
11.	Reformation and Reputation	172

Appendix I: Queries of the London Yearly Meeting	178
Appendix II: Philadelphia Meetings' Self-Condemnations	180
Bibliography	181
Index	199

Illustrations

Tables

1.	London Quaker Bridegroom Occupations	35
2.	Merchants among London Quaker Bridegrooms	35
3.	Estimates of Numbers of Enslaved Africans in Philadelphia	41
4.	Contents of London Monthly Meeting Minutes	78
5.	Contents of Philadelphia Monthly Meeting Minutes	80
6.	Sources for London Monthly Meeting Sanctions	87
7.	Insolvent/Bankrupt London Quaker Merchants	113
8.	Insolvent/Bankrupt/Fraudulent Philadelphia Quaker Merchants	126
9.	Causes for Marriage Sanctions	149
10.	Quaker Apprentice Marriages	151
11.	Quaker Apprentices training with Quaker Masters	153

Figures

1.	London Quaker Marriages	34
2.	Population of Philadelphia, European descent	39
3.	Disownments by London Monthly Meetings	93
4.	Disownments by Philadelphia Monthly Meetings	93
5.	Sanctions of Offences Related to Honesty in London	105
6.	Certificates of Removal Received by London Monthly Meetings	118
7.	Philadelphia Monthly Meetings' Testimonies of Denial Related to Honesty	124
8.	Certificates of Removal Received by Philadelphia Monthly Meetings	131
9.	Certificates of Removal Issued by Philadelphia Monthly Meetings	133
10.	Sanctions for Marriage Offences by London Monthly Meetings	149

A Note on Terms and Language

Society of Friends This term only comes into use in the late eighteenth century. Lacking an alternative, I use it whenever referring to the Friends' formal organization, or its membership as a whole, throughout the period 1650–1800.

Officers Refers to Friends who act formally on behalf of a Quaker meeting. Elsewhere in the literature these people are sometimes referred to as 'elders'. I prefer not to use that term, as it appears in the sources in reference to particular groups of senior Friends, who are not the same individuals I discuss here.

Abbreviations

LYM	London Yearly Meeting
MM	Monthly Meeting
PYM	Philadelphia Yearly Meeting
QFHSDB	Quaker Family History Society Database
SC	Self-Condemnation
ToD	Testimony of Denial

I

The Institutional Foundations of Pre-Modern Trade

Long-distance trade constituted the most dynamic sector of early modern economies. Commercial expansion increased the demand for goods, incentivizing the growth of the manufacturing and service sectors. The early modern Atlantic witnessed an unprecedented expansion of trade. It facilitated social mobility and brought prosperity in its wake. Trade increases on the scale experienced in this period require institutions that secure property rights and enforce contracts. Several influential scholars have credited the same institutions which developed to support pre-modern trade expansion with later facilitating the Industrial Revolution.[1] The Industrial Revolution, in turn, constituted the immediate cause of global inequality, providing England with the means to become the first economy to achieve sustained economic growth. It provided western Europe with the technological and financial means to conquer and colonize much of the world. In other words, long-distance trade, and the institutions governing it, are at the root of global inequality. If we want to find out why some countries are poor, and others rich, we must ask, why did trade in some times and places expand, and not in others?

As trade in the Atlantic increased, London became the biggest port in the western hemisphere. It also became home to the largest single community of Quakers, a community that for almost 400 years has enjoyed a reputation for being disproportionately successful in trade. Quakers occupied a central place in business when Britain emerged as the world's leading trading nation because, so the story goes, they were Quakers.

Long-distance trade is characterized by a time lapse between the delivery of goods and the receipt of payment. Self-interest motivates agents to break contracts and deny payment for received goods. Identifying new agents to trade with in distant locations was difficult. Even more difficult was monitoring their behaviour and forcing them to keep promises. In order for trade to take place, institutions are necessary to prevent agents from cheating their principals. The costs incurred by this are summed up under the term transaction costs.

---

[1] Eric Eustace Williams, *Capitalism and Slavery* (1944). Kenneth Morgan, *Slavery, Atlantic Trade and the British Economy, 1660–1800* (Cambridge: Cambridge University Press, 2000).

They include the costs of monitoring agents' behaviour, gathering information about trading partners and conditions, and enforcing agents' compliance with agreements. According to Douglass North and the New Institutional Economists, in early modern Europe the state emerged as the most successful organization to fulfil these tasks.[2] Early modern states agreed to enforce property rights for merchants in return for revenue from trade. States were less engaged in enforcing property rights in their colonies.[3]

In order to avoid free riding, Atlantic merchants preferred to conduct trade with individuals whom they were already connected to. Such connections could include linkages of kin, religion or local origin, with ties being reinforced by communal worship, neighbourhood and friendship.[4] A number of well-known merchant networks were based on local origin, with diaspora merchants trading with others from their home countries or towns.[5]

Perhaps the most widely discussed analysis of the link between institutions and commercial development has been offered by Avner Greif.[6] Greif analysed

---

[2] Douglass North and Robert Thomas, *The Rise of the Western World: A New Economic History* (Cambridge, Cambridge University Press, 1973).

[3] Nuala Zahedieh, *The Capital and the Colonies: London and the Atlantic Economy, 1660–1700* (Cambridge: Cambridge University Press, 2010).

[4] J. F. Bosher, 'Huguenot Merchants and the Protestant International in the Seventeenth Century', *William and Mary Quarterly* 50, no. 1 (1995); Michel Aghassian and Keram Kenovian, 'The Armenian Merchant Network: Overall Autonomy and Local Integration', in *Merchants, Companies and Trade: Europe and Asia in the Early Modern Era*, ed. Sushio Chaudhury and Michel Morineau (Cambridge: Cambridge University Press, 1999); Genevieve Bouchon, 'Trade in the Indian Ocean at the Dawn of the Sixteenth Century', in *Merchants, Companies and Trade*, ed. Sushil Chaudhury and Michel Morineau; Gershom D. Hundert, 'The Role of the Jews in Commerce in Early Modern Poland-Lithuania', in *Merchant Networks in the Early Modern World: 1450–1800*, ed. Sanjay Subrahmanyam (Aldershot: Variorum, 1996).

[5] David Hancock, 'A Revolution in Trade: Wine Distribution and the Development of the Infrastructure of the Atlantic Market Economy, 1703–1807', in *The Early Modern Atlantic Economy*, ed. John McCusker and Kenneth Morgan (Cambridge: Cambridge University Press, 2000).

[6] Avner Greif, *Institutions and the Path to the Modern Economy: Lessons from Medieval Trade* (Cambridge: Cambridge University Press, 2006). His work sparked a wave of literature on private order institutions facilitating trade expansion in different parts of the pre-modern world. Examples include Edward Stringham, 'The Extralegal Development of Securities Trading in Seventeenth-Century Amsterdam', *Quarterly Review of Economics and Finance* 43, no. 2 (2003); Saumitra Jha, 'Trade, Institutions and Ethnic Tolerance: Evidence from South Asia', *American Political Science Review* 107, no. 4 (2013); Tetsuji Okazaki, 'The Role of the Merchant Coalition in Pre-Modern Japanese Economic Development: An Historical Institutional Analysis', CIRJE Discussion Paper F 284 (2004); Janet Tai Landa, 'A Theory of the Ethnically Homogeneous Middleman Group: An Institutional Alternative to Contract Law', *Journal of Legal Studies* 10 (1981), 349-362; Janet Tai Landa, *Trust, Ethnicity, and Identity: Beyond the New Institutional Economics of Ethnic Trading Networks, Contract*

the informal institutions underlying trade expansion during the commercial revolution in the weak state environment of the medieval Mediterranean. In his classic study, the Maghrebi merchant community formed a 'coalition' in which members shared information and enforced contracts through a multilateral reputation mechanism. This enabled members to stay abreast of developments and collectively monitor each other's conduct over long distances. A breach of contract would lead to ostracism from the community, which would break its economic and social ties with the individual. The agent lost the long-term prospects of trade with the whole community. Therefore, it was in his self-interest to be honest and comply with agreements. The multilateral reputation mechanism enabled individual merchants to conduct transactions with people they did not know personally, but who they learned about from fellow community members, thus multiplying opportunities for business. Multilateral reputation mechanisms faced limitations, however. Membership of the networks operating them was based on non-economic criteria, such as ethnicity, kinship or local origin.[7] This limited the number of possible trading partners, and hence the degree of market expansion.[8] Moreover, agents were chosen for being able to be monitored and pressured, rather than their competence. Agents chosen on the basis of kinship, religious affinity or local origin might turn out to be incompetent or lazy, drink, gamble or be in other ways unsuitable as business partners.[9] This placed a constraint on the pool of talent and limited such networks' ability to support trade, and thus economic growth.

In order to explain how pre-modern merchants overcame the limitations faced by informally organized trade, work on more extensive and heterogeneous commercial environments has centred on more formal institutions. Thus, a case has been made that the inefficiencies of reputation mechanisms caused by the lack of high-quality information and the coordination of collective action were solved by medieval merchant guilds and trading fairs, where formal administrative bodies gathered, verified and distributed information.[10] They coordinated collective responses by the merchant members and ostracized offenders. More

---

Law, and Gift-Exchange (Ann Arbor: University of Michigan Press, 1994). Landa's work pre-dates that of Greif, but the debate seems to have taken off only with his publications.
7   Laura Jarnagin, *A Confluence of Transatlantic Networks: Elites, Capitalism, and Confederate Migration to Brazil* (Tuscaloosa, AL: University of Alabama Press, 2008).
8   Nuala Zahedieh, 'Making Mercantilism Work: London Merchants and the Atlantic Trade in the Seventeenth Century', *Transactions of the Royal Historical Society*, Sixth Series 9 (1999), found that 'in the early modern Atlantic religion was a particularly important basis for merchant networks'.
9   David Hancock, 'The Trouble with Networks: Managing the Scot's Early Modern Madeira Trade', *Business History Review* 79, no. 3 (2005).
10 Avner Greif, Paul Milgrom and Barry Weingast, 'Coordination, Commitment and Enforcement: The Case of the Merchant Guild', *Journal of Political Economy* 102, no. 4 (1994); Paul Milgrom, Douglass North and Barry Weingast, 'The Role of Institutions in the

recently, the debate moved towards the view that it is actually the interaction of both private and public order institutions that by complementing each other facilitated pre-modern trade expansion. Contrary to what the New Institutional Economists argued, researchers have since shown that private order institutions were not supplanted by public order ones. Instead of merchants' transactions, and thereby market expansion being restricted to private order institutions, pre-modern trading communities simultaneously accessed public order institutions such as courts. For instance, Jessica Goldberg contends that the Maghrebis 'took the trouble to use contract forms that would also allow them access to the Muslim courts, and often further secured such protection by drawing up the contract before both a Muslim and a Jewish notary'.[11] Similarly, during the early modern period, Sephardic merchants organized their trade through networks based on their common Jewish-Iberian background. When the Medici introduced economic policies aimed specifically at supporting the Sephardis' trade, a large part of the community migrated to the Mediterranean port of Livorno. They integrated the newly available public order institutions into their trading practice to the mutual advantage of the merchants and their host town.[12] At the same time, English merchant networks incorporated political and legal institutions in Bilbao in order to defend the interests of commerce, leading to a revival of the woollens trade between England and Spain.[13]

There are obvious parallels between these well-studied mercantile communities and the standard analysis of Quaker commercial success. In England, Quaker merchants could rely on public order institutions to protect their property rights. They were equally successful, however, in trade with the colonies, where public order institutions for contract enforcement were weak or lacking.[14] How was this possible?

Revival of Trade: The Law Merchant, Private Judges and the Champagne Fairs', *Economics and Politics* 2, no. 1 (1990).

11 Jessica Goldberg, *Trade and Institutions in the Medieval Mediterranean: The Geniza Merchants and Their Business World* (Cambridge: Cambridge University Press, 2012).

12 Francesca Trivellato, *The Familiarity of Strangers: The Sephardic Diaspora, Livorno, and Cross-Cultural Trade in the Early Modern Period* (New Haven, CT: Yale University Press, 2009).

13 Regina Gräfe, 'On the Spatial Nature of Institutions and the Institutional Nature of Personal Networks in the Spanish Atlantic', *Culture and History Digital Journal* 3, no. 1 (2014). See also Oscar Gelderblom and Regina Grafe, 'The Rise, Persistence and Decline of Merchant Guilds: Re-Thinking the Comparative Study of Commercial Institutions in Pre-Modern Europe', *Journal of Interdisciplinary History* 40, no. 4 (2010); Oscar Gelderblom, *Cities of Commerce: The Institutional Foundations of International Trade in the Low Countries, 1250–1650* (Princeton, NJ: Princeton University Press, 2013).

14 Frederick Barnes Tolles, *Meeting House and Counting House: The Quaker Merchants of Colonial Philadelphia, 1682–1763* (Chapel Hill: University of North Carolina Press, 1948).

Quakers in commerce

Trade in the British Atlantic was framed by the Navigation Acts, but otherwise organized privately. According to the economic history literature, Friends' commercial success in the Atlantic rested upon a collective reputation for honesty. This reputation, historians have explained, was the consequence of two institutions: first, the Quakers' distinct business ethics, and second, the Society of Friends' formal system for disciplining members who failed to settle their debts.[15] Combined, their ethical code and their church's oversight made Quaker merchants trustworthy and popular as trading partners with Friends and outsiders alike. In addition, the Quaker doctrine of religious marital endogamy supported their trade by facilitating the development of dense kinship networks.[16] These three institutions conspired to lower transaction costs for Friends and provide them with a competitive edge in trade.

The following pages set out the historiography on Quaker business ethics, Quaker meetings' enforcement of debts and Quaker marriage. They show that all three institutions, ethics, enforcement and endogamy, are generally perceived as static. Possible changes in their practice over time are not considered. Moreover, this literature treats the Society of Friends as existing in a social and economic vacuum. By extension, it assumes that its institutions developed uninfluenced by external factors. Recent work on the London Quaker community, however, shows that Friends interacted extensively with wider society. This raises the question as to whether their institutions really developed unimpaired by outside influences. In order to understand how Quaker institutions worked, and whether they are likely to have had an impact on Friends' commercial success, we need to establish their relationship with contemporary social, political and economic developments.

---

15 Tolles, *Meeting House*; Arthur Raistrick, *Quakers in Science and Industry: Being an Account of the Quaker Contributions to Science and Industry during the 17th and 18th Centuries* (London: Bannisdale Press, 1950); James Walvin, *The Quakers: Money and Morals* (London: John Murray, 1997); Isabel Grubb, *Quakerism and Industry before 1800* (London: Williams and Norgate, 1930); Ann Prior and Maurice Kirby, 'The Society of Friends and the Family Firm, 1700–1830', *Business History* 35, no. 4 (1993), 108.

16 Petra L. Doan and Elizabeth P. Kamphausen, 'Quakers and Sexuality', in *The Oxford Handbook of Quaker Studies*, ed. Stephen W. Angell and Pink Dandelion (Oxford: Oxford University Press, 2013); Pink Dandelion and Peter Collins, *The Quaker Condition: The Sociology of a Liberal Religion* (Newcastle: Cambridge Scholars, 2008), 16; Arnold Lloyd, *Quaker Social History, 1669–1738* (London: Longman), 58; Richard T. Vann, *The Social Development of English Quakerism, 1655–1755* (Cambridge, MA: Harvard University Press, 1969), 181–88; Raistrick, *Quakers in Science and Industry*, 45; Edward H. Milligan, *Biographical Dictionary of British Quakers in Commerce and Industry 1775–1920* (York: Sessions Book Trust, 2007), 588.

The literature on Quaker business ethics and its limitations

According to the historiography, Quakers' success in business was facilitated partly by a particularly strong set of values. In 1993 Maurice Kirby argued that during the eighteenth and nineteenth centuries, 'The Society of Friends ... was infused with a strong moral culture which redounded to the advantage of the Quaker businessman in terms of confidence and expectations.'[17] For the colonial period, Fredrick Tolles argued that

> Given the identical phenomenon of unusual economic success under markedly different outward conditions in England and Pennsylvania it becomes apparent that the fundamental explanation must be sought in something inherently characteristic of Quakerism and thus common to Friends on both sides of the Atlantic. Where shall we find it except in their religious and social philosophy?'[18]

While Arthur Raistrick deemed kinship networks more important, he still concluded that during the seventeenth and eighteenth centuries, 'It was this unshakeable honesty of the Quaker that made people willing to place their money in his hands when most other people were suspect, and which opened the way for the success of the Quaker bankers.'[19] Richard Grassby argued for the early modern period overall that 'Quakers ... were subject to their own strict business codes.'[20] Recently, Leslie Hannah claimed for the seventeenth to nineteenth centuries, 'Quaker values have often been linked to their economic success; and the sect certainly had an unusually demanding and relevant set of spiritual and moral requirements.'[21] Isabel Grubb, Arthur Raistrick, James Walvin, Ann Prior and Maurice Kirby, among others, have argued that the Quaker code of conduct for the pursuit of business was distinct and superior to that of contemporary mainstream society.[22] This code was based on the

---

17   Maurice Kirby, 'Quakerism, Entrepreneurship and the Family Firm in North-East England, 1780–1860', in *Entrepreneurship, Networks and Modern Business*, ed. Jonathan Brown and Mary B. Rose (Manchester: Manchester University Press, 1993), 108.
18   Tolles, *Meeting House*, 51.
19   Raistrick, *Quakers in Science and Industry*, 48.
20   Richard Grassby, *Kinship and Capitalism: Marriage, Family, and Business in the English Speaking World, 1580–1720* (Cambridge: Woodrow Wilson Center Press and Cambridge University Press, 2001), 309, citing Jacob Price, 'The Great Quaker Business Families of Eighteenth Century London', in *Overseas Trade and Traders: Essays on some Commercial, Financial and Political Challenges Facing British Atlantic Merchants, 1660–1775*, ed. Jacob Price (Farnham: Ashgate, 1996).
21   Leslie Hannah, 'The Moral Economy of Business: An Historical Perspective on Ethics and Efficiency', in *Civil Histories: Essays in Honour of Sir Keith Thomas*, ed. Peter Burke, Brian Harrison and Paul Slack (Oxford: Oxford University Press, 2000), 289.
22   Raistrick, *Quakers in Science and Industry*, 44, 47; Prior and Kirby, 'The Society of Friends and the Famliy Firm, 1700–1830', '67, 68; Walvin, *Money and Morals*, 32, 34, 35; Lloyd, *Social History*, 70; Grubb, *Quakerism*; Tolles, *Meeting House*.

virtues of honesty, reliability, risk-aversity and the prompt settlement of debts. It worked to their advantage in trade: 'because Quaker business men were known to be scrupulously honest, people were glad to deal with them'.[23] In other words, Quaker business ethics evoked trust in their trading partners. Thereby they provided Quakers with a competitive advantage in business, facilitating Friends' trade in the deceitful, low-trust environment that was the early modern economy.[24] Common elements of definitions of trust are reciprocity and positive expectations about others' intentions and behaviours.[25] It stems from 'shared rules and codes of conduct within groups'.[26] These values are introduced during childhood.[27] They regulate behaviour amongst community members, including the conduct of business. According to the literature, trading partners expected certain behaviour from Quakers because their membership in the Society of Friends implied that they subscribed to a certain set of behavioural rules. They trusted Quakers to honour their contracts and be punctual in paying their debts, as this was central to their ethical code. Therefore, Quakers were preferred as trading partners over non-Quakers.[28] The knowledge that somebody was a Quaker would have sufficed to single them out as trustworthy, thereby lowering information costs. Present-day studies indicate that perceptions of trustworthiness in exchange relationships lower transaction costs. They increase information sharing and decrease the need for safeguarding behaviours.[29] The weaker the institutional environment, the more important trust becomes for business relations. It is regarded as a 'means to decrease the costs and risks of business transactions in hostile or turbulent environments'.[30] The

23 Tolles, *Meeting House*, 59.
24 Prior and Kirby, 'Family Firm', 66.
25 Friederike Welter, 'All You Need Is Trust? A Critical Review of the Trust and Entrepreneurship Literature', *International Small Business Journal* 30, no. 3 (2012). See also Bill McEvily, Vincenzo Perrone and Akbar Zaheer, 'Trust as an Organizing Principle', *Organization Science* 14, no. 1 (2003).
26 Welter, 'All You Need Is "Trust"?', 196.
27 Mark Casson, 'Entrepreneurship and Business Culture', in *Entrepreneurship, Networks, and Modern Business*, ed. Jonathan Brown and Mary B. Rose (Manchester: Manchester University Press, 1993), 40.
28 Walvin, *Money and Morals*, 34; William Charles Braithwaite and Henry J. Cadbury, *The Second Period of Quakerism*, 2nd edition (York: William Sessions in association with the Joseph Rowntree Charitable Trust, 1961), 500; Raistrick, *Quakers in Science and Industry*, 48; Gary Stuart De Krey, *A Fractured Society: The Politics of London in the First Age of Party 1688–1715* (Oxford: Clarendon Press, 1985), 97; Tolles, *Meeting House*, 58.
29 Jeffrey H. Dyer and Wujin Chu, 'The Role of Trustworthiness in Reducing Transaction Costs and Improving Performance: Empirical Evidence from the United States, Japan, and Korea', *Organization Science* 14, no. 1 (2003). See also Casson, 'Business Culture', 41; McEvily, Perrone and Zaheer, 'Trust as an Organizing Principle'.
30 Welter, 'Trust', 194; There is a debate about the nature of trust, with some proponents arguing that it in fact veils monitoring and enforcement institutions. See for instance Timothy Guinnane, 'Trust: A Concept Too Many', *Jahrbuch fur Wirtschaftsgeschichte* 1 (2005).

early modern Atlantic was such an environment, as state institutions for the protection of property rights had yet to develop.

Among authors contending that there were distinct Quaker ethics, there is disagreement as to how important these were for Friends' business success relative to other factors. Prior and Kirby argued that honesty in trade, including the avoidance of debt, became a condition of membership of the Religious Society of Friends from its inception in the 1660s. During the eighteenth and early nineteenth centuries, their ethics conspired with the oversight of Quaker meetings over their members' businesses, as well as extensive credit networks, to facilitate Friends' business success.[31] James Walvin, discussing the seventeenth to twentieth centuries, found the most important aspect in Quaker success was the oversight practised by the meetings. However, he also discussed Quaker business ethics, arguing that 'Quakers in business were expected to conform to the principles issued from the Yearly Meeting in London and laid down in the Advices', these being honesty, risk-aversity and diligence.[32] For Leslie Hannah and Richard Grassby, business ethics also form an important reason behind the Quakers' success story.[33] These authors consider Quaker business ethics as, if not the only, certainly one important cause behind their business success.

The perception that Quakers had a special set of business ethics has begun to meet with criticism, however. Nuala Zahedieh found that Quaker merchants' 'business success is often attributed to unusual virtue'.[34] However, she suggested that the Quakers' code of conduct resembled that 'promoted in contemporary advice books and discussions of commercial reputation', and that 'Quakers were not differentiated by their ethical code, but they were differentiated by their capacity to enforce it'.[35]

Where did the notion of special Quaker ethics originate? Kirby, Walvin and Hannah did not conduct empirical studies of their own. Instead, recent studies derive their information on Quaker business ethics from literature from the early twentieth century. Kirby relied heavily on Arthur Raistrick's work, Zahedieh and Haggerty cited Fredrick Tolles, Walvin cited Braithwaite. Hannah provided no references at all for his claim, which may serve as further evidence that the idea of Quaker ethics is widely enough accepted not to require much backing up. What we need to ask, therefore, is how this earlier generation of historians, including Braithwaite, Grubb, Tolles and Raistrick, arrived at their conclusions regarding Quaker business ethics? Let us look at the sources they analyzed and the methodologies they employed.

---

31 Prior and Kirby, 'Family Firm'.
32 Walvin, *Money*, 33.
33 Hannah, 'Moral Economy'; Grassby, *Kinship*, 309.
34 Nuala Zahedieh, 'Mercantilism', 301.
35 Zahedieh, *Capital*, 109.

The main sources employed in this older historiography are publications of individual Quaker leaders or the Society itself dating from the seventeenth and eighteenth centuries. The London Yearly Meeting's annual epistles figure prominently, as do pamphlets published by the Society's early leaders including George Fox and William Penn. From these publications, authors such as Isabel Grubb, Arnold Lloyd, Arthur Raistrick and Frederick Tolles identified the virtues of industry, frugality, diligence, honesty and risk-aversity as central to the Quaker code of conduct in business.

William Braithwaite's classic works, *The Beginnings of Quakerism* and *The Second Period of Quakerism*, discuss the seventeenth and early eighteenth centuries. He used the London Yearly Meeting advices on honesty, integrity and risk-aversity in business as evidence for Quaker business ethics.[36] The widest range of sources was employed by Isabel Grubb. Focusing on the seventeenth and eighteenth centuries, she analyzed not only the epistles of the London Yearly Meeting, but also monographs and pamphlets of early Quaker leaders such as George Fox and William Penn, and arrived at the same conclusion.[37] Fredrick Tolles studied the colonial period in Pennsylvania. Based on the epistles of the London Yearly Meeting and to a smaller degree on writings by Fox and Penn, he argued that Quakerism had a distinct religious and social philosophy.[38] Similarly, discussing English Quakers in the period 1669–1738, Arnold Lloyd cited Yearly Meeting epistles and Fox's pamphlets as evidence for Quaker business ethics of integrity, simplicity and moderation.[39]

Tracing the concept of Quaker business ethics back through the literature shows that it is rooted in a flawed methodology. There are two problems: first, these works lack a comparative angle. Arguments for the uniqueness of Quaker business ethics rest upon the reading of Quaker sources alone.[40] There has so far been no systematic comparison of the business ethics of Quakers, as depicted in their records, with the business ethics of wider society. In fact, Nuala Zahedieh noted that the Quaker principles of honesty, reliability and risk-aversity appear similar if not identical to those ethics propagated by Daniel Defoe in his *Complete English Tradesman*. It is therefore worth investigating to what extent the principles of Quaker business ethics were indeed distinct. Put differently, we need to establish whether the values of honesty, frugality and diligence, which historians have identified as distinctly Quaker, were in fact unique to Friends.

---

36 Braithwaite, *Second Period*, 500.
37 Grubb, *Quakerism*.
38 Tolles, *Meeting House*, 51.
39 Lloyd, *Social History*, 70, 71.
40 The one exception is Isabel Grubb. Her comparison with Richard Baxter's work is brief, however, and her methodology remains unclear.

A second problem with these earlier studies' methodology is the gap between theory and practice. Whether the principles of Quaker business ethics in theory were different from those of mainstream ethics or not, the actual conduct of Quaker merchants in their practice of business, in their dealing with other merchants and business people, constitutes a second, separate question. The sources the historiography on Quaker business ethics rests upon discuss the rules of the conduct of business. The epistles of the London Yearly Meeting, the main source these works draw on, give directions and advice to their readers, on how to transact business. They therefore only provide information on how the Society wanted its members to act, not on how Friends actually behaved. None of the studies maintaining that Friends were exceptionally honest draw on research on the actual business practices of Quaker merchants.

The literature on the Society of Friends' formal enforcement of debts, and its limitations

The second conventional explanation for Quaker merchants' success is that Quaker meetings formally enforced contracts. They forced their members to honour promises and repay debts. Failure to do so would lead to ostracism from the Society. We find this perspective in the historiography on Quaker business throughout the twentieth century. In 1930 Isabel Grubb claimed that during the seventeenth and eighteenth centuries, 'Great care was taken by the Society to ensure that as far as possible Friends were punctual in paying their debts and in keeping their promises,' and that

> If Friends became aware that members or attenders of the meeting were defrauding the revenue, not paying their debts, or otherwise acting wrongfully, they expostulated with them, and if they did not themselves condemn their own doing, the meeting published a paper, which either expressed disapproval of the actions, or, declared that Friends were not in unity with the offender and disowned him to be of the Society.[41]

Fredrick Tolles in 1948 claimed that Philadelphia meetings during the colonial period disowned all those who refused to give up all their possessions to their creditors.[42] Arthur Raistrick in 1950, speaking of the period 1652–1800, emphasized the formal controls placed on individual business people by the meetings. He based this claim on the London Yearly Meeting's 'Advices', and argued that as these advocated honesty, Quakers must indeed have been

---

41 Grubb, *Quakerism*, 86.
42 Tolles, *Meeting House*, 90; equally Jack D. Marietta, *The Reformation of American Quakerism, 1748–1783* (Philadelphia: University of Pennsylvania Press, 1984), 23.

unshakeably honest, thus creating trust.[43] Jacob Price in 1986 argued for early modern Quakerism as a whole: 'one cannot exaggerate the importance Quakers attached to the payment of debts. Members of the most prominent families ... were disowned for failure to pay their debts.'[44] This strict policy meant that membership of the Society signalled solvency, or at least honesty. Therefore, Friends enjoyed very high credit ratings.[45] Citing Isabel Grubb, Julian Hoppit in his 1987 book, which remains the standard work on British bankruptcy in the eighteenth century, explained that

> There was a second significant, though limited, unofficial process for dealing with insolvency, constructed by the Quakers to deal with Friends who had failed. Like the law of bankruptcy, the Quakers believed that failure could result either from bad luck or from bad habits ... Where there was evidence of immorality and the good name of the Society was threatened, then the bankrupt Friends could be disowned.[46]

In 1993 Ann Prior and Maurice Kirby, relying heavily on Raistrick, argued that the meetings' oversight of Friends' business activities played a key role for the sect's success in business during the eighteenth and early nineteenth centuries.[47] Drawing on the minutes of the Leeds Friend's meetings, as well as the 'Advices', they found that meetings became involved in their members' businesses through the oversight of debt, and disownment of culpable insolvents and bankrupts. Discussing the period from the 1650s to the eve of World War I, James Walvin in 1997 argued that 'Friends had a dread of business failure and especially indebtedness', and that an 'efficient bureaucracy was put to work to ensure that even the humblest of Friends accorded with Quaker standards'.[48] He argued that the meetings helped members by offering advice, 'but it also meant that the unsuccessful – those who transgressed the Society's conventions on dealing with the consuming public – were disowned'.[49] He based this claim

---

43 Raistrick, *Quakers in Science and Industry*, 46, 47.
44 Jacob M. Price, *Overseas Trade and Traders: Essays on Some Commercial, Financial, and Political Challenges facing British Atlantic Merchants, 1660–1775* (Aldershot: Variorum, 1996), 386.
45 Equally, Richard Brown, *Society and Economy in Modern Britain 1700–1850* (London: Routledge, 1990), 209: 'In the 18th century the Quakers would cut off from membership all Friends who had deviated to the extent of going bankrupt, a form of sanction experienced by Charles Lloyd, uncle of the founder of the bank, in the 1720s.' Provides no references.
46 Julian Hoppit, *Risk and Failure in English Business 1700–1800* (Cambridge: Cambridge University Press, 1987), 31.
47 Prior and Kirby, 'Family Firm'.
48 Walvin, *Money and Morals*, 33, 72–73; equally Milligan, *Dictionary*, 582; Raistrick, *Quakers in Science and Industry*, 46.
49 Walvin, *Money and Morals*, 208.

on the 'Advices' and anecdotal evidence from the secondary literature. Finally, in 2000, Leslie Hannah argued that from the seventeenth century onwards, 'Quaker discipline was direct, relentless, comprehensive and intrusive,' and that 'the power to enforce implicit contracts through the ... meeting gave a special competitive advantage in ... long-distance trade'.[50]

However, the empirical basis for these views is remarkably thin. For example, neither Hannah nor Tolles included references to cases of disownments for debts. Jacob Price referred to only one such case. Walvin largely relied on Pressnell's *Country Banking* for evidence that in Norwich, sixty insolvencies became subject to investigation from 1701 to 1773.[51] Pressnell in turn named as a reference A. Eddington's transcript of the Norwich monthly meeting's eighteenth-century minutes.[52] Upon consultation, it appeared that there were in fact only twenty-nine cases of dealings for debts, insolvency or bankruptcy in the Norwich meeting's minutes, which involved thirty-three individuals. Just twenty-two of these cases led to disownments. Only two cases fell into the period before 1750, and neither led to a disownment.[53] Norwich's first disownment for debt occurred in 1755. Beyond this, Walvin narrated three further instances of York Quakers who in the eighteenth century were pressured by their meeting to repay their debts.[54] Similarly, Lloyd provided one example of a meeting's investigation into debt from 1673.[55] Grubb cited two cases in which a monthly meeting became involved in a member's business, one from Dublin in 1702 and one from Surrey in 1786.[56] Prior and Kirby cited four cases during the eighteenth century in which a Leeds meeting oversaw the repayment of debts. Only one of them took place before the mid-century, in 1721.[57]

Two problems appear with this literature. First, the Society's involvement in business is treated as static. Thin evidence from across the seventeenth to nineteenth centuries is used indiscriminately. Second, there have been no studies of Quaker meetings' capacity to capture misconduct. We do not know whether meetings sanctioned all bankrupt and insolvent Friends, or only a small fraction of them. Therefore, Prior and Kirby's conclusion that 'the close internal control

---

50 Hannah, 'Moral Economy', 290, 293.
51 Walvin, *Money and Morals*, 73.
52 L. S. Pressnell, *Country Banking in the Industrial Revolution* (Oxford: Clarendon Press, 1956); A. Eddington, Minutes of the Norwich Monthly Meeting (1701–1771), and Minutes of the Norwich Monthly Meeting (1776–1800), Typescript, 1935, Library of the Society of Friends.
53 Pressnell, *Country Banking*; Eddington, Norwich MM minutes (1701–1771 and 1776–1800).
54 Walvin, *Money and Morals*, 74, 75.
55 Lloyd, *Social History*, 37.
56 Grubb, *Quakerism*, 70.
57 Prior and Kirby, 'Family Firm', 74, 75.

exercised by the meeting in the oversight of debt is of considerable importance to the Quaker success story' seems premature.[58]

The literature on Quaker marriage patterns, and its limitations

A third explanation for Quaker commercial success points towards Friends' doctrine of marriage. Marriage was an important institution in the conduct of early modern business in general, and long-distance trade in particular. It served as a foundation for business through facilitating capital accumulation and the creation of kinship networks. Kinship networks were important in early modern trade because a firm's survival depended on its access to credit. Kin were an important investor in early modern firms. A greater kinship network meant a greater number of potential investors, and therefore more capital for the firm to do business with.

Access to credit could be made and unmade by the partners' reputation for sound character.[59] A merchant, or partner in a firm, might acquire a reputation for being unreliable, not good with money or generally untrustworthy. In such a case, creditors would demand their money back, or refuse to lend or give credit for goods in the first place. This would rob the merchant or firm of its ability to trade and cause their bankruptcy. As there was no limited liability for firms before the later nineteenth century, a bankruptcy meant not only the end of a business, but also the loss of most property the merchant's family owned. Marriage to kin provided an answer to these challenges. It constituted a means of recruiting partners and agents for a firm whose behaviour was easy to monitor.[60] A staff member or partner who was also a relative could be observed in their personal life at family gatherings, church or other occasions that were not immediately tied to the conduct of business. Hence, junior partners married the daughters of senior colleagues, masters married apprentices' sisters and partners married into the same family. In the English Levant Company relation through marriage was extremely common, and most East India servants were related.[61]

---

58 Prior and Kirby, 'Family Firm', 73, similarly Walvin, *Money and Morals*, 79.
59 Leonore Davidoff and Catherine Hall, *Family Fortunes: Men and Women of the English Middle Class 1780–1850* (London: Hutchinson, 1987), 201.
60 Gabor Gyani, 'Middle-Class Kinship in Nineteenth-Century Hungary', in *Kinship in Europe: Approaches to Long-Term Developments (1300–1900)*, ed. David Warren Sabean, Simon Teuscher and Jon Mathieu (New York: Berghahn Books, 2007). Naomi Tadmor, 'Early Modern English Kinship in the Long Run: Reflections on Continuity and Change', *Continuity and Change* 25, no. 1 (2010), 29; Davidoff and Hall, *Family Fortunes*, 201.
61 Grassby, *Kinship*, 306–7.

Marriage furthermore served as a way to transfer resources between generations and families. It helped obtain funds for business ventures. This transfer could take the form of dowries, portions, bride prices or inheritance. Depending on local property and inheritance legislation, marriage could be beneficial or detrimental to the accumulation of individual families' wealth. Marrying a spouse from a wealthy family provided access to that family's assets. Under English common law, married women were not allowed to sign contracts, were not liable for their own debts and therefore did not become partners in firms. They were not usually able to hold property. Hence, their marriage meant a one-way transfer of property from their families into the purses and businesses of their husbands.

In this setting, historians have argued, Quakers held an advantage because of the Society of Friends' doctrine of marital endogamy. Friends were supposed to marry only fellow Quakers. Historians of Quakerism have argued that monthly meetings enforced this rule, and that early modern Friends followed it closely. Economic historians trying to explain Quaker business success argued that the doctrine limited the number of possible spouses for Quakers, and thereby led to the growth of exceptionally close kinship networks, which included an unusual frequency of marriages between close kin. These supplied Quaker merchants and other business men with exceptionally good access to credit.

Jacob Price in 1996 published a study of the fourteen leading English Quaker merchant and banking families of the eighteenth century. He found that by the late eighteenth century, they had all become related through intermarriage. This included repeated marriages between the same families, and cousin marriages.[62] This was noteworthy, as since the early middle ages, kin marriages were considered a great taboo across Europe. The law banned marriages between individuals related up to the fourth degree of kinship. This included both consanguineal kin, which are 'relationships of shared blood', and affinal kinship, i.e. relationships through marriages, for instance to deceased spouses' siblings.[63] The London Yearly Meeting also advised against 'marriage with near kindred' several times between 1691 and 1730.[64] Price and others argued that Friends were forced to break this taboo, as the doctrine of marital endogamy severely limited the choice of marriage partners. As Quakers made

---

62 Price, 'Business Families'.
63 Ralph A. Houlbrooke, *The English Family, 1450–1700* (London: Longman, 1984), 39. The rules were set out in the Church of England's 'Table of Kinship and Affinity'.
64 Society of Friends, *Epistles of the Yearly Meeting of Friends Held in London* (London, 1818), epistle 1691, 59; epistle 1714, 181; epistle 1727, 192; epistle 1730, 202. The 1691 epistle refers to 'This Meeting's former advice against marriage with near kin' – this advice is however not included in any of the meeting's earlier epistles. It is interesting to note that this advice ceases as kin marriages in wider society increase from the mid-eighteenth century onwards.

up only a small fraction of society, they soon ran out of potential spouses. This forced them to either remain single, or marry Friends they were already related to. Endogamy thereby led directly to kin marriages, and the creation of close-knit and geographically far-flung kinship networks. These linkages provided Friends with contacts and funds, which allowed them to prosper in business and especially long-distance trade. Thus, the practice of endogamy gave Friends a competitive advantage in business.[65]

However, research in historical demography shows that kin marriages observed by the literature for eighteenth-century Quakers were not actually that unusual. Rather, they reflect a cross-European trend. While there is little evidence in England and other parts of Europe for repeated consanguineal marriages in the seventeenth century, marriages between close relatives multiplied in various parts of Europe in the eighteenth and nineteenth centuries – exactly the period for which Quaker kin marriages have been recorded. David Sabean, Simon Teuscher and Jon Mathieu in 2007 found that previously frowned upon or even prohibited marriages became 'part of the overall strategies of noble, middle class, and peasant families'.[66] Swiss marriage dispensations, for instance, included few petitions for exceptions to marriage laws in order to marry relatives until the middle of the eighteenth century, but accelerated in the last quarter of the century.[67] Across Europe this development peaked in the nineteenth century, when 'enormous energy' was spent on the creation of 'extensive, reliable and well-articulated structures of exchange among connected families over many generations'.[68]

The deep-reaching transition of doctrine surrounding incest and marriage patterns across Europe was driven by increased commercialisation.[69] As trade became ever more important to European economy and society, need for credit grew, too. Merchants needed advances, industrialists required capital. 'The issue for those undertaking risky adventures in mining, metallurgy, textile production, and international trade was ... how to bring ... investment capital through credit and assemble reliable staff or correspondents.'[70] The conse-

---

65 Prior and Kirby, 'Family Firm', 67; Rosemary Moore, 'Seventeenth-Century Context and Quaker Beginnings', in *The Oxford Handbook of Quaker Studies*, ed. Pink Dandelion and Stephen W. Angell (Oxford: Oxford University Press, 2013), 25; Raistrick, *Quakers in Science and Industry*, 44; Milligan, *Dictionary*, 588; Price, 'Business Families'.
66 Sabean, Teuscher and Mathieu (eds), *Kinship in Europe*, 21.
67 Jon Mathieu, 'Kin Marriages: Trends and Interpretations from the Swiss Example', in Sabean, Teuscher and Mathieu (eds), *Kinship in Europe*, 193–210.
68 Sabean, Teuscher and Mathieu, *Kinship in Europe*, 3. On intermarriage for business interests since later eighteenth century in England in general, see idem, 18.
69 Sabean, Teuscher and Mathieu (eds), *Kinship in Europe* also discuss the extension of the nation state increasing its reach into communities as a second driving force.
70 Sabean, Teuscher and Mathieu, *Kinship in Europe*, 17.

quence was a growth of marriage-based kinship networks – Friends' practice of marrying kin in this period therefore was not exceptional, but the norm.

The assumption that the doctrine of marital endogamy set limits upon the choice of spouse also serves as the basis for Richard Vann and David Eversley's monumental demographic study of British and Irish Friends from the seventeenth to nineteenth centuries, published in 1992. Based on Quaker marriage records and family reconstitution, it delineates the development of Quaker marriage patterns throughout this period. The authors found a distinct Quaker marriage pattern.[71] Friends stood apart from the general population in two respects: they married late, and an unusually large number of female Friends never married at all. From the late seventeenth to the late eighteenth century, the average age at first marriage among English women declined from just under twenty-seven years to just under twenty-four years. Those of female Friends, however, remained high throughout this period, ranging from 28.05 to 28.77 years. These ages were higher even than those of the next highest group, peers' daughters.[72] The average population began to catch up with them only in the second half of the nineteenth century.[73] Furthermore, female Friends displayed extremely high celibacy rates. The celibacy rates of English women overall dropped between the late seventeenth and late eighteenth century, from almost a quarter of the total female population to roughly 6 per cent. The celibacy rates of urban Quaker women, in contrast, rose in the same period from 3.5 per cent to 20 per cent. What is more, while celibacy rates for urban Quaker men were similar to those of English peers (1.2 to 3.5 per cent), those of Quaker women bear no resemblance to those of any other group in the population.[74]

No equally comprehensive demographic study exists for colonial Friends. The few smaller-scale studies that we do have, however, depict trends very similar to those Vann and Eversley identified for Friends in Britain and Ireland. Colonial marriage patterns in general differed in some ways from western European ones. Their most distinct feature is the lower age at first marriage, compared to the higher ages typical to the European marriage pattern. However, as in England and Ireland, Quaker women's age at first marriage in the colonies increased over the course of the eighteenth century.

Based on the records of ten Quaker meetings in New Jersey, New York and Pennsylvania, Robert Wells and Michael Zuckerman showed that female Friends born before 1730 married at an average age of twenty-two years. Female

---

71 As did the children of peers. We have no explanation for their marriage behaviour.
72 Richard T. Vann and David Eversley, *Friends in Life and Death: The British and Irish Quakers in the Demographic Transition, 1650–1900* (Cambridge: Cambridge University Press, 1992), 103.
73 Vann and Eversley, *Friends*, 101.
74 Ibid., 108.

Friends born after 1750 were an average age of 23.4 years when they first wed.[75] They found no particular variation between urban and rural meetings. Male Friends' age at first marriage remained fairly stable over the course of the colonial period and into the early nineteenth century.[76]

Female colonial Friends display the same trend of rising celibacy rates as their European sisters. In Philadelphia, rates of marriage varied greatly between different ethnic and religious groups. Quaker women in the city stood out in that they displayed exceptionally high celibacy rates in the later eighteenth and early nineteenth centuries.[77] Susan Klepp found that among women of the Philadelphia gentry, a great number of whom were Friends, 24 per cent of those born in the last quarter of the eighteenth century and 27 per cent of those born in the first quarter of the nineteenth century remained unmarried at age fifty. By the latter period nearly three times as many women as men remained celibate.[78] Studies of various rural meetings in the Delaware Valley show a similar trend: Barry Levy found that in the Welsh Tract, just west of Philadelphia, in the late seventeenth and early eighteenth century, 7 per cent of Quaker men and 14 per cent of Quaker women never married. Female Quaker celibacy in the region increased over the course of the eighteenth century, towards the end of which 23 per cent of Quaker women in New Jersey never married.[79] Wells and Zuckerman's study of ten meetings across the middle colonies, cited above, showed a similar trend: among Quaker women born before 1786, 9.8 per cent remained single; among those born after 1786, 23.5 per cent did.[80]

How can Friends' distinct marriage patterns be explained? Controlling for occupational distribution, Vann and Eversley found that the 'common fact of being Quakers had more to do with the ages of marriage than the particular occupation which was followed'.[81] They explained Friends' high ages at marriage with a cultural norm of late marriage. This norm was enforced through the Quaker marriage procedure, which required permissions and certificates from various parties and meetings. This was time-consuming and thereby served to delay marriage. Moreover, the meeting's requirement of parental consent for a

---

75 Robert V. Wells and Michael Zuckerman, 'Quaker Marriage Patterns in a Colonial Perspective', *William and Mary Quarterly* (1972), 431.
76 Wells and Zuckerman, 'Marriage Patterns', 421.
77 Karin A. Wulf, *Not All Wives: Women of Colonial Philadelphia* (Ithaca, NY: Cornell University Press, 2000), 12, citing Susan E. Klepp, 'Fragmented Knowledge: Questions in Regional Demographic History', *Proceedings of the American Philosophical Society* 133, no. 2 (1989), 120.
78 Klepp, 'Fragmented Knowledge', 233.
79 Wulf, *Not All Wives*, 13.
80 Wells and Zuckerman, 'Marriage Patterns', 426.
81 Ibid., 115.

wedding deterred Friends who may have married at younger ages against their families' will.[82]

Regarding female Friends' high celibacy rates, scholarship provides two types of explanations. The first may be termed demographic, the second economic. Vann and Eversley hypothesized that the immediate cause for the high celibacy rates of European Quaker women after 1750 was a sex imbalance among the Society's membership. In other words, there were more female Friends than male Friends. This sex imbalance was itself the result of two factors. First, before 1750, Quaker meetings disowned more men than women, a tendency that Vann and Eversley observed through the disownment records of London's Horsleydown monthly meeting. This led to a shortage of possible Quaker husbands for Quaker women after 1750. As a consequence, Vann and Eversley argued, Quaker women began marrying non-Quakers. They see evidence for this in the increase in the meeting's disownments of women for marriage delinquencies after 1750.[83] Similarly, Wells and Zuckerman suggested that in America, the decrease of immigration toward the end of the eighteenth century, combined with increased migration from the eastern shoreboard to the west, led to a shortage of men, and thereby limited Quaker women's opportunities to marry.[84]

While Vann and Eversley's study in particular remains extraordinarily impressive, it is not clear that their analysis of marriage trends, and celibacy in particular, is well founded. One key assumption that they make, which Wells and Zuckerman share, is that Quaker monthly meetings captured all marriages, either in the meetings' marriage records or among the sanctions for irregular marriage. In other words, all marriages were registered, and all marriages outside the community were followed by sanctions. They do not consider that the meetings may not have captured or sanctioned all cases of exogamous marriages, or that their interest in or ability to enforce the doctrine may have changed over time. As a result, they conclude that women in their reconstitution for whom they observe a death, but have no observation of a marriage, must have remained single.[85]

Furthermore, the emphasis that Vann and Eversley, Price, Wells and Zuckerman, and others, placed on marital outcomes being driven by opportunities to marry – women being squeezed out of the marriage market by the lack of potential spouses – is rooted in demographic determinism. This assumes that early modern women always preferred marriage, as it provided them with financial security. If women remained single, as we saw many early

---

82 Ibid., 84.
83 Ibid., 124–25.
84 Wells and Zuckerman, 'Marriage Patterns', 434.
85 Vann and Eversley, *Friends*, 108.

modern women did, this must have been due to a lack of men.[86] Some scholars of women's history have challenged the assumption that marriage was necessarily desirable as a means of gaining financial security. They argue that due to the law of coverture, marriage could be detrimental to a woman's fortunes, even if she were poor. In 1994, Barbara Todd argued that poor women were likely to only have the opportunity of marrying equally poor men. Given the restrictions coverture placed on married women's property rights, rather than providing a woman with financial security, it made her vulnerable to losing what income she had to her husband.[87]

The demographic line of reasoning further sits uneasily with subsequent scholarship. More recent research suggests that rates of marriage were not determined primarily by the number of potential partners available. Rather, research on the historical development of marriage patterns shows that in Europe, first ages at marriage and overall rates of marriage were determined by institutions. Particularly important were institutions governing the transfer of wealth, and household formation.[88] Young couples married only if they could afford to set up a household of their own. This dependence of marriage on couples' economic situation means that ages at marriage reflect the economic conditions of the time. Rates of marriage in England were strongly correlated with the development of male real wages. The increasing prosperity that accompanied the period before and during the onset of industrialization was reflected in both dropping ages at first marriage and declining celibacy rates. Related to this, scholars have suggested that rising female celibacy rates in North America were partly due to women's improved ability to own property after the revolution, making marriage for financial security less necessary.[89] It

---

86 Jeremy Boulton, 'London Widowhood Revisited: The Decline of Female Remarriage in the Seventeenth and Early Eighteenth Centuries', *Continuity and Change* 5, no. 3 (1990).
87 Barbara Todd, 'Demographic Determinism and Female Agency: The Remarrying Widow Reconsidered ... Again', *Continuity and Change* 9, no. 3 (1994).
88 Lawrence Stone and Jeanne C. Fawcier Stone, *An Open Elite? England 1540–1880* (Oxford: Clarendon Press, 1984); Judith J. Hurwich, 'Marriage Strategy among the German Nobility, 1400–1699', *Journal of Interdisciplinary History* 29, no. 2 (1998); J. P. Cooper, 'Patterns of Inheritance and Settlement by Great Landowners from the Fifteenth to the Eighteenth Centuries', in *Family and Inheritance: Rural Society in Western Europe, 1200–1800*, ed. Jack Goody, Joan Thirsk and E. P. Thompson (Cambridge: Cambridge University Press, 1976); Olwen H. Hufton, *The Prospect before Her: A History of Women in Western Europe. Vol. 1, 1500–1800* (London: HarperCollins, 1995); Gillian Hamilton and Aloysius Siow, 'Class, Gender and Marriage', *Review of Economic Dynamics* 10, no. 4 (2007); Maristella Botticini and Aloysius Siow, 'Are there Increasing Returns in Marriage Markets?', Boston University Department of Economics, Working Paper WP 2006-050 (2006); Vivienne Brodsky-Eliott, 'Single Women and the London Marriage Market: Age, Status and Mobility, 1598–1619', in *Marriage and Society: Studies in the Social History of Marriage*, ed. R. B. Outhwaite (New York: St Martin's Press, 1982).
89 Wells and Zuckerman, 'Marriage Patterns', 437. See also Wulf, *Not all Wives*, 16.

is likely that Friends' ages at, and rates of, marriage were equally determined by factors other than the size of the marriage market. We therefore need to explain the role institutions played for the Quaker marriage pattern.

Finally, Vann and Eversley's sample of 'urban Quakers' is made up to two-thirds of Friends from Bristol, and one-sixth each of Friends from Norwich and London.[90] Both London's labour and marriage market, however, were distinct.[91] As we have seen that marriage was strongly determined by economic factors, the metropolis's Quaker marriage market merits its own study.

What this book does

The literature on Quakers in trade suffers from two major limitations. First, contextualization: practices observed among early modern Friends are assumed to have been unique to Quakers, and rooted in a distinct Quaker doctrine. These studies pay little if any attention to contemporary developments that may have influenced what Friends thought and did. Economic historians have so far failed to actually compare Quaker business ethics to mainstream business ethics. The demographic studies relying on Quaker records pre-date more recent findings on the development of kinship and marriage patterns in Europe more generally. This suggests that Quaker practices were not as distinct as theretofore assumed. Their conclusions regarding the distinctness of Quaker marriage practices therefore need to be reviewed. Second, authors writing about the Society of Friends' enforcement of its doctrine, be it in respect to honesty in business or endogamous marriage, have assumed that this engagement was both static over time, and comprehensive. Without conducting empirical studies of Quaker meetings' practice of enforcing the discipline, they took this to have remained constant over the roughly 150-year period from Quakerism's inception to 1800. No attention has been paid to possible changes in the Society of Friends' understanding and execution of its rules regarding debts or marriage. What is more, the meetings' sanctions are assumed to have been complete. Again without testing for this, historians have argued that meetings not only aimed to sanction misbehaviour comprehensively, but also managed to do so. This book addresses these shortcomings. Based on the records of the London Quaker meetings, as well as to a lesser extent the Philadelphia Quaker community, it undertakes the first comparative and empirical study of Quaker business ethics, the Society of Friends' enforcement of debts, and Quaker marriage patterns. Its aim is to establish the actual nature of these three aspects of Quakerism, which economic

---

90   Vann and Eversley, *Friends*, 37.
91   Boulton, 'Widowhood'.

historians have credited with such great influence over both Quaker merchants' success in trade, and British economic development as a whole.

As will be discussed in detail later, few personal papers of individual London Friends from this period survive. This limits our ability to study individual Quakers' responses to meetings' actions, as well as processes that took place in the community outside the meeting house. On the other hand, the surviving records of the Society of Friends' meetings are unusually extensive. They provide rich information on the meetings' activities and how these changed over time. In order to make the best use of the available sources, and be able to draw substantiated conclusions, this book therefore focuses on the Quaker meetings. Through these, it reconstructs the institutional development of the Society of Friends from the 1660s to 1800. It offers a detailed empirical study of London monthly meetings' enforcement of Quaker discipline in areas which economic historians consider important for the conduct of trade.

Chapter two provides an overview of the origins and early history of the Society of Friends. Chapter three introduces the Quaker communities of London and Philadelphia. A special emphasis is placed on what we know about the Quaker merchants of these two ports. Chapter four investigates the nature of Quaker business ethics. Based on the epistles of the London Yearly Meeting and publications of early Quaker leaders including George Fox and William Penn, as well as non-Quaker sermons, it undertakes the first comparative study of Quaker and non-Quaker business ethics. Its aim is to establish whether Quaker business ethics were indeed distinct, and superior to contemporary business ethics of the British mainstream, and whether they may therefore explain Friends' success in trade.

Chapter five shifts the focus onto the means by which meetings enforced Quaker doctrine among their congregations. This and the subsequent chapters make use of the London and Philadelphia monthly meetings' records. Chapter five explains how Quaker discipline was supposed to work, and gives an overview of how Quaker meetings' methods of enforcing discipline developed over the course of the eighteenth century in both cities.

Chapter six introduces the Quaker reform movement of the mid-eigthteenth century and explains how this is reflected in the meeting records. Chapters seven to nine look at how Quaker meetings implemented sanctions for delinquencies against the Quaker discipline regarding the conduct of business, and marital endogamy. These two aspects were chosen for having been identified by the literature as crucial to Quaker commercial success. In chapters seven and eight, I conduct empirical studies of meetings' sanctioning of indebtedness and bankruptcy in the two largest Quaker communities, London and Philadelphia. These were also located in the period's largest Atlantic ports in England and the colonies respectively. Therefore, findings from these studies are significant for Quakers' involvement in trade in general. The records of the meetings in these two locations are unusually complete and supply a wealth of information on their involvement in sanctioning, including that of business offences. I also test the comprehensiveness of the meetings' responses. In other words, did the monthly meetings capture all business failures in their territories? Did they even try to do this? This study faces certain challenges due to the nature of early modern records. The main difficulty lies in identifying Quakers in the non-Quaker records, which frequently provide a person's name only, without any additional information about them. This makes it challenging to link individuals from different records and identify them safely. I do this for a sample of merchants from both London and Philadelphia. Finally, I analyze the surviving papers of London Quaker merchants to try to establish whether Friends feared repercussions from the Society for misconduct in business, and whether this fear led them to act more honestly and diligently.

Chapter nine offers a large-scale study of Quaker marriages and disownments for marrying out, as well as how these developed over time. This is made possible by a unique source available for this community: a database compiled by the Quaker Family History Society. It contains information on almost 10,000 Quaker marriages from the mid-seventeenth to the early eighteenth century. This is complemented by London meeting records of disownments. The study is limited by the scarcity of Friends' personal papers. The sources that do survive provide interesting and colourful insight into the motivation behind marriages and the concerns Friends had about their own and their peers' choices of partners. These sources, however, are too few to allow general conclusions. It also proved difficult to trace individuals who were disowned beyond the actual disownment records themselves, as these often provide only the person's name, but no further information which would make it possible to link them to other records. This made it impossible to establish whom the disowned Friends did marry. The surviving records, however, do show that both Quaker meetings' attitudes towards marital endogamy, and those of the Quaker population as a whole, changed over time, partly explaining the driving forces underlying the Quaker marriage pattern.

By this point in the book, it will have become clear that contrary to what the historiography argues, Quaker institutions changed dramatically between the mid-seventeenth and the end of the eighteenth century. Chapters ten and eleven explain these changes by contextualizing them within contemporary political developments. The book closes by outlining the causal relationship between political crises in colonial Pennsylvania and institutional changes within the Society of Friends. It discusses their impact on the Quakers' reputation and public perception of Friends' honesty in business.

2

The Society of Friends

Quakerism emerged from the most chaotic and violent period in English history: the Civil Wars of the 1640s. For centuries, European monarchs had justified their rule through the 'divine right of kings'. This doctrine held that God himself endowed aristocrats with the right to govern, thus legitimizing the political order in a way that made it impossible for faithful Christian subjects to argue with. From the sixteenth century onwards, the protestant reformation began to call this right into question. Martin Luther translated the Bible into German in 1534. This was not the first translation of the holy book into a European vernacular language. However, the recent invention of the printing press, also in Germany, meant that the Holy Book now became accessible to a large audience. It marked a turning point in Europeans' relationship with their faith. Instead of relying on the interpretation of priests, literate people could now read the Bible for themselves. This led to some interesting discoveries. Readers found that quite a few of the doctrines espoused by the Church had no actual basis in scripture. For instance, it contained very little, if any, basis for the divine right of kings. This discovery fired up unprecedented debate on the distribution of political power across Europe. It set in motion a process culminating in severe political violence. On the continent, protestant and catholic alliances fought each other and ravaged the land in the Thirty Years' War. In the British Isles, the Civil Wars raged from 1641 to 1652. Supporters of the monarchy on the one hand, and of Parliament on the other, had their armies fight over supremacy in the state. The Parliamentarians won. In 1649, they manifested their victory over the monarchists, and their rejection of the divine right of kings, by beheading Charles I. The monarchy turned republic under the leadership of Oliver Cromwell.

These events demonstrate an important feature of early modern European society: in this period, the political and the religious spheres were not separated. It was a deeply religious society that suffered the Civil Wars and which shaped the world in its aftermath. The political transformation England underwent then was the most dramatic imaginable. The divine right of kings represented a strong relationship between worldly and divine power. Parliamentarians, men, had executed the king, supposed bearer of divine endorsement. This act introduced a previously inconceivable fragility of political authority.

Parliamentarian and royal armies had ravaged the country for almost a decade, leaving behind a traumatized population. After experiencing much violence and death, ordinary people set about rebuilding their lives. At the same time, those in power reconstructed the country's political and religious order. These experiences of instability and radical change created a vacuum. In addition to the desire for safety and security, it offered an opening for the creation of a new political and religious order.

During the years immediately following the wars this vacuum was filled by countless new religious sects and movements. The hundreds of groups that sprang up, and the concepts they promoted, reflect the social turmoil seventeenth-century English women and men found themselves in. The new movements were strongly influenced by millennialism, the belief that the world was corrupted and coming to an end. This prospect led believers to aim for a radical reform of society and church. They promoted new ideas about what the relationship between God and people ought to look like, and what form worship ought to take. As the authority of Crown and Church had been challenged and overthrown, the notion that social hierarchies might be reordered did not appear far-fetched. This included not only the relationships between people of different stations, but also that between the sexes. In some of the new groups, women held unusually high and autonomous positions. They further expressed their rejection of traditional authorities and social structures by refusing to doff hats before supposed superiors, or addressing each other with 'thee' and 'thou', instead of the more formal 'you'. Some would not swear oaths. Based on scripture, they argued that swearing oaths implied that one did not speak the truth in other instances. Actually being truthful all the time made oaths obsolete. Changing the names of the days and months to purify them from pagan notions was also popular. Many of these groups rejected academic interpretations of the Bible – their way of rebelling against elite Church leadership and 'experts'. Following this logic, professional clergy became obsolete.

One of the groups sharing these ideas were the Quakers. The Quaker movement started in the English East Midlands, through the linking of a number of local religious groups with similar ideas. Quakerism's core belief since its beginning has been the immediate relationship between individuals and God. Friends believe that direct communication with the divine is possible for everyone.[1] Therefore, the individual religious participation of those 'convinced' was central. At meetings, they might sit completely silent for as long as two or three hours, each listening for the voice of God within.[2] Alternatively,

---

[1] Carole Dale Spencer, 'Quakers in Theological Context', in *The Oxford Handbook of Quaker Studies*, ed. Angell and Dandelion; Stephen W. Angell, 'God, Christ, and the Light', in *The Oxford Handbook of Quaker Studies*, ed. Angell and Dandelion.

[2] Rosemary Anne Moore, *The Light in Their Consciences: Early Quakers in Britain, 1646–1666* (University Park: Pennsylvania State University Press, 2000), 144.

they 'quaked'. Early Friends trembled, shook and spoke in tongues. For these believers, 'quaking' was an outward manifestation of the inward workings of the power of God. Following the idea of immediate communication between believer and God further, Friends of the 1650s wanted to abolish the Church of England as obsolete and oppressive. They refused to support it through paying tithes. What is more, they began a kind of guerrilla war, interrupting services and verbally attacking ministers.[3] Friends recognized, however, that they did require certain services the Church had so far provided, and sought to offer their followers an alternative. Quaker meetings began providing for their poor, as the parish usually did. They also started to solemnize marriages. But early Friends not only rejected the authority of the church, they took issue with secular power as well. While civil government was to be respected, they argued, it had no rights over the church (themselves). Essentially, they insisted on choosing which laws they would obey, while rejecting all those they did not agree with. Unsurprisingly, this attitude towards the law did not endear them to the authorities.

From the 1650s onwards, Quaker lay ministers travelled between meetings in order to preach. Their journeys took English Friends through their own counties, as well as to continental Europe and the Americas. American Friends, in turn, visited meetings across the colonies and in England.[4] How many of these women and men there were is difficult to tell, as the records are incomplete. What sources survive suggest that on average about 100 ministers were active per decade during the seventeenth and early eighteenth centuries.[5] These ministers stemmed from a broad range of socio-economic backgrounds, and included both women and men.[6] They financed their trips from various sources. Often their home meetings contributed towards the costs of their journey.[7] Moreover, during the 1650s, several funds were set up to support Friends' causes. Most prominent among these was the Kendal Fund, part of whose purpose was the financing of travelling ministers.[8] Finally, and importantly, ministers funded

---

3 Barry Reay, *The Quakers and the English Revolution* (London: Temple Smith, 1985), throughout, examples 35–37.
4 Margaret Hope Bacon, 'Quaker Women in Overseas Ministry,' *Quaker History* 77, no. 2 (1988).
5 Naomi Pullin, *Female Friends and the Making of Transatlantic Quakerism, 1650–1750* (Cambridge: Cambridge University Press, 2018), 13; Jordan Landes, *London Quakers in the Trans-atlantic World: The Creation of an Early Modern Community* (2015), 41–47, offers a detailed discussion of the Morning Meeting's records regarding travelling ministers up to c. 1720.
6 Sarah Crabtree, *Holy Nation: The Transatlantic Quaker Ministry in an Age of Revolution* (Chicago: University of Chicago Press, 2015), cited in Pullin, *Female Friends*, 189.
7 Pullin, *Female Friends*, 101.
8 Kate Peters, 'The Dissemination of Quaker Pamphlets in the 1650s', in *Not Dead Things* (Leiden: Brill, 2013), 221; see also Landes, *London Quakers*, 26; Moore, *Light in Their Consciences*, 24, 25.

their trips by combining them with business.⁹ Evidence suggests that George Fox traded iron on his trip to Europe in 1677. William Penn is often thought to have used his missionary trip to the Rhine valley the same year to find investors for his newly chartered colony in America.¹⁰

Together, these 'public Friends' helped tie the individual meetings together and create a single, transatlantic community. Thanks to their efforts, the Quaker movement spread rapidly. By the mid-1650s, Quakerism had taken root all over England and Wales.¹¹ The missionaries also succeeded in founding various small Quaker communities in northern Germany and the Dutch Republic, but most of these were short-lived. More successful were their efforts to recruit new Friends and set up meetings in the American colonies. Soon there were Quaker communities in Barbados, Jamaica, New England and, importantly, Pennsylvania.

Within a decade, between 35,000 and 40,000 women and men had turned Quaker, making the movement the most successful among the revolutionary sects.¹² They were as numerous as or larger than other major religious minorities, such as Catholics, Fifth Monarchists or Baptists. Meetings increasingly connected and began to grow into a formal organization. The first headquarters were at Swarthmoor Hall, the home of early Quaker leader Margaret Fell, in the far north of England. While Friends still constituted less than 1 per cent of the total population, their rapid increase in numbers combined with their attitude towards Crown and Church alarmed the authorities. As Barry Reay put it, Quakerism became 'a national problem rather than a regional nuisance'.¹³ Early Friends thought they represented the one true way of believing, and that all other religious bodies had it wrong. They attacked ministers and disrupted sermons, and some engaged in rather erratic behaviour. This included cases of individual Quakers 'walking naked as a sign'. One Friend is even reported to have dug up a corpse, commanding it, 'in the name of the living God, to arise and walk'.¹⁴ The most prominent of these erratic instances, however, was when James Nayler, one of the movement's leaders, rode into Bristol on a horse on Easter Sunday in 1656, apparently emulating Jesus's entry into Jerusalem.¹⁵

---

9 S. Juterszenka, 'Meeting Friends and Doing Business: Quaker Missionary and Commercial Activities in Europe, 1655–1720', in *German Historical Institute London, Bulletin, Supplement no. 2: Cosmopolitan Networks in Commerce and Society, 1660–1914*, ed. Andreas Gestrich and Margit Schulte-Beerbuehl (London: German Historical Institute London, 2011), 198.
10 Ibid., 198, 199.
11 Moore, *Light in Their Consciences*, 131.
12 Reay, *The Quakers and the English Revolution*, 11.
13 Ibid., 10.
14 Ibid., 108.
15 Moore, *Light in Their Consciences*, 39.

These incidents provoked a lot of negative reactions and added to the popular animosity that met Friends during the 1650s. Barry Reay summed this up as 'a mixture of xenophobia, class hatred, ignorance and a superstition that merged with the world of witchcraft ... Quakers were hated as political radicals, as social and religious deviants, and in some cases as economic middlemen.'[16] In the face of the severe reputational damage acts such as Nayler's caused the movement, the meeting organization took a genius step: it introduced the Society of Friends' first public relations campaign. The seventeenth century's prime medium for disseminating information and ideas was the pamphlet. Friends used these expertly to improve their reputation. During their first decade, the Quakers produced over 1000 pamphlets. The meeting organization carefully controlled their content, printing and distribution. The pamphlets targeted audiences where they might have the greatest possible impact. One of its greatest successes was the appropriation of the term 'Quaker'. This was initially derogatory. It referred to early Friends' pentecostal forms of worship, which included shaking and speaking in tongues. In their campaign, Friends made sure the term appeared immediately visible in large print on all their publications.[17]

In 1660 the Commonwealth came to an end, and Charles II ascended the throne. England was a monarchy once more. The new king immediately ordered a crackdown on religious extremists. The Church of England set about redefining its identity by taking stock and ordering its beliefs. As part of this process, it ejected parish ministers who were insufficiently conformist to the new canon. In January 1661 another sect, the Fifth Monarchists, staged an uprising in London and tried to take control of the capital. In response, the government came down hard on dissenters. Authorities across the country arrested Quakers at meetings, their homes, their places of work and off the streets. By March nearly 5,000 Friends were in prison, and hundreds died there. Old Elizabethan and Jacobean statutes, intended originally for use against Catholics, were revived to deal with the movement. In addition, the Quaker Act of 1662 and the better-known Conventicle Act of 1664 aimed at consolidating the primacy of the Church of England and the Crown. They forbade religious assemblies of more than five people outside the structure of the Anglican Church. They demanded all subjects swear an oath of loyalty to the Crown. Quakers would not swear, and as a consequence many were fined, imprisoned or transported to the colonies.[18] In order to protect Friends in this situation of increased persecution and suffering, their leadership issued a number of letters and statements

---

16 Barry Reay, 'Popular Hostility towards Quakers in Mid-Seventeenth-Century England', *Social History* 5, no. 3 (1980).
17 Kate Peters, *Print Culture and the Early Quakers* (Cambridge: Cambridge University Press, 2005).
18 Reay, *The Quakers and the English Revolution*, 106.

in which they emphasized Quakerism's peaceful nature. Over the course of the following two centuries, these ideas would be developed into what is now known as the Quaker Peace Testimony. Particularly important among the publications of the Restoration period was George Fox's aptly titled 'Declaration from the Harmless and Innocent People of God, Called Quakers'.[19] Through such publications the movement sought to assure the government that they were a non-violent community that respected state authority and posed no threat. They formally declared their loyalty to the monarch.

Also in order to meet the challenge of persecution, over the course of the 1660s, Friends expanded their rudimentary organization of meetings in order to help suffering Quaker communities to stay in touch and support each other, both spiritually and financially.[20] Furthermore, this allowed Friends to respond to persecution by collecting information about victims and using that information to lobby politically for Quaker interests. The organization grew into a sophisticated, hierarchical structure spanning from Danzig on the Baltic to the West Indies. At the lowest tier stood the local meetings for worship. They dispatched representatives to the monthly meetings, or meetings for business. These in turn sent emissaries to the quarterly meetings, who in turn chose members to represent them at the highest body, the Yearly Meetings. The first of these was London Yearly Meeting, which first sat in 1668. It would play an important role in coordination and church government. Friends in their meetings everywhere read its epistles, and it acted as an attorney for Quaker concerns. From 1682 onwards, it monitored the development of the community by requesting all quarterly meetings submit annual reports in which they responded to three queries. These concerned the number of Friends within the quarterly meetings' jurisdiction imprisoned for their faith, how many had been released since the previous year, and how many died in prison.[21] These questions reflect that persecution was the Quakers' greatest concern at the time. As the community's circumstances changed in the following decades, the

---

19 J. Stubbs, G. Fox and R. Hubberthorn, *A Declaration from the Harmless & Innocent People of God, Called: Quakers Against All Plotters and Fighters in the World. For the Removing Of the Ground of Jealousie and Suspition from Both Magistrates and People in the Kingdome, Concerinig Wars and Fightings. And Also Something in Answer to that Clause of the King's Late Proclamation, which Mentions the Quakers, to Clear Them from the Plot and Fighting, which Therein is Mentioned, and for the Clearing Their Innocency. This Declaration was Given Unto the King, Upon the 21st Day of the 11th Month, 1660* (J. Bringhust, 1684).
20 Sylvia Stevens, 'Travelling Ministry', in *The Oxford Handbook of Quaker Studies*, ed. Angell and Dandelion.
21 R. E. Stagg, 'Friends' Queries and General Advices: A Survey of their Development in London Yearly Meeting, 1682–1860', *Journal of the Friends Historical Society* 49 (1961), 229.

queries were amended and updated according to the context in which Quakers found themselves at the time.[22]

Additional Yearly Meetings followed in different parts of the British Empire, including Philadelphia in 1685. The organization also included a number of meetings specializing in resistance and fighting persecution. Among these, the Meeting for Sufferings and the Second Day's Morning Meeting deserve special attention. As the London Yearly Meeting convened for only a few days annually, the Meeting for Sufferings and the Morning Meeting served as its standing representative organs throughout the year.

Friends founded the Meeting for Sufferings in 1675. Its task was to defend Quaker interests vis-à-vis external threats, especially those issuing from political authorities. It did this by gathering information about Quaker victims of persecution and then taking political action against it. Regional and local meetings submitted reports about members of their congregations being imprisoned for their faith or having their property confiscated to the Meeting for Sufferings. The Meeting used the information the organization provided to lobby Parliament for the relief of persecuted Friends, until in 1689 it adopted the Toleration Act. The Meeting furthermore instigated defensive actions against bills about to be introduced to Parliament which were expected to disadvantage or discriminate against Quakers. In addition, positive action was taken.[23] The Meeting pursued a seven-year campaign for the Affirmation Bill, which from 1695 onwards allowed Friends to replace oaths with affirmations, when dealing with official business. Moreover, there were attempts to organize the Quaker vote in Parliamentary elections through the meeting network. The Meeting for Sufferings continued its work as a political lobby for Friends' interests throughout the eighteenth century.[24]

While the Meeting for Sufferings was in charge of defending the Society on the political front, the Second Day's Morning Meeting managed the movement's message. The first records detailing its activities stem from 1673. Its tasks included the oversight over travelling ministers. It issued certificates confirming that the minister had the approval of the Society to travel and preach. It also followed these Friends' progress through correspondence and receiving reports after they returned. The Meeting further censored all publications by Friends respecting the Society. Everything had to be approved by the Meeting before it could be printed.[25] Through these efforts, the Meeting unified the growing

---

22 David J. Hall, 'What Should Eighteenth Century Quakers Have Read?,' *Journal of the Friends Historical Society* 62, no. 2 (2018).
23 Ethyn Williams Kirby, 'The Quakers' Efforts to Secure Civil and Religious Liberty, 1660–96', *Journal of Modern History* 7, no. 4 (1935).
24 Alison Olson, 'The Lobbying of London Quakers for Pennsylvania Friends', *Pennsylvania Magazine of History and Biography* 117, no. 3 (1993).
25 Landes, *London Quakers*, 26.

and dispersed Quaker communities into a single movement, and consolidated its beliefs into a coherent message.

The multitude of different Quaker meetings kept closely in touch with each other. The London Yearly Meeting kept the congregations abreast of developments through annual epistles which it sent to all monthly meetings. They included reports on the state of different Quaker communities all over the Western world, especially in respect of state persecution. By 1700 the number of Quaker meetings had grown substantially. In the British Empire alone the Society of Friends counted about 50,000 members.[26]

The largest single Quaker community throughout the seventeenth and eighteenth centuries was that of London. The second most important community of the period was located in Philadelphia. Political and religious events taking place in these two locations influenced the development of Quakerism as a whole. Moreover, London was the world's biggest port in this period. During the eighteenth century, Philadelphia's trade expanded to a degree that made it surpass both Boston and New York as commercial hubs, and become North America's primary port. Thus, studying the institutional development of the Society of Friends in these two communities is crucial to understanding the relationship between Quakers, trade and economic development. The next chapters therefore introduce the London and Philadelphia Quaker communities in more detail.

---

26 Fredrick Tolles, 'The Trans-atlantic Quaker Community in the Seventeenth Century', *Huntington Library Quarterly* 14, no. 3 (1951), 243. Quaker population numbers have long been controversial. Andrew Fincham sums up the debate, and estimates that in c. 1700 overall Quaker numbers were between 45,000 and 50,000. However, the data on which he bases his projections suffers from several weaknesses. For instance, the nineteenth-century census he uses to extrapolate from does not include Friends of Gracechurch Street Monthly Meeting in London, which was one of the largest meetings. I therefore think 50,000 more likely than 45,000. Andrew Fincham, 'Faith in Numbers: Re-quantifying the English Quaker Population during the Long Eighteenth Century', *Religions* 10, no. 2 (2019).

3

The Quaker Communities of London and Philadelphia

London Friends

Londoners first encountered Friends in the autumn of 1654, when Quaker missionaries to the city reported successes among groups of Seekers and Baptists.[1] During 1657 and 1658 the Quaker headquarters moved from Swarthmoor, Cumbria, to the capital. London presented an ideal base for an Atlantic-wide faith. Together, the metropolis's political and economic pre-eminence would shape the Quaker community – and vice versa. Home to the emerging empire's political leadership, it allowed the Meeting for Sufferings to lobby Parliament and the Crown on behalf of Friends' interests. The city's centrality for the growing colonial trades facilitated easy communication with Friends in the Americas.

London had held a central place in the English economy for centuries.[2] Its prosperity was based on the presence of the court, Parliament and the central law courts. It was the country's biggest manufacturing centre as well as a hub for local and foreign trade.[3] During the early modern period the city emerged as first the nation's, and then Europe's pre-eminent port. London merchants led England's participation in long-distance trade in the second half of the seventeenth century. Particularly important became trade with the American colonies.[4] During the 1640s, colonists introduced sugar into Barbados. It proved a huge success. European indentured servants and an ever-increasing number of enslaved Africans worked the plantations.[5] Over the course of the

---

1   Reay, *Revolution*, 10.
2   Perry Gauci, *Emporium of the World: The Merchants of London, 1660–1800* (London: Hambledon Continuum, 2007), 12.
3   Zahedieh, *Capital*, 21; A.L. Beier, 'Engine of Manufacture: The Trades of London', in *London, 1500–1700: The Making of the Metropolis*, ed. A. L. Beier and Roger Finlay (London: Longman, 1986).
4   Zahedieh, *Capital*, 21.
5   Ibid., 29.

following decades, England expanded its possessions in the Caribbean, and with this grew the production of sugar and tobacco. As demand for plantation produce grew, so did the enslaved population in the Caribbean: while in 1660 there were 34,000 enslaved African men, women and children toiling in the English West Indies, by 1700 their number had grown to 115,000.[6] By that time, almost 20 per cent of London's imports consisted of plantation produce, part of which was re-exported to continental Europe.[7] In exchange, London merchants exported English manufactured goods to the Caribbean. These made up 15 per cent of the metropolis's total exports.[8]

The plantation economies continued to expand over the course of the eighteenth century. To supply them with cheap labour, Britain became the world's largest slave trading nation. The trade in slaves and slave-produced goods fuelled the growth of the middle class. This group forged a communal identity through consumption. They adopted the habit of drinking Asian tea, which they supplemented with Caribbean sugar. Friends were part of this emerging socio-economic group. They rose to respectability and wealth by trading in slave-produced goods, and firmly established themselves among the middling sorts by joining in the consumption habits that slavery enabled, and that scholars have since termed the 'consumer revolution'.[9]

The growth of London's trade was closely linked to its demographic developments. The city experienced a population boom in the mid- to late seventeenth century, which was fuelled by migration. With higher wages and affordable bread prices, London was an attractive destination. The city provided apprenticeships and training for migrants from the provinces, as well as employment. In 1650 it counted about half a million inhabitants; by 1700 there may have been as many as 757,000. By the turn of the nineteenth century, close to a million called London home.[10] The large population meant that merchants had a large market right on their doorsteps. As the city was also a centre of manufacturing, goods for export were easily available, too.[11]

These same reasons that made the city attractive to migrants also applied to Friends. Community support additionally made settlement easier. Early modern London was home to six Quaker monthly meetings. The Bull & Mouth, later Gracechurch Street, and Devonshire House were the oldest, dating back as some form of Quaker gathering places to Friends' first appearance in the capital in the

---

6   Ibid., 33.
7   Gauci, *Emporium*.
8   Zahedieh, *Capital*, 10.
9   See for instance Maxine Berg and Elizabeth Eger, *Luxury in the Eighteenth Century: Debates, Desires, and Delectable Goods* (Basingstoke: Palgrave Macmillan, 2003).
10 E. A. Wrigley, 'A Simple Model of London's Importance in Changing English Society and Economy 1650–1750', *Past & Present* 37 (1967).
11 Gauci, *Emporium*, 13.

1650s.[12] Both were located quite close to each other, in the City. They were at the heart of Quaker 'colonies', areas with particularly dense Quaker populations.[13]

Horsleydown monthly meeting was located in Southwark, just to the southern end of London Bridge. Judging by the extent of its records, together with Devonshire House and Gracechurch Street, it constituted the largest meeting in the capital. Three smaller meetings included the Peel, in Clerkenwell, and Westminster and Ratcliff monthly meetings, which were named for the neighbourhoods they were located in to the west and east of the City respectively. Starting in the 1750s, each of these meetings set up separate women's monthly meetings. Until then, male and female Friends appear to have worked in the monthly meetings together.[14] Between them, these meetings shared the task of administering the community.

The Society of Friends did not clearly define membership at this point. It was regular for individuals to attend meetings for worship of several denominations at the same time, or move back and forth between them. Quaker meetings registered marriages, the births of Friends' children and burials. The six London monthly meetings' extensive birth, marriage and death records survive. They allow rough estimates of the size of the congregations from the seventeenth to early nineteenth centuries. Similar in form to parish registers, the Quaker vital records are considered by demographic historians to be the best available for the early modern period. The London Quaker meetings' records suggest that the number of those in some way associated with the Society peaked in the late 1670s and 1680s at between 5,000 and 8,000 Friends. From around 1700 these numbers declined steadily until the 1720s, which saw a pronounced drop.[15] They then plateaued until the nineteenth century. This trend, depicted in figure 1, is in line with the most recent estimates of the development of the English Quaker population as a whole during the eighteenth century.[16] Moreover, the overall population of London tripled from roughly half a million in the 1670s to c. 1.5 million in 1815. Hence, the Quaker community shrank not only in absolute numbers, but even more so relative to the population of the city as a whole.

As the community's size changed, so did its socio-economic composition. Seventeenth-century London Friends were represented in all occupational

---

12 William Beck et al., *The London Friends' Meetings: Showing the Rise of the Society of Friends in London; Its Progress, and the Development of Its Discipline; with Accounts of the Various Meeting-Houses and Burial-Grounds, Their History and General Associations* (London: Pronoun Press, 2009).
13 Gary Stuart De Krey, 'Trade, Religion, and Politics in London in the Reign of William III' (doctoral thesis, 1979), 144.
14 Beck et al., *London Friends' Meetings*, 353, 354; see also Pullin, *Female Friends*, 96.
15 Simon Dixon, 'Quaker Communities in London, 1667–c. 1714' (doctoral thesis, University of London, 2006), 42, 43.
16 Fincham, 'Numbers'.

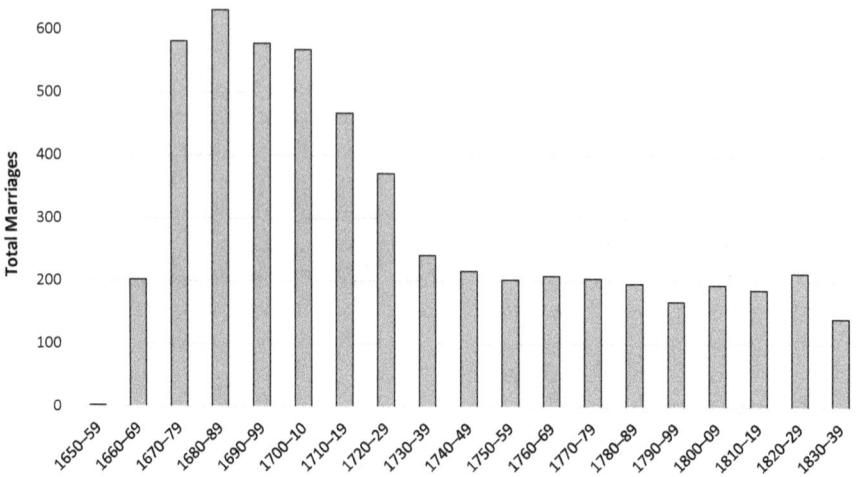

Figure 1. London Quaker Marriages
Sources: Quaker Family History Society Database (QFHSDB)

groups except the learned professions.[17] However, Simon Dixon found that 'Quakers in the humbler industrial trades far outnumbered those from the commercial strata.'[18] In this they matched their non-Quaker contemporaries. A comparison with the 1692 Poll Tax, levied to finance military expenses, showed the distribution of Friends among different occupations to have been 'remarkably close' to that of the overall population. The distribution of occupations changed over time. Until the 1690s, more Friends engaged in 'making' activities than in 'dealing'. This focus shifted in the period 1690–1719, when Friends became increasingly involved in 'dealing', a trend which continued throughout the eighteenth century.[19] The occupations of Quaker bride grooms as registered in marriage certificates show ever fewer Friends making their living in manufacturing, while ever more earned their living in commerce. What is more, the share of merchants increased from less than 0.5 per cent in the

17 The socio-economic background of early English Quakers was long subject to debate, but the question appears to be settled now. They stemmed predominantly from the lower middling strata of society. The debate is summed up in Dixon, 'Quaker Communities'. Individual publications which were important in the debate include Adrian Davies, *The Quakers in English Society, 1655–1725* (Oxford: Clarendon Press, 2000); Judith Hurwich, 'The Social Origins of the Early Quakers', *Past & Present* 48 (1961); Vann, *Social Development*.
18 W. A. Cole, 'The Quakers and Politics, 1652–1660' (doctoral thesis, University of Cambridge, 1956), 115.
19 Dixon, 'Quaker Communities', 87.

1660s to 6.5 per cent by the mid-eighteenth century, from when it stagnated. In general, we consider occupations that focus on dealing to belong to higher-income groups than occupations that focus on making. The occupations the Quaker marriage records list therefore indicate that the London community grew increasingly prosperous as the eighteenth century went by.

Table 1. London Quaker Bridegroom Occupations

Years	Dealers (%)	Makers (%)	Other (%)	Total Known Cases
1720–29	29.4	59.2	11.4	306
1730–39	27.6	50.8	21.6	181
1740–49	27.3	53.6	19.0	179
1750–59	30.0	54.7	15.3	150
1760–69	31.6	57.0	11.4	158
1770–79	36.9	51.0	12.1	149
1780–89	41.6	48.9	9.5	137
1790–99	43.1	36.7	20.2	109
1800–09	36.5	47.5	16.1	137
1810–19	58.7	28.6	12.7	126
1820–29	55.8	31.8	12.4	129
1830–39	51.5	31.7	16.8	101

Source: Quaker Family History Society Database, Marriages. The category 'other' includes employment in agriculture, building, services, transport and miscellaneous.

Table 2. Merchants among London Quaker Bridegrooms

Years	Marriage Total	Merchants	% of Merchants out of total marriages
1660–70	225	1	0.4
1695–1705	632	23	3.6
1745–1755	199	13	6.6
1795–1805	193	12	6.2

Source: Quaker Family History Society Database, Marriages.

The diverse ways in which London Friends made their living furthermore suggests that they did not keep to themselves. We have evidence that seventeenth- and eighteenth-century Friends took part in community life beyond the meeting house, and that economic and social interactions between Quakers and followers of other beliefs were common. For example, the records of the London livery companies, who until the mid-eighteenth century held important economic as well as political influence, provide evidence for Friends' integration into London society. At least 600 male Friends were freemen, and about two-thirds of London Quaker apprentices trained with non-Quaker masters. As being an apprentice involved living in the household of one's master, this is evidence that London Friends enjoyed strong cross-religious ties. What is more, we often find Friends holding parish offices. This occurred not only in London, but from the 1660s onwards across England and Wales.[20]

The relationship between Friends and others is significant as it speaks to the community's ability to influence and control the lives and conduct of its members. The more cut off the community was from its surroundings, the costlier exit would have been for individual Friends, thus increasing the community's power over the individual. That London Friends had close cross-religious ties is also indicated by their experiences with persecution. Research has shown that this varied greatly across England.[21] London Friends appear to have been comparatively lucky. During periods of persecution between the 1660s and the 1680s, metropolitan Quakers frequently received assistance from their neighbours. When Friends' houses were raided and goods confiscated in lieu of fines, neighbours sometimes bought the goods back and returned them to their owners. What is more, officers of the parish, who were drawn from the neighbourhood, sometimes refused to carry out orders to disperse Quaker meetings. Simon Dixon concluded that 'By the 1680s entire parishes were adopting a policy of non-cooperation with the London authorities with regard to enforcing the conventicle legislation.'[22]

The limited surviving records of individual Friends, especially for the seventeenth century, allow only small glimpses into their daily lives.[23] Extant are the journals of clothier Norris Purslow, c. 1690–1737, tobacconist Peter Briggins,

---

20 Dixon, 'Quaker Communities', 238.
21 Bill Stevenson, 'The Social Integration of Post-Restoration Dissenters, 1660–1725', in *The World of Rural Dissenters 1520–1725*, ed. Margaret Spufford (Cambridge: Cambridge University Press, 1995) and Davies, *The Quakers in English Society*, 185–88, argue that Friends were well integrated with wider society. John Miller, '"A Suffering People": English Quakers and their Neighbours, c. 1650–c. 1700', *Past and Present* 188, no. 1 (2005), is more critical but leaves some room for integration; for London see Dixon, 'Quaker Communities', 238.
22 Dixon, 'Quaker Communities', 235.
23 Ibid., 275.

from 1706 to 1708, and an account book of apothecary Thomas Mayleigh from roughly the same period. These records contain information on the business and social networks of the three men. All three drew on contacts who were co-religionists, but were also in touch with non-Quakers. Purslow joined an astrological society, and even became its president. At least one close contact of Briggins can be safely identified as non-Quaker. Evidence from records of the chancery court additionally shows that Friends were frequently involved, either as plaintiffs or as defendants, in commercial litigation with non-Quakers.[24] The source situation is slightly better for the mid- and later eighteenth century, when correspondence and diaries of several London Friends survive. They equally demonstrate that the writers had cross-religious ties, and will be discussed in more detail later. The diary of seventeen-year-old Betty Fothergill presents an exception. It shows that she spent much of her time socializing, and all her contacts appear to be fellow Friends. This is the only source of a female Friend we have for London. Men and women had different patterns of social interaction. It is possible that among Quakers, these included differences in the extent of cross-religious social ties. Finally, as we will see in chapter seven, it was not uncommon for Friends to marry outside the Society. Taken together, the evidence from personal and court records suggests that the contacts of Quakers, either socially or commercially, were not restricted to their co-religionists.

Philadelphia Friends

While persecution in England continued, Friends successfully sought ways to escape. One of their own, William Penn, managed to obtain permission to found a colony in America. Penn was the son of an influential admiral and friend to King Charles II, who borrowed heavily from the elder Penn. When he passed away, William inherited these outstanding debts. William Penn and Charles II reached an agreement: to settle his debts, Charles granted William a charter in 1681 for his very own colony in America: Pennsylvania. The first ships carrying Quaker colonizers laid anchor in the Delaware River in 1682. Their goal was to live peacefully and undisturbed in the 'way of truth'.

In order to fund the venture, Penn presented it not only as a religious endeavour, but also as an investment opportunity.[25] He founded a joint-stock company.[26] The 'free society of traders' was invested with privileges in trade

---

24 For instance Bankruptcy Commission Docket Books: Peter Briggins, 1716; John Eliot and Philip Eliot 1723, 1731, 1733; John Eliot Jr 1730; John Eliot 1726, 1731, 1736, 1737, 1743; Joseph Ormston 1706, 1710, 1716, 1741.
25 Gary B. Nash, 'The Free Society of Traders and the Early Politics of Pennsylvania', *Pennsylvania Magazine of History and Biography* 89, no. 2 (1965), 149.
26 Ibid., 148.

and the economic exploitation of the Delaware Valley. Penn and his associates needed to raise £20,000. They advertised the project in England, Ireland and Scotland. Initially very successful, stocks sold rapidly in 1682.[27] Both Friends and non-Friends invested in the company. Some planned to settle in Pennsylvania themselves, others remained in London and regarded the colony purely as a business opportunity.[28] A significant part of the investors were wealthy Quaker merchants.[29]

As one if its first tasks, the Free Society organized for indentured servants to be brought as agricultural labour to the colony, to produce goods to export to other American colonies. The company was further to engage in whaling, fishing, manufacturing linen and exploring mining opportunities.[30] However, the company from the beginning suffered from mismanagement by its officers in Philadelphia. Rumours of this got back to London, leading subscribers to withhold payments. This resulted in financial shortages, which further inhibited the company's success. It proved unable to enforce the privileges its charter granted against individual merchants, who soon flocked to the Delaware Valley from other colonies in the Americas.[31] Within less than a decade, the company failed miserably. By the end of 1686, the Free Society of Traders 'was all but defunct'.[32] While the Free Society of Traders failed, however, the colony itself proved a great success.[33]

European conquest and African slavery

The area that was to become Pennsylvania was initially inhabited by native Americans. The Lenni Lenape, whom the Europeans called the Delaware Indians, had long settled in what is today south-eastern Pennsylvania and southern New Jersey. European colonists, especially Swedes, had started moving into their land in the early seventeenth century. When the English began claiming the area, European colonization accelerated. Over time, the Europeans would deprive the Indian population of ever greater parts of their land, sometimes through purchase, often by means of deceit and violence.[34]

The first European colonists in Pennsylvania included both Friends and followers of other faiths. As the first great wave of immigration ended in 1685,

27 Ibid., 154, 155.
28 Mary K. Geiter, 'Notes and Documents: London Merchants and the Launching of Pennsylvania', *Pennsylvania Magazine of History and Biography* 121, no. 1/2 (1997), 101.
29 Nash, 'The Free Society of Traders', 156.
30 Ibid., 154.
31 Ibid., 158–62.
32 Ibid., 173.
33 Gary B. Nash, *Quakers and Politics: Pennsylvania, 1681–1726*, new edn (Boston: Northeastern University Press, 1993), 56.
34 Brycchan Carey, *From Peace to Freedom: Quaker Rhetoric and the Birth of American Antislavery, 1657–1761* (New Haven, CT: Yale University Press, 2012), 11.

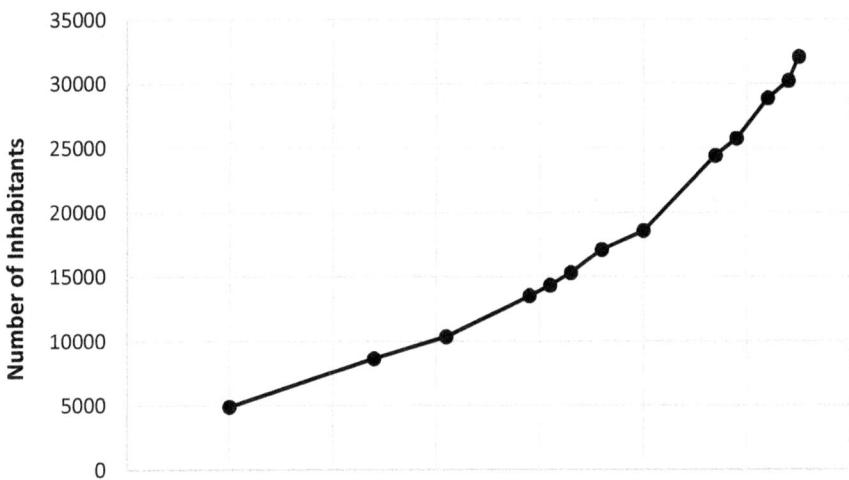

Figure 2. Population of Philadelphia, European descent
Source: Billy Smith, Death and Life in a Colonial Immigrant City

almost 8,000 migrants had arrived in Pennsylvania. Roughly a third of these early colonists were indentured servants.[35] Those who arrived in the colony as free women and men made their living as artisans and yeomen. Around the year 1700, Friends in the colony became outnumbered by Europeans of other denominations. However, they continued to dominate its political and economic life until the mid-eighteenth century. For instance, the majority of Philadelphia's mayors, and large numbers of the colony's overseas merchants, were Friends.[36]

The European population of the colony's capital, Philadelphia, is estimated to have been around 2,000 in 1690. Probably a little over half of them were Quakers. Population numbers remained steady for the next twenty years. Then, they began to grow exponentially, climbing to almost 5,000 in 1720. In 1760 Philadelphia monthly meeting registered 2,250 members, about 12 per cent of the city's overall population. On the eve of the Revolution, Philadelphia counted 32,000 inhabitants.[37]

35 Nash, *Quakers and Politics*, 50–52.
36 Tolles, *Meeting*, 12, 64; Richard Bauman, *For the Reputation of Truth: Politics, Religion, and Conflict among the Pennsylvania Quakers, 1750–1800* (Baltimore, MD: Johns Hopkins University Press, 1971), 1,2.
37 Billy G. Smith, 'Death and Life in a Colonial Immigrant City: A Demographic Analysis of Philadelphia', *Journal of Economic History* 37, no. 4 (1977).

From the very beginning, African slavery was a part of everyday life in Pennsylvania. The colony's Quaker founders unquestioningly planned to use forced African labour to build their 'holy experiment'. The first arrivals brought enslaved Africans with them. When preparing his move to Philadelphia in 1683, London Quaker merchant James Claypoole wrote to his brother Edward in Barbados with a request for slaves:

> I think I must have 2 Negroe men, strong fellows and a boy and Girle, so I advise thee, yt when thou meets with such as may be proper (?) for ye Country and my occasion to keep them for mee: The boy & girl may bee from 12 to 17 years old or between 10 and 15.[38]

Similarly, Quaker merchant Jonathan Dickinson brought ten enslaved Africans from Jamaica when he first sailed for Philadelphia.[39]

In December 1684, two years after Friends first began building the city, a shipload of 150 enslaved Africans had been brought to Philadelphia.[40] Thus, Africans made up at least 7.5 per cent of Philadelphia's population from its earliest days. Friends were the largest slave owners in Pennsylvania during the seventeenth century, and Friends and enslaved Africans lived and worked in close proximity with each other in Philadelphia.[41] We lack reliable statistical data for slavery in Pennsylvania for the years following this first shipment.[42] The scattered evidence we do have stems from inventories of estates and burial records. These sources provide an insight into the general development of slavery and slave ownership in the city. They suggest that about one in fifteen Philadelphia families owned slaves during the seventeenth century.[43] In the summer of 1712, a slave revolt in New York taught white Pennsylvanians to fear violence from captive Africans. In response, they demanded the import of enslaved workers be limited, or abolished entirely. The Pennsylvania assembly thereupon raised the import duties on slaves to £20 per capita. The same revolt also led some Pennsylvania Quakers to address the Philadelphia Yearly Meeting, unsuccessfully requesting that it force all Friends to withdraw from the slavery business.[44]

---

38 James Claypoole to his brother Edward Claypoole, London, 27th of the fourth month 1682, James Claypoole, Letter book 1681–84, Historical Society of Pennsylvania, 227.
39 Darold D. Wax, 'Quaker Merchants and the Slave Trade in Colonial Pennsylvania', *Pennsylvania Magazine of History and Biography* 86, no. 2 (1962), 148.
40 Gary B. Nash, 'Slaves and Slaveowners in Colonial Philadelphia', *William and Mary Quarterly* 30 (1973), 255.
41 Jason Daniels, 'Protest and Participation: Reconsidering the Quaker Slave Trade in Early Eighteenth-Century Philadelphia', *Pennsylvania History* 85, no. 2 (2018), 239, 247.
42 Nash, 'Slaves and Slaveowners', 247.
43 Ibid., 226.
44 Daniels, 'Protest', 247.

Table 3. Estimated Numbers of Enslaved Africans in Philadelphia

Year	Estimated number of enslaved people	% of total population
1767	1,392	8.8
1769	1,270	7.9
1772	1,069	5.9
1773	945	5.1
1774	869	4.5
1775	672	3.4

Source: Gary Nash, *Slaves and Slaveholding in Philadelphia*, 237.

As a consequence of the higher import duties, the African population probably did not grow much over the following years. After it was abolished in 1731 slave imports seared for about a decade, then dropped off again for reasons we cannot yet explain.[45] The beginning of the Seven Years' War in 1756 marked a turning point in the development of African slavery in Philadelphia. European indentured labourers became scarce as they were recruited into the British military. Pennsylvanians responded to the succeeding shortage of labour by importing unprecedented numbers of enslaved Africans.[46] The decade from 1755 to 1765 saw the peak of slave trading in Philadelphia. While before this point enslaved Africans had reached the Delaware Valley individually or in small groups, now large cargoes of African captives were brought to Philadelphia. Rather than relying on the inter-colonial trade to supply forced labour as before, Philadelphians now sent ships directly to the West African coast to purchase captives to meet the city's demand for labour.[47] As table 3 shows, the city's enslaved population grew accordingly. In the early 1760s, enslaved people may have comprised as much as 90 per cent of the unfree labour force in Philadelphia.[48] In 1767, possibly the peak of enslaved presence in the city, there were about 1,400 enslaved Africans living in Philadelphia, constituting about one-twelfth of the population.[49]

In 1758 the Philadelphia Yearly Meeting agreed to exclude Friends who bought or sold slaves from meetings for business. It also appointed a committee which visited slave-owning households and tried to convince them to free their slaves.

45 Nash, 'Slaves and Slaveowners', 226, 227.
46 Ibid., 229.
47 Wax, 'Slave Trade', 145.
48 Nash, 'Slaves and Slaveowners', 245.
49 Ibid., 236.

Still, slave ownership was not a reason for disownment and would only become so in 1774. Their efforts do not seem to have had much effect. Manumissions were rare, and towards the end of the eighteenth century, Friends were still over-represented among slave owners in Philadelphia.[50] Quakers only ceased to buy enslaved Africans as German and Irish workers became available again after the Seven Years' War ended in 1763. The numbers of Africans brought to the city dropped off to an average level of sixty-six annually, continued to diminish year by year, and by 1770 had all but disappeared.[51]

Socio-economically, most enslaved workers were legally owned by upper middle-class and upper-class Philadelphians. However, artisans, shopkeepers and mariners also frequently appear as legal owners in the records.[52] Accordingly, the occupations we find enslaved Africans in are also diverse. They worked in all sectors of the economy, from agriculture to manufacturing, and service in white people's households.[53] William Penn relied on enslaved labour to work his large landholdings.[54] A survey of the *Pennsylvania Gazette* found advertisements offering the services of enslaved Africans, qualified 'as carpenters, millers, distillers, bakers, shipbuilders, blacksmiths, sailmakers, and manager of a bloomery'.[55]

Besides the enslaved, there also developed a small population of free blacks in the city, with the first free African woman appearing in a baptism record in 1717. Sixty-four black couples married at Anglican churches in Philadelphia between 1727 and 1780. Jean Soderlund found that 'In one-quarter of these marriages, both partners were free, and another 14 per cent were marriages between a free black and a slave.'[56] Unfortunately, we know little about this group of people. Manumissions in Philadelphia were rare until late 1775, even among Quakers. Hence the free black community remained small. Gary Nash estimated that by 1770 it comprised 150 individuals, growing to about 250 on the eve of the Revolution.[57]

Economic development
The early Quaker immigrants included a great number of merchants. These arrived from other colonies as well as from England.[58] They brought their

50   Ibid., 252, 253.
51   Ibid., 232.
52   Ibid., 249, 250.
53   Daniels, 'Protest', 247.
54   Elizabeth Cazden, 'Quakers, Slavery, Anti-slavery, and Race', in *The Oxford Handbook of Quaker Studies*, ed. Angell and Dandelion, 349.
55   Nash, 'Slaves and Slaveowners', cited in Jean R. Soderlund, *Quakers and Slavery: A Divided Spirit* (Princeton, NJ: Princeton University Press, 2014), 62.
56   Soderlund, *Quakers and Slavery*, 81.
57   Nash, 'Slaves and Slaveowners', 241.
58   Tolles, *Meeting House*, 43; Nash, *Quakers and Politics*, 55.

existing commercial networks with them and thereby connected Philadelphia to the Atlantic trade. The fertile Delaware Valley soil quickly produced large agricultural yields. These were enough to feed the colonists and export provisions to other colonies. They provided the main export goods. Thus, within three years of the first ships' arrival, Philadelphia 'was firmly established in the Barbados provisioning trade and had cut deep inroads into New York's control of the middle-Atlantic fur and tobacco markets'.[59] Almost from the beginning, Philadelphia merchants were not only involved in slavery by providing foodstuffs for enslaved Africans working the Barbadian plantations; they also participated in the slave trade directly by purchasing and selling enslaved Africans as part of their inter-colonial commercial relationships.[60] The Pennsylvania economy continued to follow this pattern for the rest of the century. What changed were the volume of trade and the relative importance of different goods. Well into the eighteenth century, tobacco and skins constituted Pennsylvania's most important export products. Then furs, lumber and especially flour came to dominate.[61] In return, the city's merchants received bills of exchange. These were used to purchase English manufactured goods via the New England colonies.[62]

During its first four decades, Pennsylvania suffered from religious, political and legal instability.[63] During the 1690s, Philadelphia Friends had to overcome a religious schism, which led a considerable number of Friends to leave the Society.[64] Historians still disagree about its causes. Jerry Frost and Jon Butler argue that the reasons were purely theological. Gary Nash offers an interpretation based on economic interests of different factions within colonial society, while John Smolenski regards the schism as a sign of a crisis of creolization

---

59 Nash, *Quakers and Politics*, 56.
60 Daniels, 'Protest', 248.
61 Arthur Louis Jensen, *The Maritime Commerce of Colonial Philadelphia* (Madison, WI: State Historical Society of Wisconsin, for the Department of History, University of Winsconsin, 1963), 7, 8.
62 James F. Shepherd and Gary M. Walton, *Shipping, Maritime Trade, and the Economic Development of Colonial North America* (London: Cambridge University Press, 1972), 112.
63 Marylynn Salmon, 'Notes and Documents: The Court Records of Philadelphia, Bucks, and Berks Counties in the Seventeenth and Eighteenth Centuries', *Pennsylvania Magazine of History and Biography* 107, no. 2 (1983); A. Laussat, *An Essay on Equity in Pennsylvania* (Philadelphia, 1826); Carli Conklin, 'A Variety of State-Level Procedures, Practices,and Policies: Arbitration in Early America', *Journal of Dispute Resolution* 55 (2016); Edwin B. Bronner, 'Philadelphia County Court of Quarter Sessions and Common Pleas, 1695', *American Journal of Legal History* 1, no. 1 (1957); Lawrence Lewis, 'The Courts of Pennsylvania in the Seventeenth Century', *Pennsylvania Magazine of History and Biography* 5, no. 2 (1881); Bronner, 'Philadelphia County Court of Quarter Sessions and Common Pleas, 1695'.
64 Jon Butler, '"Gospel Order Improved": The Keithian Schism and the Exercise of Quaker Ministerial Authority in Pennsylvania', *William and Mary Quarterly* 31, no. 3 (1974).

within colonial society.⁶⁵ Most recently, Madeleine Ward has made a strong case that the issue was in fact a theological one, concerning the nature of Christ and the 'light within'.⁶⁶ Whatever sparked the controversy, it led Friends to split into two factions, the separatists following the newly arrived George Keith. Keith had been an important Quaker missionary in Europe before coming to America in 1685. He arrived in Philadelphia in 1689.⁶⁷ Keith observed his fellow Friends' way of worship in the colonies, and thought it too far removed from traditional protestant practices. Colonial Quakers, in his view, focused too much on mystical elements of their faith, such as the light within, while neglecting the Bible. He was also sceptical of the close relationship between the Society of Friends and Pennsylvania government.⁶⁸ In particular, he criticized certain leading Friends for acting as ministers for the Society while also holding high political offices in the colony.⁶⁹ He wrote and circulated a pamphlet titled 'Gospel Order Improved', in which he made suggestions for a stricter and more sophisticated form of church government.⁷⁰ Keith gained many followers who set up separate meetings in Philadelphia. Friends in Philadelphia and London discussed the separation and the issues Keith and his supporters raised. Philadelphia's Meeting of Public Friends disowned Keith in 1692.⁷¹ The larger part of the conflict, however, was not negotiated in Friends' meetings. In particular the monthly meetings, which as we will see would become responsible for discipline later, had no part in it. Instead, the conflict was resolved first and foremost in Pennsylvania courts. The reason for this was exactly one of the points Keith had criticized about the Pennsylvania brethren: that Quaker ministers also held public office. The fact that some of the public Friends he attacked were also office holders served as a reason to take him to court. In October 1692, a grand jury charged Keith and some of his followers for 'reviling civil magistrates' as well as printing and distributing seditious literature.⁷² Keith

---

65 Jerry William Frost, *A Perfect Freedom: Religious Liberty in Pennsylvania* (Cambridge: Cambridge University Press, 1990), 19, and Butler, 'Gospel Order', on theological reasons; Nash, *Quakers and Politics*, on economic and political causes. See also John Smolenski, *Friends and Strangers: The Making of a Creole Culture in Colonial Pennsylvania* (Philadelphia: University of Pennsylvania Press, 2011).
66 Madeleine Ward, 'The Christian Quaker: George Keith and the Keithian Controversy', *Brill Research Perspectives in Quaker Studies* 2, no. 1 (2019). Ward's article also contains an excellent discussion of the historiography.
67 Andrew R. Murphy, 'Persecuting Quakers? Liberty and Toleration in Early Pennsylvania', in *The First Prejudice: Religious Tolerance and Intolerance in Early America*, ed. C. Beneke and C. S. Grenda (Philadelphia: University of Pennsylvania Press, 2011), 150.
68 Murphy, 'Persecuting Quakers', 150.
69 Ibid., 151.
70 Ibid., 151; Butler, 'Gospel Order', 435.
71 Murphy, 'Persecuting Quakers', 151, 152.
72 Ibid., 153.

travelled to London to explain his case, where London Yearly Meeting also disowned him in 1694.

Not only religious but also political crisis shook Pennsylvania during its early years. The colony's frame of government changed repeatedly.[73] The colonial assembly frequently passed laws, only to have them repealed by the Crown. William Offutt found that Pennsylvania suffered 'the highest percentage of disallowed colonial legislation'.[74] For instance, in 1706 the Privy Council revoked 52 of 105 laws submitted by the Assembly.[75] The functioning of the courts was further impeded by the 'oath controversy' from the 1690s to about 1720.[76] The English legal system required the swearing of oaths throughout. As part of their beliefs, Friends refused to swear. In Pennsylvania, therefore, Friends replaced oaths with affirmations. However, from the outset, Pennsylvania colonists included other protestants as well. Soon, a power struggle between Friends and non-Quaker colonists emerged, centring around the use of oaths. Anglicans argued that the lack of oaths made the justice system unfit to deal with crime, lobbying for a replacement of affirmations by oaths both locally and with the government in England. They repeatedly brought all legal processes to a halt.[77] Losing the option of affirming would have put Quakers at a serious disadvantage in the legal system, making it impossible for them to litigate, and excluding them from acting as judges or jurors.

Political instability in the colony further increased as William Penn was twice arrested. The first time was immediately after the Glorious Revolution under charges of treason, due to his close relationship with former King James II. Between 1692 and 1694 the colony came under Crown control, as it failed to take measures to defend itself against the French in the War of the League of Augsburg.[78] In 1708 Penn again was imprisoned, this time for debts. Close to bankruptcy, he prepared to sell the colony to the Crown. These plans hung

---

73 William M. Offutt, Jr, *Of 'Good Laws' and 'Good Men': Law and Society in the Delaware Valley, 1680–1710* (Urbana: University of Illinois Press, 1995).
74 William M. Offutt, Jr, 'The Atlantic Rules: The Legalistic Turn in Colonial British America', in *The Creation of the British Atlantic World: Anglo-America in the Trans-Atlantic World*, ed. Elizabeth Mancke and Carole Shammas (Baltimore, MD: Johns Hopkins University Press, 2005), 43.
75 Jack D. Marietta and G. S. Rowe, *Troubled Experiment: Crime and Justice in Pennsylvania, 1682–1800* (Philadelphia: University of Pennsylvania Press, 2006), 20.
76 William H. Lloyd, 'The Courts of Pennsylvania in the Eighteenth Century Prior to the Revolution', *University of Pennsylvania Law Review and American Law Register* 56, no. 1 (1908), 34; J. William Frost, 'The Affirmation Controversy and Religious Liberty', in *The World of William Penn*, ed. Richard S. Dunn and Mary Maples Dunn (Philadelphia: University of Pennsylvania Press, 1986); Marietta and Rowe, *Troubled Experiment*, 21, 22.
77 Frost, 'Affirmation', 171. Also Marietta and Rowe, *Troubled Experiment*, 30.
78 Offutt, 'Good Laws', 3; on defence finances: Bronner, 'Philadelphia County Court of Quarter Sessions and Common Pleas, 1695', 459.

over Pennsylvania until his death in 1718. Penn's heirs held on to the colony and appointed governors to represent their interests vis-à-vis the Pennsylvania Assembly. The legal and political situation improved dramatically from about 1722 onwards.[79] Political unrest calmed down, laws remained in place and courts sat regularly. From this point on, Philadelphia's trade increased greatly and over the course of the following decades, the city emerged as North America's primary port. Friends continued to constitute one of the major communities of Philadelphia merchants during this period.[80]

From the mid-seventeenth to the late eighteenth century, Quakerism evolved from a radical, revolutionary movement to a peaceful, established sect. Friends survived persecution in England and founded a successful colony in America. London Friends grew into a prosperous commercial upper middle-class community. Philadelphia Friends transformed their colonial experiment into North America's primary port. Commerce was an important avenue for income and advancement, and we find many merchants in the London and Philadelphia Quaker meeting records. Exchange in the British Atlantic in this period grew a great deal, and Friends were at the centre of this development. The next section therefore takes a closer look at Quakers in trade.

Friends as merchants

Quakers have enjoyed a reputation among historians for being disproportionately successful in trade. Fredrick Tolles traced this perception back to statements by seventeenth-century Quaker authors such as George Fox.[81] Fox recorded in his Journal that Friends gained customers 'when people came to have experience of Friends' honesty and faithfulness ... and that they would not cozen and cheat them'.[82] Later historians made similar assertions. Leslie Hannah, for example, speaks of 'very high Quaker incomes'. He furthermore argues that Quaker business success substantially contributed to Britain's overall economic development in this period.[83] The basis of such claims, however, has rarely been set out in detail. There simply are no empirical studies comparing Quaker merchants' fortunes to those of overseas traders of other denominations.

Contemporaries perceived London overseas merchants as wealthy, an impression that is reflected in the fact that in the Poll Tax of 1692 they were forced to pay a surcharge. Greater merchants were estimated to make about

---

79 Marietta and Rowe, *Troubled Experiment*, 33.
80 Thomas M. Doerflinger, *A Vigorous Spirit of Enterprise: Merchants and Economic Development in Revolutionary Philadelphia* (Chapel Hill: University of North Carolina Press, 1986), 59.
81 Tolles, *Meeting House*, 59,60.
82 George Fox, Journal I, 186, cited in Tolles, *Meeting House*, 59.
83 Hannah, 'Moral Economy', 296.

£400 per year, lesser merchants about £120. This put even the lower-income group of merchants at a wealth level well above those of 'persons in the law' or 'eminent clergymen'. More recent historical research confirms this overall impression of the prosperity of the merchant community.[84]

Quakers began to join the Atlantic trade during the late seventeenth century. This sector of the economy was dominated by the plantation complex, i.e. most business related to the Atlantic trade was in the last instance dependent on African slavery. While few London Friends seem to have personally owned enslaved people, they traded in plantation produce such as sugar and tobacco, which was grown by enslaved African labourers. They also owned slave ships which transported captives from Africa to the Americas.[85] Their involvement in the slave trade increased in 1711, as the 'Company of Merchants of Great Britain, trading to the South-seas, and other parts of America' was set up. It held the monopoly on the trade in enslaved Africans into South America. Given the expansion of the plantation economies there, contemporaries considered it a great opportunity for fast profit. Friends shared in this enthusiasm and partook in the opportunities the venture seemed to offer. Their hopes were disappointed, however. In 1720, share prices first soared sky-high, then collapsed. Jordan Landes found that in that year alone, London Quaker merchants had invested at least £24,750 in the company. During the financial crisis that followed, many former investors were ruined, others at least suffered great losses.[86]

Records that provide insight into individual London Quaker merchants' businesses are scarce. No such papers survive from the seventeenth century. We have evidence only of a handful of merchants from the mid-eighteenth century. While this data is not sufficient to establish whether Quaker merchants in general were more or less successful than others, it is helpful to review some of the evidence that does survive to illustrate the kind of information which can be derived from their papers, as well as the challenges that make definitive conclusions about Quaker business success so elusive.

The earliest London Quaker merchant for whom business records survive is John Eliot (1683–1762). He inherited land and tin interests in Cornwall and traded with the Mediterranean and the West Indies. His principal income, however, came from insurance underwriting. His accounts survive from 1722 onwards. At this point, his net personal estate was £11,230.2.7. By 1740 this had increased to £39,596. At his death in 1762 he was worth £97,989.[87] Samuel Hoare, a merchant's son from Cork, Ireland, inherited some money from his

---

84 Perry Gauci, *The Politics of Trade: The Overseas Merchant in State and Society, 1660–1720* (Oxford: Oxford University Press, 2001), 24.
85 Landes, *London Quakers*, 168.
86 Ibid., 100.
87 Jacob M. Price, *Capital and Credit in British Overseas Trade: The View from the Chesapeake, 1700–1776* (Cambridge, MA: Harvard University Press, 1980), 32.

father. Born in 1716, by 1743 he appears to have been worth about £11,510. In 1744, with his marriage to Grizell Gurnell, who brought a dowry of £4,000 to the marriage, he moved to London and joined his father-in-law's firm. They were active in the Irish, Portuguese and Dutch trades, and also had connections to Pennsylvania. Hoare seems to have benefited greatly from the Seven Years' War, as the increase in his annual living expenses from £1,434 in 1764–78 to £1,891 in 1778–90 suggests. His estate kept growing, and by 1795 he was worth £82,651.[88] Robert Plumsted was another substantial merchant of the eighteenth century. Two of his letter books from the mid-1750s survive. They contain copies of Plumsted's correspondence with his business partners overseas. Trading predominantly with Philadelphia and the Caribbean, he dealt in plantation produce, agricultural tools and machinery. His main trading partners overseas were fellow Quakers. His two most important contacts, however, were not only religious brethren but also relatives, making it more difficult to determine the importance of membership in the Society for his business.[89] Another London Quaker merchant for whom we have sources is Plumsted's contemporary and kinsman James Farmer. Farmer acted as the London representative of the Birmingham gun manufacturers Farmer & Galton. The gun industry expanded greatly during the long eighteenth century, fed by Britain's many wars in that time. The Galton firm was among the oldest and most prominent in the business. It supplied the English state, as well as the English overseas trading companies with weapons for their military ventures overseas. Farmer & Galton were the main suppliers of guns to the African Company.[90] British slave traders used their weapons as barter, exchanging them for enslaved Africans on the West African coast.[91] Hence, James Farmer's business, like so many at the time, drew its capital primarily from African slavery. As member of the firm he supplied arms to the Royal African Company, while on his own account he traded substantially with Lisbon. We know few details of the precise extent of his interests there, or the goods he dealt with. However, his involvement was enough to cause him to go bankrupt after the Lisbon Earthquake of 1755. He recovered, however, and by 1766 his share in the partnership with Galton

---

88 Price, *Credit*, 34, 35.
89 S. D. Smith and T. R. Wheeley, '"Requisites of a Considerable Trade": The Letters of Robert Plumsted, Atlantic Merchant, 1752–58', *English Historical Review* 124, no. 508 (2009).
90 W.A. Richards, 'The Birmingham Gun Manufactory of Farmer & Galton and the Slave Trade' (MA thesis, University of Birmingham, 1972).
91 Priya Satia's 2018 study of the British gun industry in the long eighteenth century discusses the Galton firm and its ties to the African trade in great detail. Priya Satia, *Empire of Guns: The Violent Making of the Industrial Revolution* (Stanford, CA: Stanford University Press, 2019).

was placed at £13,862.[92] Yet another contemporary, John Hanbury, became the leading tobacco merchant of the period. His finances were considered so solid that he was made principal contractor for monetary remittances to North America at the start of the Seven Years' War. At his death in 1758, he is estimated to have been worth well over £100,000. Note that this was after he had already settled £300,000 on his daughter Anna.[93] Finally, the chemist and drugs merchant Thomas Corbyn traded medical ingredients with the New World. His correspondents were based in Boston, Connecticut, New York, Rhode Island, Philadelphia and throughout the Caribbean. A letter book of his is extant, covering the period 1742–55.[94] His trade seems to have thrived and he became the leading supplier of medicine to Barbados. However, the book does not contain enough information to estimate the extent of his wealth.[95]

As discussed above, Pennsylvania was partly founded as an investment opportunity for Quaker merchants. Hence, it is not surprising that we find many Friends among the colony's merchant class. In Philadelphia, at the time of the Revolution, a major merchant was worth about £35,000, and anyone worth over £20,000 was considered rich. The majority of merchants, however, possessed only a few thousand pounds. These were rather small sums, compared to merchants in the West Indies or England.[96] To put these numbers into perspective, it may help to note that at the same time, a 'good-sized ship cost roughly £2,000 and a fine town house £3,000–£4,000'.[97] For the mid- and late eighteenth century, Thomas Doerflinger's study on the Philadelphia merchant community provides some information on individual Quaker merchants' wealth. The dry goods merchant Henry Drinker was worth £35,559 in 1784, for example.[98] Joshua Fischer and Sons, who kept a vessel in the English trade, became financially involved in iron manufacturing, in order to mitigate risk. They supplied lots of short-term credit to iron works.[99] In 1770 their company was worth £31,225.[100]

While London merchants participated in the transatlantic slave trade by investing in the South Sea Company and providing guns for the African

92   Karl Pearson, *The Life, Letters and Labours of Francis Galton* (Cambridge: [s.n.], 1914), 40.
93   Price, *Credit*, 21.
94   Richard Palmer, 'Thomas Corbyn, Quaker Merchant', *Medical History* 33 (1989), 373.
95   Ibid.
96   Doerflinger, *A Vigorous Spirit of Enterprise*, 139.
97   Ibid., 129.
98   Ibid., 130.
99   Ibid., 153; Thomas Clifford, active in the England trade, equally provided financing for iron production.
100 Ibid., 130; Kenneth Morgan, *An American Quaker in the British Isles: The Travel Journals of Jabez Maud Fisher, 1775–1779* (London: Published for the British Academy by Oxford University Press, 1992). 2. Other Quaker merchants listed by Doerflinger, but not discussed in any more detail, include John Head (p. 88), Daniel Wister and Owen Jones (p. 96).

company, their brethren in Philadelphia had more direct links to slavery. Starting in the colony's earliest years, Quaker merchants in the City of Brotherly Love bought and sold enslaved Africans. The trade in human beings formed part of Friends' commercial relationships with the Caribbean.[101] Most of the enslaved workers arrived on consignment from merchants in Barbados, Jamaica and the Leeward Islands.[102] In practice, this meant that a West Indian trading partner of a Philadelphia merchant would send an enslaved person over, and ask their partner to sell her, in return for a percentage in the profit.

Since the seventeenth century, there had been among Pennsylvania Quakers some who opposed slavery on moral grounds. Most famously, the German Town Declaration of 1688 condemned slavery as well as all 'social hierarchies based on race'.[103] The 'Exhortation and Caution to Friends concerning Buying or Keeping of Negroes', published by William Bradford in 1693, equally condemned slavery based on moral reasoning, and called upon Friends to end slavery.[104] A discourse on the injustice of enslaving fellow human beings continued into the eighteenth century. Proponents of abolitionism campaigned among their peers and published pamphlets arguing against the enslavement of both Africans and native Americans.[105] Some of these Friends were sanctioned or even disowned for their efforts.[106] The most radical among the early abolitionists was undoubtedly Benjamin Lay. Working people from rural England, Lay and his wife Sarah had first encountered slavery during a two-year sojourn in Barbados in 1718–20. The excessive violence with which their fellow colonists, including Friends, treated the island's enslaved African population turned the Lays into vehement abolitionists.[107] When immigrating to Pennsylvania years later, they took up the cause again, with more fervour than ever. While slavery was less common in the Quaker colony, and the degree of violence possibly less excessive than in the Caribbean, Sarah and Benjamin recognized that in essence the condition of bondage was the same. They campaigned uncompromisingly against the practice. Benjamin repeatedly staged what we would now call performance art to highlight the evil of slavery and the hypocrisy of his fellow, slave-keeping Friends. The most famous instance of this was Benjamin's appearance at Philadelphia Yearly Meeting in 1738, which involved

---

101 Daniels, 'Protest', 253.
102 Ibid., 248.
103 Katharine Gerbner, 'Antislavery in Print: The Germantown Protest, the Exhortation, and the Seventeenth-Century Quaker Debate on Slavery', *Early American Studies* (2011), 564.
104 Ibid., 553.
105 Carey, *From Peace to Freedom*, argues for an ongoing discourse, with the different publications against slavery issued in Pennsylvania during the seventeenth and eighteenth centuries being part of the same conversation.
106 Daniels, 'Protest'.
107 Marcus Rediker, *The Fearless Benjamin Lay: The Quaker Dwarf who Became the First Revolutionary Abolitionist* (Boston: Beacon Press, 2017), 36.

the piercing of a Bible with a sword and splattering of fake 'blood' all over the – slave-owning – Quaker leadership.[108] Pennsylvania Friends disowned him.[109] However, these early campaigners' work was not in vain. Having witnessed their activism during the 1730s and 1740s, a younger generation of Friends would facilitate a cultural shift within the Society when they came to hold religious offices in the 1750s.[110] Better-known, second-generation abolitionists, such as John Woolman and Anthony Benezet, would continue the efforts of the Lays and their allies.[111] Abolitionist ideas would gradually become more acceptable, eventually culminating in the staunch policies we still associate with the Society of Friends today.

The efforts of the small number of activists who, like the Lays, laboured to change the hearts and minds of their fellow Friends, however, had little influence on the merchant class. Philadelphia Quaker merchants, for the most part, were not enthusiastic about slave trading. Their qualms were less ethical than economic. Researchers have found no evidence of ethical concern over trading in enslaved Africans among the papers of Philadelphia Quaker merchants. The surviving correspondence of Quaker merchants Jonathan Dickinson and Isaac Norris shows them complaining about the 'bad quality' of the African arrivals, and the difficulties they encountered selling them.[112] As Norris reported to a correspondent who had sent him several enslaved Africans to sell in Philadelphia:

> Ye Negro woman being bigg wth child is not of ready Sale – I have offer'd here to several & hitherto hold ye price P40 for I think her worth it – the boy I have not yet gott a Mastr. For – There is here Generally 5 or P10 Difference between offering to sell & wanting to buy a Negro.[113]

Similarly, Jonathan Dickinson in 1700 wrote to his brother in law in Barbados about a consignment of enslaved Africans he had received from him:

> As to Jack both I and Isaac have Endeavoured to make Sale of him – but Cannot get the Money to answer thy Value of P45 here. The boy Carro is not much Bigger then [sic] one of ye Two boys I rot. Wth mee and is not Soe likely for a Market.[114]

108 Ibid., 2.
109 Ibid., 68.
110 Rediker sums up the conclusions reached by Carey and Soderlund in this respect: Rediker, *Benjamin Lay*, 134.
111 There has been a lively debate on the nature and development of Quaker abolitionist ideas. For recent examples, see Carey, *From Peace to Freedom*; Gerbner, 'Antislavery in Print'; Cazden, 'Quakers'.
112 Wax, 'Slave Trade', 151.
113 Isaac Norris to Richard Sleigh, May 20, 1701, cited in Wax, 'Slave Trade'.
114 Jonathan Dickinson to Isaac Gale, June 25, 1700, cited in Wax, 'Slave Trade'.

About 1730, the organization of the Philadelphia slave trade changed. Instead of receiving enslaved individuals or small groups of Africans upon consignment, Philadelphia merchants began importing large cargoes of captives directly from the West Indies.[115] This cut out middlemen such as Friends Isaac Norris and Dickinson, whose participation in the trade rested on their networks with the West Indies.[116] While the trade of enslaved people overall increased in the following decades, it was carried out primarily by merchants of other denominations. Quakers no longer played a dominant part in it.[117] While a few individuals continued to buy and sell slaves into the 1750s, the summit of the Philadelphia slave trade during the Seven Years' War, when local merchants sent vessels directly to Africa to obtain slaves, appears to have taken place without Quaker participation.[118]

Perhaps the best argument for the Quakers having an unusual degree of success in commerce is their numerical prominence among traders. There is evidence that a surprising number of Quakers were active as merchants. During the 1690s, fewer than 8,000 Friends lived in London. They accounted for at most 1.6 per cent of the city's total population. Nuala Zahedieh identified ten Quakers among the fifty-nine leading merchants of the 1686 London port books. That makes 16.9 per cent of the total. Perry Gauci compiled a database of 850 London merchants based on tax returns in the 1690s, when wealthy merchants had to pay an extra levy. Out of the metropolis's wealthiest traders, he identified twenty-two as certain, and one as a possible Friend. That makes at least 2.6 per cent of the total.[119] At the same time, perhaps 0.19 per cent of Londoners were full-time merchants, versus a Quaker share of 0.28 per cent.[120] Moreover, as we saw in table 2, the percentage of merchants among London Quaker bridegrooms was multiple times this number, increasing further over the course of the eighteenth century. Hence, a much greater proportion of Friends acted as merchants than among the general population.

---

115 Wax, 'Slave Trade', 145.
116 Daniels, 'Protest', 256.
117 Ibid., 242.
118 Wax, 'Slave Trade', 145.
119 I arrive at these numbers by comparing the findings of various authors: Perry Gauci, Merchant Database, Centre for Metropolitan History; Simon Dixon, 'Quakers and the London Parish, 1670–1720', *London Journal* 32 (2007) estimated that there were at most 8,000 Quakers in London in 1700; Zahedieh, 'Mercantilism'. See also Jordan Landes, 'The Role of London in the Creation of a Quaker Transatlantic Community in the Late Seventeenth and Eighteenth Centuries' (doctoral thesis, University of London, 2011). On Quaker success in commerce see Lloyd, *Social History*; Paul Herman Emden, *Quakers in Commerce: A Record of Business Achievement, etc.* (London: Sampson Low & Co., 1940); Walvin, *Money*, 207.
120 Gauci estimated that in the late seventeenth century, there were about 1,000 merchants in the city. The population for the same period is estimated at 527,000. Perry Gauci, *The Politics of Trade: The Overseas Merchant in State and Society, 1660–1720*.

Perhaps unsurprisingly, the available evidence for Philadelphia suggests an even greater over-representation of Friends among the merchant class. According to Fredrick Tolles, merchants made up 17.8 per cent of Quaker bride grooms in the period 1683–1708, a greater proportion than we observe in London.[121] From about 1700 the percentage of merchants among Philadelphia Quakers increased steadily.[122] Gary Nash found that in the period 1682–1740, at least 42.7 per cent of Philadelphia merchants were Friends.[123]

Quaker merchants were furthermore set apart from others by the scale of their networks. Nuala Zahedieh found that the vast majority of English Atlantic merchants in the late seventeenth century focused their trade on either the northern colonies, or the West Indies. Zahedieh suggests that 'This strong specialisation by port stemmed from the overwhelming necessity of firm, reliable credit networks dependent on little more than the fragile ties of reciprocity and reputation and the difficulty of maintaining more than very few such relationships.' In contrast, Quaker merchants traded with unusually diverse destinations. She suggests that this was due to the fact that religious minorities, including the Quakers, could resort to 'ready-made trust networks' based on religious ties. Indeed, the destinations Quaker merchants traded with were correlated strongly with the presence of Quaker communities and meeting structures.[124] Zahedieh explains that 'By the late seventeenth century there was a Quaker meeting in almost every colony as well as in every county of England with a Yearly Meeting in London acting as the hub for both information and regulation.' The meeting structure provided channels of communication, through which 'Distant Quakers would not only provide detailed business information about their own members but also good general intelligence.'[125] This conclusion fits with what we know about Philadelphia Quaker merchants' networks. Fredrick Tolles found that 'By virtues of their commercial, religious, personal, and family contacts, the Philadelphia Quakers were in close touch with the entire north Atlantic world from Nova Scotia to Curacao and from Hamburg to Lisbon.' He thought that Philadelphia's trade developed out of pre-existing Quaker merchant networks.[126] Indeed, in 1702, George Keith argued that Philadelphia Friends' prosperity stemmed from their 'keeping their Trade within themselves and maintaining a strict correspondence and intelligence over

---

121 Tolles, *Meeting House*, 41.
122 Ibid., 41–2, 116, based on analysis of Quaker marriage records. For the development of the socio-economic status of Philadelphians in general, and merchants of all congregations in particular, see Doerflinger, *A Vigorous Spirit of Enterprise*.
123 Gary B. Nash, 'The Early Merchants of Philadelphia: The Formation and Disintegration of a Founding Elite', in *The World of William Penn*, ed. Richard S. Dunn and Mary Maples Dunn (Philadelphia: University of Pennsylvania Press, 1986).
124 Zahedieh, 'Mercantilism', 155.
125 Ibid., 156.
126 Tolles, *Meeting House*, 89–91.

all parts where they are'.[127] Tolles agreed that to a large extent this was true.[128] Thomas Doerflinger argued the same, saying that not just the Quakers but most Philadelphia merchants traded predominantly within their own religions and ethnic communities.[129] Examples of Philadelphia Quaker merchants whose networks support these arguments are Samuel Carpenter and James Claypoole. Carpenter had already acted as a merchant for a decade in Barbados, before migrating to Philadelphia in early 1683. He built the first wharf in Philadelphia, which could accommodate ships of 500 tons. By 1685 he had invested in several grain mills, timber lands and a lime burning business. His trade with the West Indies was extensive. He also speculated in land in Pennsylvania and New Jersey. Within ten years of his arrival, he had become the wealthiest merchant in the province.[130] Similarly, James Claypoole traded from London before migrating to the Quaker colony in the 1680s. He already had commercial ties to the Baltic and the West Indies.[131] Once in Philadelphia, he continued his business. He imported beef, pork, dairy products, a variety of dry goods and tools from England. In return, he sent pipe staves, timber, silver, furs and whale oil.[132]

These individual examples offer some illustration of the breadth and scale of individual Quaker merchants' businesses. They suggest that a disproportionate number of Friends were active in overseas trade and that their trade was unusually broad in scope, but not that they became disproportionately rich. All the merchants we have details on counted fellow Friends among their trading contacts. These relationships may have arisen from encounters within the context of the Society. It is equally possible, however, that they were based on kin relationships. We can therefore not easily determine the importance of the Society of Friends for these merchants' businesses. These examples furthermore show that as traders, Quaker merchants were not isolated from other parts of society. John Hanbury's relationship with the State during the Seven Years' War is a clear illustration of this. We notice moreover that these merchants traded with a wide variety of goods, ranging from agricultural products and drugs to weapons. Several of them spread risk by investing in businesses aside from overseas trade, such as land speculation and underwriting.

127 George Keith and Protestant Episcopal Historical Society, *Collections of the Protestant Episcopal Historical Society for the Year 1851* (New York, 1851).
128 Tolles, *Meeting House*, 89.
129 Doerflinger, *A Vigorous Spirit of Enterprise*, 59.
130 Nash, *Quakers and Politics*, 61.
131 Ibid., 15.
132 Ibid., 62.

4

Quaker Business Ethics

The most obvious possible explanation for Quakers' reputation for exceptional honesty in business is that they had a distinct, superior set of business ethics. Indeed, Quaker historians have traditionally argued this.[1] Quaker business ethics are supposed to have evoked trust in their trading partners. Thereby they provided Friends with a competitive advantage in business, facilitating Friends' trade in the deceitful, low-trust environment that was the early modern economy.[2] These claims however lack empirical substantiation, and have begun to meet with scepticism.[3] This chapter investigates the content of Quaker business ethics and compares them to those of the contemporary British mainstream.

The historical development of business ethics
The comparative literature on the historical development of business ethics is still limited.[4] Max Weber famously argued that Calvinism introduced to Europe a rational, methodical and controlled thriving for individual economic betterment, including the virtues of reliability, honesty and punctuality in business, thereby supporting the development of capitalism.[5] His work on the protestant ethic has fuelled scholarly debates for almost a century, incurring a fair amount of criticism.[6] R. H. Tawney argued that Weber under-

---

[1] Kirby, 'Entrepreneurship', 108; Price, 'Business Families'; Hannah, 'Moral Economy', 289; Raistrick, *Quakers in Science and Industry*, 44–47; Prior and Kirby, 'The Society of Friends and the Family Firm, 1700–830', 67, 68; Walvin, *Money*, 32, 34, 35; Lloyd, *Social History*, 70; Tolles, *Meeting House*, 59.
[2] Prior and Kirby, 'Family Firm', 66.
[3] Sheryllynne Haggerty, *'Merely for Money'?: Business Culture in the British Atlantic, 1750–1815* (Liverpool: Liverpool University Press, 2012), 69; Zahedieh, *Capital*, 109.
[4] Gabriel Abend, *The Moral Background: An Inquiry into the History of Business Ethics* (Princeton, NJ: Princeton University Press, 2014), 15.
[5] Max Weber, *The Protestant Work Ethic and the Spirit of Capitalism* (New York: Scribner, 1958).
[6] R. H. Tawney, *Religion and the Rise of Capitalism: A Historical Study* (London: Murray, 1926). For more recent studies dealing with Weber's theory see for instance Leonard Dudley and Ulrich Blum, 'Religion and Economic Growth: Was Weber Right?', *Journal of Evolutionary Economics* 11, no. 2 (2003); Sasha Becker and Ludger Woessman, 'Was Weber

estimated the evolution of Calvinism from community-enforced asceticism to highly individualistic cultures encouraging the pursuit of wealth through industry, thrift and diligence.[7] As he argued, Puritanism gave these virtues 'a supernatural sanction, [and] turned them from an unsocial eccentricity into a habit and a religion'.[8] While Weber proposed that Calvinism pioneered the idea of diverting humans' 'passions' towards the individual pursuit of wealth, Hirschman located this in a different source.[9] He argued that early modern philosophers, including Montesquieu and Stewart, proposed the economic virtues of frugality, moderation, work, order, regularity and individual pursuit of wealth as a means of achieving political stability, and that these virtues preceded Calvinism. However, while influenced by Calvinist and Puritan ideas, Quakerism in fact rejected their core belief in predestination. Instead Quakers emphasized individual agency as the route to salvation.[10]

The Dissemination of Business Ethics

Norms are instilled, beginning in childhood, through social networks, kinship groups, or religious or ethnic communities.[11] While much of this process is informal and difficult to study for historical communities, there are formal processes of dissemination of norms which can be traced. Early modern print culture plays an important part here.

Of particular importance for the dissemination of business ethics in early modern Europe were business advice manuals. Some 12,000 commercial advice manuals were published in Europe between 1470 and 1820.[12] The seventeenth century especially witnessed a steady increase in commercial titles. In England, ten such texts were published in the first decade of the century, and seventy-two in the last. In the period after the Restoration, this type of publication emerged as an important genre.[13]

Manuals were frequently published either under pseudonyms or anonymously. Of those authors who can be identified, most were writing masters

---

Wrong? A Human Capital Theory of Protestant Economic History', *Quarterly Journal of Economics* 124, no. 2 (2009).
7 Tawney, *Religion and the Rise of Capitalism*, 111, 115, 227, 272.
8 Ibid., 272.
9 Albert O. Hirschman, *The Passions and the Interests: Political Arguments for Capitalism before Its Triumph* (Princeton, NJ: Princeton University Press, 1977), 71.
10 Peters, *Print Culture and the Early Quakers*, 2.
11 Janet Tai Landa, *Trust, Ethnicity, and Identity: Beyond the New Institutional Economics of Ethnic Trading Networks, Contract Law, and Gift-Exchange* (Ann Arbor: University of Michigan Press, 1994); Casson, 'Business Culture', 40.
12 Daniel Rabuzzi, 'Eighteenth Century Commercial Mentalities as Reflected and Projected in Business Handbooks', *Eighteenth Century Studies* 29, no. 2 (1995–96), 170.
13 Natasha Glaisyer, *The Culture of Commerce in England, 1660–1720* (London: Royal Historical Society, 2006), 104.

or accountants.[14] While some authors claimed to be merchants, the secondary literature argues that most probably were not. Hence, they do not present a source for actual mercantile conduct.[15] However, they do provide evidence on the reading public's perception of merchants, and the behaviour ascribed to them.

We cannot be sure who the readers of these manuals were.[16] Some authors advertised their books for the use in writing schools, others addressed merchants and tradesmen.[17] Manuals included advice and instruction about accounting, bills of exchange and letter writing. Others included dictionaries of commercial terms, details of coaches and fairs and general business affairs, such as procedures at a custom house.[18] Moreover, they contain large amounts of 'opaque, useless' data, such as lengthy lists of goods and sales catalogues of trading companies.[19] This suggests that they were really aimed less at merchants than at readers with a general interest in trade.

Trade was the great transformer of early modern society. It made the world smaller and larger at the same time. The import of an unprecedented array of goods from far-away places broadened Europeans' horizons: there was more out there than people had realized before, and the existence of the Far East in its vastness began to sink in. The East India Companies brought tea and cotton, porcelain and silk from India and China. These goods were beautiful, exotic, exciting. Still items of luxury in the 1600s, over the course of the eighteenth century they became more widely dispersed. These goods brought far-away places within reach of those who did not go on trading voyages to India or China but stayed at home. The growing middling class began consuming these goods, and Asian imports came to play a key role in shaping their social and cultural identity.

At the same time, trade with these distant lands was a vehicle for the middling sorts to move up the social ladder. Commerce and its associated sectors provided the incomes, which middling sort consumers used to purchase foreign goods and signal their identity as those who were in touch with these foreign places. Long-distance trade became associated with a new, fashionable lifestyle of the middling sorts. The number of merchant manuals grew with the onset of the consumer revolution.[20] They were frequently written in a style conducive to

---

14 Ibid., 113.
15 Rabuzzi, 'Business Handbooks', 170.
16 Ibid., 173–75.
17 Glaisyer, *The Culture of Commerce in England*, 116.
18 Ibid., 100–3.
19 Rabuzzi, 'Business Handbooks', 170.
20 Ibid., 179.

spectators and 'arm chair merchants'.[21] This suggests that they served to let readers partake in and understand this new world developing around them.

Finally, the instruction provided by the manuals was not merely technical. They include advice on how to act as a merchant, and what behaviour was considered conducive to success in trade.[22] The manuals 'attempted to infuse their readers with values and a rationale to go along with the techniques required by a given task'.[23] This makes them an excellent source for business ethics.

A second important source for contemporary ethics are sermons. They were ubiquitous. Most people heard at least one sermon a week, on Sundays. They were also published.[24] Europe in this period was a deeply religious society. Faith was woven into the fabric of everyday life. It constituted a fundamental component of human existence, shaping family and work lives, the law, the guilds, government and leisure time. Hence, early modern people read printed religious texts with great interest, and sermons constituted a major part of the early modern book trade.[25] Printed sermons were available in a wide range of prices, from two penny chapbooks to expensive folio editions. Some were bestsellers, others printed at the expense of their authors.[26] From the 1640s onward, the reading of sermons by individuals began to be seen as a sign of seriousness.[27]

All sermons shared a set of generic conventions that made them a recognizable category for contemporary readers: they were headed by a scriptural text, and consisted of its explanation and application.[28] The published sermons of moderate nonconformist minsters were very similar to those of Anglican clergy. They were 'similar in content, published in similar books by the same printers, sold by the same booksellers, and presumably marketed in the same way to similar audiences'.[29] This chapter therefore does not distinguish between conformist and non-conformist sermons.

---

21 Glaisyer, *The Culture of Commerce in England*, 142.
22 Rabuzzi, 'Business Handbooks', 175.
23 Ibid., 171.
24 John Gordon Spaulding, *Pulpit Publications, 1660–1782* (New York: Ross Publishing, 1996).
25 William Gibson, 'The British Sermon 1689–1901: Quantities, Performance, and Culture', in *The Oxford Handbook of the British Sermon, 1689–1901*, ed. Keith C. Francis and William Gibson (Oxford: Oxford University Press, 2012).
26 Rosemary Dixon, 'Sermons in Print 1660–1700', in *The Oxford Handbook of the Early Modern Sermon*, ed. Peter McCullough, Hugh Adlington and Emma Rhatigan (Oxford: Oxford University Press, 2011).
27 James Rigney, 'Sermons into Print', in *The Oxford Handbook of the Early Modern Sermon*, ed. Adlington, McCullough and Rhatigan, 205.
28 Dixon, 'Sermons in Print', 461.
29 Ibid., 471.

The majority of sermons dealt with practical subjects, including Christian life and doctrine. They touched upon all areas of everyday life, including the conduct of business. Moreover, sermons frequently constituted reactions to contemporary developments, forming the 'religious response to political events'.[30]

Not all sermons that were preached were also published. Those that were published were sometimes edited and altered for publication. Moreover, sermons were published that had never been preached. This, however, does not limit their usefulness as a source for ethics. The published sermons were widely circulated. Hence, they reflect what people read and thought about the issues they addressed.

Within the Society of Friends, we can assume that values were disseminated informally, as in society in general, within communities and families. Moreover, Quakers from the earliest times onwards used print extensively to communicate their ideas both to the public and within their community. As discussed above, since the 1650s, Friends published numerous pamphlets to share their beliefs with a wide audience. In addition, they disseminated ideas formally through their organization of meetings. Evidence for this is found in the Quaker publications. These frequently include advice on the raising of children, and wielding a positive influence over servants, apprentices and young people in general, who were regarded as being in danger of getting 'ensnared by worldly things'. In addition, leading Friends published monographs on their ideas. Some of these deal with the conduct of business. They include George Fox's 1658 *Warning to All Merchants in London and Such as Buy and Sell*, which is a key document for early Quaker history as well as Quaker business ethics.[31] Further sources include *A Brief and Serious Warning to Such as Are Concerned in Commerce and Trading, Who Go under the Profession of Truth* by the Quaker minister Ambrose Rigge, first published in 1678, and William Penn's *No Cross, No Crown* and his *Fruits of a Father's Love: Being the Advice of William Penn to His Children*.[32] The Society promoted these works through the meeting structure. Throughout the eighteenth century, monthly meetings' minutes contain references to subscriptions for and ordering of several copies of different Quaker leaders' publications.

The most important Quaker publications for the study of norms, including business ethics, are the annual epistles that London Yearly Meeting began issuing

---

30   Keith A. Francis, 'Sermons: Themes and Developments', in *The Oxford Handbook of the British Sermon, 1689–1901*, ed. Francis and Gibson, 10.
31   George Fox, *A Warning to All Merchants in London and Such as Buy and Sell* (1658).
32   Ambrose Rigge, *A Brief and Serious Warning to Such who Are Concerned in Commerce and Trading* (London, 1678); William Penn, *No Cross, no Crown* (London, 1669); William Penn, *Fruits of a Father's Love: Being the Advice of William Penn to his Children* (London, 1726. First published 1669.).

in 1675. The Meeting occasionally sent out letters to individual meetings, or upon special occasions, as well. Its annual epistles however present its most frequent and coherent communication with the Society's membership. They therefore serve as our main source. London Yearly Meeting sent its annual epistles to all monthly meetings. They served to disseminate the Society's values. They are preserved for almost every year, with the exception of the period 1677–81. Throughout, these included 'advices' regarding good conduct on issues Friends discussed during these annual gatherings. Philadelphia Yearly Meeting also issued annual epistles. These however consisted for the most part of a copy of that year's London Yearly Meeting epistle. Therefore, the London epistles are a good source for the Atlantic Quaker community as a whole. They served as a means of disseminating the Society's doctrine, its values and norms.

In 1681 the annual epistle instructed that 'every Quarterly Meeting enter this, and all such other papers and epistles as they may have had from the Yearly Meetings, in their book, to be read every Quarterly Meeting; that Friends be reminded of services therein desired'.[33] There is evidence on the practice of this for the London community. Copies of the epistles are included regularly among the London monthly meetings' minutes. Horsleydown monthly meeting in 1750 noted: 'This being monthly Quarterly Meeting, the last Yearly Meeting epistle was read, and verbal exhortations delivered; recommending to keep in humility, in the fear of the lord & c which we hope will be remembered.'[34] It is also frequently noted that the epistles were read out in the monthly meetings themselves. Ratcliff monthly meeting in fourth month 1700 noted that 'The Yearly Meeting Paper was read & c.'.[35] A hundred years later the practice was still ongoing: Devonshire House monthly meeting in seventh month 1800 noted that 'the Yearly Meeting epistle is to be read'.[36] Peel monthly meeting in third month 1800 noted that the 'Yearly Meeting advices were read'.[37] Finally, there is evidence that epistles were to be read in meetings of worship as well. Ratcliff monthly meeting in 1750 noted: 'This meeting directs that the Yearly Meeting epistle be read in the Meetings for Worship at Ratcliff by Thomas Ollive, and at Wapping by Daniel Weston.'[38] The Peel in 1800 even decided to distribute

---

33 Society of Friends, *Collection of Epistles from the Yearly Meeting of Friends in London* (New York: Samuel Wood & Sons, 1821), 1681, 12; 1713, 108.
34 Horsleydown MM minutes, 2/v/1750, 279. See also Westminster MM minutes v/1750, 171.
35 Ratcliff MM minutes, iv/1700, 154.
36 Devonshire House MM minutes, vii/1800, 431; see also Peel MM minutes, 12/iv/1750, NP.
37 Peel MM minutes, iii/1800, 144; also vii/1800, 167; Westminster MM minutes, iv/1700, 115; vii/1800, 316.
38 Ratcliff MM minutes, v/1750, NP.

copies of the epistle 'among the families of friends'.³⁹ This indicates a wide distribution and awareness of their content amongst pious London Friends at least. There is no reason to doubt that similar practices were followed by other Quaker communities across the Atlantic world.

The content of Quaker business ethics
The sources reveal four key themes of Quaker business ethics. The first and most dominant is a general concern about covetousness, and its implications for business. These implications appear increasingly refined over time as issues specific to the business community. They are debts, taxes and fraud.

Covetousness is an important theme in the Bible, and its prohibition is set out in the tenth commandment. William Penn defined it as

> the love of money or riches; which, as the apostle has it, is the root of all evil. It branches itself into these three parts: first, desiring of unlawful things; secondly, unlawfully desiring of lawful things; and lastly, hoarding up, or unprofitably with-holding the benefit of them from the relief of private persons, or the publick.⁴⁰

Quakers distinguished between wealth earned through hard work, and covetousness. They called industry 'praise worthy' and 'indispensable'. Rather it is 'the desire of great things, and the engrossment of the time and attention, from which we desire that all our dear Friends may be redeemed'.⁴¹ Concern arose only when the drive for accumulating wealth distracted Friends from the pursuit of Truth.

The London Yearly Meeting identified covetousness as the 'common, destructive cause ... of many particulars of deviation'.⁴² To emphasize this point, Friends' publications frequently cite the Bible verses 1 Tim. 6.9–11:

> They that will be rich, fall into temptation, and a snare, and into many foolish and hurtful lusts, which drown men in destruction and perdition. For the love of money is the root of all evil; which while some coveted after, they have erred from the faith, and pierced themselves through with many sorrows.

In this vein, the 1720 epistle warned to 'take heed against pride, covetousness, and hastening to be rich in the world'.⁴³ The following year the meeting

---

39 Peel MM minutes, viii/1800, 176. Similarly Westminster MM minutes, vii/1800, 183: LYM epistle 'hath now been read, the following friends are appointed to distribute them amongst our members'.
40 Penn, 'Cross'.
41 Friends, *Epistles* 1787, 393.
42 Ibid., 1797, 282, 283.
43 Ibid., 1720, 128.

lamented that 'last year's advice has not been duly heeded'.[44] This verse is referenced in epistles from the 1740s and 1750s.[45]

Prominent among the deviations covetousness caused were debts and financial ruin. The 1754 epistle argued that covetousness, and 'the love of money being the root of all evil', 'hath been verified in the ruinous consequences of an earthly, ambitious spirit, pushing men forward, in the pursuit of greatness, upon hazardous attempts, which have too often issued in the fall and ruins of themselves and families'.[46] In the sources, covetousness, and related to this extravagant lifestyles, are frequently held responsible for causing an inability to pay one's debts.[47] Fox, in an early epistle, warned all those engaged in trading to 'keep out of debts … Go not beyond your estates, less thy bring yourselves to trouble, and cumber, and a snare.'[48] Later Quaker writings on debts are basically repetitions of this idea. Quaker minister Ambrose Rigge in his 1678 pamphlet warned Friends not to borrow what they would not be able to pay back, especially not from vulnerable people such as orphans or widows. In particular, he warned them not to borrow in order to finance an expensive lifestyle.[49] In a further pamphlet, Fox quoted Romans 8.8: 'Owe no man anything, but to love one another: for he that loveth another, hath fulfilled the law' in an epistle to 'all of what trade or calling soever, keep out of debts; owe no man anything but love … For a man that … runs into debt, and lives highly of other men's means; he is a waster of other men's [goods] and a destroyer.'[50] He interpreted the verse to mean that one ought to pay all one's debts diligently and punctually, the love owed to one's neighbours being the one debt one can never settle.

The epistles contain twenty-seven references to debts between 1692 and 1797. The first epistle dealing with debts elaborated further on Fox and Rigge's ideas. It recommended that

> the payment of just debts be not delayed … nor any to overcharge themselves with too much trading and commerce beyond their capacities to discharge a good conscience towards all men: and that all Friends concerned be very

---

44 Ibid., 1721, 129, 130.
45 Ibid., 1741, 191; 1744, 201; 1746, 208; 1749, 217; 1752, 228; 1753, 232; 1759, 257.
46 Friends, *Epistles* 1753, 240–41; equally 1746, 209; 1759 259–60; 1759 reproduced in 1786, 353; also 1781, 337–38; 1783, 345; for this verse see also 1740, 191, related not to financial ruin but 'fall from your own stedfastness'.
47 Ibid., 1778, 328; 1797, 382–83; 'All these things shall be added unto you', 'Your heavenly father knoweth that ye have need of all these things' Matt. 6.32, 33; Friends, *Epistles* 1697, 71; 1724, 138; 1732, 159.
48 George Fox, *The Line of Righteousness and Justice Stretched Forth over all Merchants* (London, 1661).
49 Rigge, *Commerce and Trading*.
50 Fox, *Line of Righteousness*.

careful not to contract extravagant debts, to the endangering the wronging others and their families; which some have done, to the grieving the hearts of the upright: nor to break their promises, contracts, or agreements, in their buying and selling (or in any other lawful affairs), to the injuring themselves and others, occasioning strife, contention, and reproach to truth and Friends. And it is advised that all Friends that are entering into trade, or that are in trade, and have not stocks sufficient of their own to answer the trade they aim at, be very cautious of running themselves into debt, without advising with some of the ancient and experienced Friends among whom they live; and more especially such trading as hath its dependence upon sea adventures.[51]

Warnings not to break one's debts or launch further into trade than one can afford recur in the epistles from the 1730s to the 1750s. In 1735 the meeting advised 'that Friends everywhere take diligent care to prevent, as much as possible, persons professing with us defrauding their creditors of their just dues'.[52] In 1753 it reminded Friends to 'be careful and exact in performing their contracts, words, and promises ... to which end we advise you, as we have often done, to avoid an inordinate pursuit after riches, and not to launch into trade or business above your abilities'.[53] In 1755 they warned that 'an eager desire after riches hath ruined many, by pushing them in the pursuit thereof upon dangerous attempts'.[54]

London Yearly Meeting began to discuss the danger of financial ruin as a consequence of covetousness explicitly in 1727. In its epistle of that year it expressed the hope that Friends 'may be preserved from the two extremes of covetousness on the one hand, and extravagancy on the other; the latter of which has been the occasion of the failings of some among us, in the non-payment of their just debts'.[55] In 1771 the Yearly Meeting referred to 'divers instances of scandalous failures [that] have of late appeared amongst some in profession with us'.[56] The 1781 epistle found that 'some have not been sufficiently concerned to keep themselves clear of unadvised and imprudent adventures in trade and business'.[57] Bankruptcies as the consequence of covetousness are mentioned twice. In 1767, with a reminder of the positive example of 'ancient friends, presently forgotten', Yearly Meeting found that 'many have entered large schemes of trade, which has reduced them in their circumstances, but unwilling to lessen their standard of living, they used indirect means to procure

---

51   Friends, *Epistles* 1692, 50; 1703, 84 refers also to not defrauding the government; 1708, 97; 1724, 138.
52   Ibid., 1735, 171.
53   Ibid., 1753, 235.
54   Ibid., 1755, 245.
55   Ibid., 1727, 145.
56   Ibid., 1771, 302.
57   Ibid., 1781, 337, 378; 1783, 345.

temporary support, which has led to failures and bankruptcies'.[58] Similar is the 1793 epistle, which found that 'Many have been of late the overturnings and failures in the commercial world'.[59]

In 1788 the London Yearly Meeting criticized a lack of risk adversity. It asked 'were all thus awakened, what place would be found for extensive schemes in trade, nor fictitious credit to support them?', implying that this advice came as a reaction to contemporary practice of using 'fictitious credit'. This referred to accommodation bills.[60] In the last decades of the eighteenth century, Britain experienced a whole series of financial crises. According to Julian Hoppit, these were caused 'by the extensive use of credit, in the form of bills of exchange and accommodation notes, to fund expansion'.[61] In the last third of the eighteenth century, complaints about 'fictitious bills' were commonplace.[62] This epistle therefore likely constitutes a reaction to these crises.

The second major theme of business ethics in the Quaker literature is that of the evasion of taxes and customs out of covetousness. Penn reasoned that covetousness was an enemy to the state, as it bred corruption. It led people to abuse and defraud the government:

> by concealing or falsifying the goods they deal in: as bringing in forbidden goods by stealth; or lawful goods, so as to avoid the payment of dues, or wonting the goods of enemies for gain; or that are not well made, or full measure; with abundance of that sort of deceit.[63]

Between 1693 and 1786, eleven epistles dealt with this topic. The 1693 epistle referred to the duty of paying taxes and tributes with reference to the Bible, reminding Friends that they were subjects of 'Caesar's kingdom', and therefore ought to pay their 'taxes, tribute, &c.'.[64] References to the kingdoms of God and Caesar, and the respective obligations membership in them held for their subjects, were evoked repeatedly throughout the period. In 1703 the meeting explicitly advised to 'avoid all indirect and unwarrantable methods, in trade and merchandize, by which the government may be defrauded of its due'.[65] The same advice was repeated throughout the century. In 1709 Yearly Meeting specified:

---

58 Ibid., 1767, 289.
59 Ibid., 1793, 374–75.
60 Ibid., 1788, 361.
61 Julian Hoppit, 'Attitudes to Credit in Britain, 1680-1790', *Historical Journal* 32, no. 2 (1990), 133.
62 Hoppit, 'Attitudes to Credit', 137.
63 Penn, 'Cross', 202.
64 Friends, *Epistles* 1693, 56.
65 Ibid., 1703, 84; 1709, 99.

not to defraud or wrong any, in any way of commerce, trade, trust, or dealing; much less to put any abuse on the government, by endeavours to diminish any of the customs, excise, or any other publick civil dues. Yet if any, going under our profession, should happen to be so far tempted, through covetousness, and the love of unrighteous gain, as to be drawn into such evil...

Friends should 'deal with such persons, to make them sensible of such corrupt and pernicious practices'.[66] In 1719, London Yearly Meeting added that the buying and selling of 'goods reasonably expected to be run' was forbidden, and that monthly meetings ought to testify against offenders.[67] In 1721, it referred Friends to the 1719 epistle.[68] The same warning reappeared in 1733, this time supported by the scriptural quote 'Render therefore unto Caesar the things that are Caesar's'.[69] In the following year it referred to the same biblical text again.[70] In 1762, it added that 'in maritime counties especially, some may be exposed to the temptation of buying run goods for private use'.[71]

The third major aspect of business ethics that Quaker authors derived from the perceived risk of covetousness was an incentive to commit fraud. In the seventeenth and early eighteenth centuries, 'fraud' had two meanings. First, it could mean the same thing it does today, criminal deception. Additionally, the term also included any behaviour that was in some way misguiding or insincere.[72] In other words, seventeenth- and early eighteenth-century English people considered as fraudulent not only illegal practices, but also ones they deemed immoral.

Fox admonished London merchants for their 'deceitful merchandize, and cozening, and cheating, and defrauding one another'. Alluding to the sermon of the mount, he appealed to them to 'keep to yea and nay to all people in their common occasions, for whatsoever is more than these, cometh of evil'. Fox's warning was wordy and angry, and he painted the local practice of trading in the darkest colours, claiming that 'this City hath a name and a bad report of deceitful Merchandize'.[73] Equally, the epistles warned 'not to defraud or wrong any, in any way of commerce, trade, trust, or dealing'.[74] They expressed

66 Ibid., 1709, 99.
67 Ibid., 1719, 123.
68 Ibid., 1721, 130.
69 Ibid., 1733, 163; Matt. 22.21.
70 Ibid., 1734, 167; 1736, 175; 1757, 251.
71 Ibid., 1726, 269–70.
72 Ann M. Carlos, Edward Kosack and Luis Castro Penarrieta, 'Bankruptcy, Discharge, and the Emergence of Debtor Rights in Eighteenth-Century England', *Enterprise & Society* (2018), 12, 13.
73 Fox, *Warning*, 1,2.
74 Friends, *Epistles* 1709, 99.

particular concern that Friends might be 'defrauding their creditors of their just debts, and not performing their word and promise'.[75]

The key business-specific themes of Quaker ethics – debts, taxes and fraud – emerged from a general concern with covetousness. Quakers understood covetousness as a thriving towards wealth that eclipses good sense and the importance of living in the way of Truth. It leads to endangering one's own and others' wellbeing by leading into taking risks in the pursuit of wealth. Related to risk-aversity is the payment of debts, as being risk-averse is necessary in order to ensure that one will be able to pay them. The same logic applies to taxes and customs, i.e. fraud committed against the government, as well as fraud committed against private individuals. In spite of the nature of Quakerism as a faith based on revelation rather than the reading of the Bible that is central to other forms of Protestantism, Quaker authors drew on scripture to support their arguments. Key Bible sections for Friends were 1 Tim. 6.9–11, including 'The love of money is the root of all evil', and verses from the gospels referring to the tributes owed to God and Caesar respectively.

The distinctiveness of Quaker business ethics

After establishing the contents of Quaker business ethics, we can now enquire whether these were distinct from the general business ethics being propounded in English society. The Presbyterian minister John Abernethy defined covetousness as having two meanings: first, the desire of another person's possessions, and second, 'an immoderate desire of worldly possessions in whatever way they are to be acquired, even supposing it should be without injustice of any kind'.[76] Just as we saw in the Quaker epistles, Abernethy distinguished between acquiring wealth through diligence, in order to supply for one's family, and endeavours which go beyond this. 'I do not say moderate industry, but the exorbitant passion which is properly called covetousness.' These same commonalities between Quaker and other views are visible in other writings on covetousness.[77] Church of Scotland minister David Lamont used similar words, explaining that 'Industry, or proper application to business, does not constitute covetousness.'[78] John Bradford, Church of England clergyman and Independent minister, also acknowledged that gaining wealth through lawful methods and hard work is acceptable, even to a degree greater than required to answer one's own necessities, if it promotes the wellbeing of society as a

---

75   Ibid., 1729, 150; 1735, 171.
76   John Abernethy, *Sermons on Various Subjects* (1751), 295; see also Henry Stebbing, *Sermons on Practical Christianity* (London, 1759), 79.
77   Abernethy, *Sermons*, 316; also William Enfield, *Sermons for the Use of Families* (London, 1772); David Lamont, *Sermons on the most Prevalent Vices* (London, 1780), 131; Stebbing, *Practical Christianity*, Sermon V, 78–94, at 80.
78   Lamont, *Prevalent Vices*, 130.

whole.⁷⁹ Church of England clergyman Henry Stebbing argued that 'it makes a very essential Difference in this case, whether a Man gathers wealth by honest or dishonest means'.⁸⁰

Presbyterian minister Edmund Calamy's 1709 sermon titled 'A sermon at the merchants' lecture in Salters' Hall, upon occasion of the many late bankrupts' directly linked covetousness to financial ruin.⁸¹ The sermon is based on the same Bible verse, 1 Tim. 6.9–11, which appeared so prominently in Quaker epistles between the 1720s and 1750s: 'The love of money is the root of all evil'. It argues that covetousness is the common cause for financial ruin. He opened by stating that

> Among the many complaints of the times we live in, hardly any one is more commonly in the mouths of all, than against the breaking of tradesmen, and that sometimes in such circumstances, as that a great Scandal is brought upon our Holy Religion, and such Enormities are discover'd, as even Heathens themselves would have been ashame'd of.⁸²

This verse is employed to the same end in sermons by Milbourne in 1709 and William Sheridan, Bishop of Kilmore and Ardagh among others.⁸³ Similarly, the Bishop of Ely's 1717 sermon on 'The justice of paying debts' attributed 'the late failures of some eminent citizens' to covetousness.⁸⁴ Bradford, in a 1720 sermon titled 'The honest and dishonest ways of getting wealth', argued that recent 'disorder and confusion' was caused by an 'irregular pursuit' of wealth. In other words, covetousness.⁸⁵

Warnings about being risk-averse to avoid failure of the kind found in the Quaker epistles are ubiquitous in business advice literature and sermons. In 1726, popular journalist and author Daniel Defoe attributed the South Sea crisis

---

79 Samuel Bradford, *The Honest and Dishonest Ways of Getting Wealth. A Sermon Preach'd in the Parish Church of St Mary le Bow, on Sunday, November 20th, 1720* (London, 1720), 21; also Thomas Wheatland, *Twenty-six Practical Sermons on Various Subjects* (London, 1739), 43; James Foster, *Sermons* (London, 1744), 183–84; Edmund Calamy, *A Sermon at the Merchants' Lecture in Salters' Hall, on December 7th 1708, upon Occasion of the Many Late Bankrupts* (London, 1709).
80 Stebbing, *Practical Christianity*, 85.
81 Calamy, *A Sermon at the Merchants' Lecture in Salters' Hall*; also Bradford, *The Honest and Dishonest Ways of Getting Wealth*, 3; Luke Milbourne, *Debtor and Creditor Made Easy; or, The Judgement of the Unmerciful Demonstrated in a Sermon* (London, 1709); William Sheridan, *Practical Discourses upon the Most Important Subjects* (London, 1720).
82 Calamy, *A Sermon at the Merchants' Lecture in Salters' Hall*, 3.
83 Milbourne, *Debtor and Creditor*.
84 William Fleetwood, *Two Sermons, the One before the King ...... the Other Preach'd in the City, on the Justice of Paying Debts* (London, 1718).
85 Bradford, *The Honest and Dishonest Ways of Getting Wealth*.

to tradesmen's lack of risk-aversity.[86] He warned traders 'not to launch out in adventures beyond the compass of their stocks; and withal, to manage those things with due wariness'.[87] The anonymously published *Compleat Tradesman* of 1684 also advised readers 'not to engage in too many businesses, lest so many Irons burn, nor in too great Affairs, lest thy loss prove Irrepairable'.[88] Delany argued that

> this habit of running thoughtlessly into debt, draws many other worse habits after it: lying, swearing, cheating, and all kinds of vice and villainy, are its sure attendants; nay, sometimes, even murder, and an open defiance of public justice, as hath been seen in more than one unhappy and dreadful instance.[89]

Citing Romans 13.8 – 'Owe no man anything but to love one another' – as Fox had done, Delaney argued that 'the duty of paying debts' was 'a duty of as great consequence to the wellbeing of society, as any other whatsoever; as comprehending under it one great and important branch of commutative justice.' He explained that this was important as trade was interlinked, and 'the failure of one man here may affect many others in the remotest regions of the earth'.[90] Yet he lamented that the duty of paying debts was 'utterly and openly disregarded, as if neither the laws of God, nor Man, nor Nature, exacted it of us'.[91] Berriman's 1763 sermon also discussed Romans 13.8: 'Owe no man any thing but to love one another.' In his interpretation it forbade 'such borrowing and dealing with one another, as will sometimes bring men unavoidable in debt', hence he warned of taking risks in business.[92] He applied a broad definition of debts to include taxes and customs owed to the government. He appealed to his readers to 'Render therefore to all their dues: tribute to whom tribute is due, custom to whom custom … owe no man anything, but to love one another'.[93]

As Berriman illustrates, sermons discuss the duty of paying taxes and customs as well, perhaps unsurprisingly given the ties between church and state in this period. The Plymouth vicar John Gilbert in a 1699 sermon 'on the sin of stealing custom and the duty of paying tribute' supported his argument by

---

86   Daniel Defoe, *The Complete English Tradesman…* (London: C. Rivington, 1738), 48.
87   Defoe, *Complete English Tradesman*, viii; also William Berriman, 'Sermon XIV: The Guilt and Danger of Making Haste to Be Rich', in *Christian Doctrines and Duties Explained and Recommended* (London, 1751); Patrick Delany, *Twenty Sermons on Social Duties, and their Opposite Vices* (London, 1747), 240.
88   N. H., *The Compleat Tradesman, or, the Exact Dealer's Daily Companion* (London, 1684), 78.
89   Delany, *Social Duties*, 243, 254.
90   Ibid., 250.
91   Ibid., 240.
92   Berriman, 'Sermon XIV', 227.
93   Ibid., 334.

citing Romans 13.7, 'Render to all their dues, tribute to whom tribute, custom to whom custom'. He defined custom as meaning 'the legal taxes which are appointed for the support of the government, under which we live, and enjoy protection and safety' as well as the 'tax laid upon trade'.[94] An anonymous 1795 sermon on 'The rights of Caesar' made the same point, defining the 'things that are Caesar's' as all taxes intended for the maintenance of government, and for the benefit of the country as a whole.[95] The sermon on 'The sinfulness of buying run-goods' by the Anglican deacon and governor of London's Christ's Hospital School, William Unwin, made the same arguments.[96] Unwin argued that the government required revenue for its maintenance and offices, and that 'by purchasing run goods, you wrong the public body'.[97]

Finally, several extant sermons warn against fraud, closely shadowing Quaker discourse on this issue. They range from general warnings not to defraud anyone to detailed discussions of what fraud entails. Samuel Clarke in a 1660 sermon argued that 'the foundation of this crime was covetousness'.[98] Enfield explained that 'The seller defrauds his neighbour, when he takes advantage of the ignorance or mistakes of the purchaser, or makes use of arts to impose upon his judgement.'[99] Thomas Wilson argued, 'I do not mention false weights and measures; oppressing the poor; buying or selling of stolen goods; using oaths and lies to deceive those with whom they deal. Those that do any of these things know that they do ill.'[100] Moreover, taking advantage of others' 'ignorance, oversights, negligence or drunkenness in commercial transactions' was condemned.[101]

The above section has shown that non-Quaker sources discuss the key themes of Quaker business ethics at great length, too. Covetousness was the subject of countless sermons. These authors defined it not as general ambition to better one's position by acquiring wealth through hard labour, but as more extreme

---

94 John Gilbert, *A Sermon on the Sin of Stealing Custom, and the Duty of Paying Tribute* (Plymouth, 1699), 3.
95 A friend to peace and good order, *The Rights of Caesar: A Sermon. In which the Scripture-Doctrine of Magistracy is Opened Up and Enforced* (Edinburgh, 1795).
96 William Unwin, *The Sinfulness of Buying Run-Goods, Attempted to Be Shewn* (London, 1773).
97 Ibid., 10; also Berriman, 'Sermon XIV', 224; Thomas Gisborne, *An Enquiry into the Duties of Men in the Higher and Middle Classes of Society in Great Britain* (London, 1797), 244.
98 Samuel Clarke, *One Hundred and Seventy Three Sermons, on Several Subjects*, Sermon CLCXI, 'Of sin and deliberate fraud' (Dublin, 1751), 360.
99 Enfield, *Sermons for the Use of Families*, 57–58.
100 Thomas Wilson, *Sermons* (London, 1785), 32.
101 Richard Fiddes, *Fifty-two Practical Discourses Preached on Several Subjects* (London, 1720); also Wilson, *Sermons*, 23–40; Clarke, 'Sermon CLCXI', 357–72.

thrift that outbalances other, more important concerns of religion, just as in the Quaker literature.

The Quaker and non-Quaker authors' preoccupation with covetousness reflects a contemporary public debate on the dangers of luxury that continued through much of the eighteenth century. Scholars have argued that the debate was connected to the expansion of trade, especially in luxury goods, and increased consumerism.[102] In the early eighteenth century, luxury was regarded as sinful, but as Maxine Berg and Elizabeth Eger argue, it 'gradually lost its former associations with corruption and vice'.[103] Important in this development was Mandeville's 1705 'Fable of the Bees', which depicted trade and luxury as both vicious, and beneficial to the nation.[104] Mandeville summed up contemporary ideas of luxury as follows:

> It is a receiv'd Notion, that Luxury is as destructive to the wealth of the whole Body Politic, as it is to that of every individual Person who is guilty of it, and that a National Frugality enriches a Country in the same manner as that which is less general increases the Estates of private Families ... What is laid to the Charge of Luxury besides, is, that it increases Avarice and Rapine: And where they are reigning Vices, offices of the greatest Trust are bought and sold; the Ministers that should serve the Public, both great and small, corrupted, and the Countries every Moment in danger of being betray'd to the highest Bidders: And lastly, that it effeminates and enervates the People, by which the Nations become as easy Prey to the first Invaders.

Mandeville then introduced the argument that consumption, in spite of its negative image, was beneficial to the wellbeing of the nation, through increasing demand and thereby trade, which caused great controversy.[105]

From the mid-1760s onwards denunciations of luxury declined.[106] The traditional moral perspective increasingly came to be replaced by an economic one. Even the clerical contributors to the debate focused more on the economic impacts. Luxury was understood to be closely linked to corruption. Corruption in turn was linked to national debt, stock-jobbing and the moneyed companies.[107] However, it was no longer only a vice. It was also regarded as beneficial to the country, as it supported trade.[108]

---

102 Paul Langford, *A Polite and Commercial People: England 1727–1783* (Oxford: Oxford University Press, 1989, 1998), 577; Berg and Eger, 'Luxury', 11.
103 Berg and Eger, 'Luxury', 7.
104 Ibid., 10.
105 Bernard Mandeville, *The Fable of the Bees, etc.* (London: T. Ostell, 1806).
106 John Sekora, *Luxury: The Concept in Western Thought, Eden to Smollett* (Baltimore and London: Johns Hopkins University Press, 1977), 65.
107 Ibid., 64.
108 Ibid., 113.

Denunciations of luxury declined in Quaker and non-Quaker sources alike in the second half of the eighteenth century, reflecting Berg and Eger's view that by this point luxury was regarded as a sign of 'production [and] trade' that had a 'civilising impact' and benefited the country.[109] The 1750s and 1760s saw broad public debate in periodicals, books, sermons and pamphlets on the topic of luxury.[110] Early in the 1750–1770 period, authors described it as a 'common current vice', and potentially a threat to the state.[111] In the process of the debate, the definition of luxury 'gradually lost its former associations with corruption and vice, and came to include production, trade and the civilising impact of superfluous commodities'.[112] The term itself was redefined. While in the beginning of the eighteenth century, luxury was understood to include everything that was not a basic necessity for survival, by the end of the century more goods were categorized as necessities, including those 'of the mind', i.e. reading, education, and politeness.[113] An economic and nationalist perspective replaced the traditional moral one.

The sources consulted for this chapter reflect the currency of this debate, but they do not relax in their condemnation of covetousness. They worry that people live beyond their means in order to afford luxuries and therefore borrow more than they could hope to repay and engage in risky business transactions. Hence, they regarded being modest and plain in one's life style as a way of meeting the challenge of covetousness. William Penn, for example, in his 'advice to his children', warned readers to 'avoid pride as you would avoid the devil, remembering you must die, and consequently those things must die with you that could be any temptation to pride; and that there is a judgment follows, at which you must give an account both of what you have enjoyed and done'.[114] In references spread throughout the period, the epistles mentioned pride, luxury and extravagance thirty-two times between 1688 and 1798, referencing 'outward habits and fashions', 'words, ways, fashions and customs of the world' and the 'glittering gaiety of this vain world'.[115] In 1734, the London Yearly Meeting issued a particularly long epistle regarding the 'vain

---

109   Berg and Eger, 'Luxury', 7.
110   Sekora, *Luxury*, 66.
111   Ibid., 64–66. Sekora places the peak of the controversy between 1753 and 1763. Margaret Hunt, *The Middling Sort: Commerce, Gender, and the Family in England, 1680–1780* (Berkeley: University of California Press, 1996), 50, also found that luxury was 'routinely condemned in the eighteenth century'.
112   Berg and Eger, 'Luxury', 7.
113   Christopher Berry, *The Idea of Luxury: A Conceptual and Historical Investigation* (Cambridge: Cambridge University Press, 1994), 125.
114   Penn, *Father's Love*, 42.
115   Friends, *Epistles* 1688, 329; 1703, 85; 1712, 107; 1704, 87; 1718, 122; 1719, 124; 1721, 129; 1724, 137; 1739, 185.

fashions and corrupt customs of the world'.¹¹⁶ In 1763, it warned the affluent not to get carried away 'into pride, indolence, and extravagance' as this had led to debts and ruin.¹¹⁷ In 1768 it reprinted and distributed Quaker minister Ambrose Rigge's 1678 epistle quoted above warning tradesmen not to borrow in order to finance an expensive lifestyle.¹¹⁸ This was nothing unusual: in the same period Patrick Delany of the Church of Ireland warned that a 'spirit of extravagance' and living above one's fortune was dangerous.¹¹⁹ Defoe named extravagant living as a frequent cause for tradesmen's financial ruin.¹²⁰ Many more examples could be given.

As we have seen, non-Quaker authors also made an explicit connection between covetousness and the issues of risk-aversity and debts, taxes and fraud identified as its offshoots by Friends. It is interesting that non-Quaker authors appear to attribute as much importance to the duty of paying taxes and customs as did Friends. The concern for taxes can be seen in the context of the early modern theme of subject duty. Obedience to authority had been a common element in business ethics since the Middle Ages.¹²¹ One might expect that Friends put more emphasis on this point due to their refusal to pay tithes. This caveat in their pursuit of being regarded as good citizens might have motivated them to make up for this by appearing particularly loyal to the Crown, if not to the ecclesiastical authorities. Yet the thrust of their arguments about governmental dues is the same as that of non-Quaker authors. Moreover, they base them on the same authorities from the New Testament, especially 1 Timothy and Jesus's instructions on giving Caesar his dues.

The metaphorical framework of Quaker and non-Quaker ethics

The fundamental conceptual overlap between Quaker and non-Quaker business ethics can also be seen in the way that writers of all denominations used the same set of metaphors to illustrate their arguments. The sources frequently liken the related issues of luxury, pride and covetousness to an illness or epidemic. For Penn luxury was

> A disease as epidemical, as killing: it creeps into all stations and ranks of men; the poorest often exceeding their ability to indulge their appetite; and

---

116 Ibid., 1734, 66, similar content in 1735, 170; 1736, 174; 1737, 178; 1738, 180, including Bible reference Romans 13.2; 1747, 213; 1755, 245; 1771, 301; 1781, 339; 1789, 364; 1715, 112; 1717, 119 refers to Epistle of 1715; 1732, 160; 1720, 128; 1727, 145; 1721, 129; 1741, 194; 1754, 40; 1719, 124; 1735, 170; 1736, 174; 1789, 364; 1798, 385.
117 Ibid., 1763, 273.
118 Ibid., 1768, 292.
119 Delany, *Social Duties*, 243–45.
120 Defoe, *Complete English Tradesman*, 87.
121 Barrington Moor, *Moral Aspects of Economic Growth, and Other Essays* (Ithaca, NY: Cornell University Press, 1998), 10.

the rich frequently wallowing in those things that please the lusts of their eye and flesh, and the pride of life.[122]

Moreover, he found the covetous man to be 'a disease to the body politick, for he obstructs the circulation of blood'.[123] Lamont also used the analogy of the sick human body to explain the danger covetousness posed to society:

> A man is covetous, when his heart is set upon keeping money. Money is to the world what blood is to the body. When the blood circulates properly, the body is in health; when it flows irregularly, the body is in pain: so when money circulates with sprightliness, the world prospers; when money stagnates, the world declines.[124]

In a similar vein, the 1709 epistle described pride as a 'leprosy':

> And let the aged remember, and the youth know, that when apparent signs of the plague of leprosy appeared on the walls in the houses of Israel, it was the care of the priest under the law, to have the houses cleansed, and the lepers also. And surely Christ's priesthood should not fall short of their care to endeavour to stop and remove the manifest tokens of the leprosy of the great sin of pride, and all superfluity of naughtiness. And therefore let all concerned be earnestly stirred up to sincere obedience to this light of Christ, our great high priest; that he may cleanse the hearts and houses of that growing plague, which tends to the ruin of families and posterity.[125]

The Yearly Meeting used the same basic metaphor again in 1773, when it warned of luxury as a 'spreading contagion'.[126] Similarly, Thomas Mun called luxury a 'general leprosie'.[127] Calamy termed covetousness 'a fatal contagion', which loosened 'all the bands of society ... introducing general confusion'.[128] In 1710, Laurence Hacket, in a sermon to the Levant company merchants, called pride a 'tumour'.[129] Charles Brent in a 1728 sermon before a merchant audience in Bristol referred to the love of money, i.e. covetousness, as 'an evil disease'.[130]

---

122 Penn, *Cross*, 218.
123 Ibid., 206.
124 Lamont, *Prevalent Vices*, 135.
125 Friends, *Epistles* 1709, 99.
126 Ibid., 1773, 311.
127 Thomas Mun, *England's Treasure by Forraign Trade, or: The Balance of our Forraign Trades Is the Rule of our Treasure* (London, 1664), 180.
128 Calamy, *A Sermon at the Merchants' Lecture in Salters' Hall*, 6.
129 Laurence Hacket, *A Sermon Preached at St Bennet-Finct Church [sic]* (London, 1707), 31.
130 Charles Brent, *Money Essay'd; or, the True Value of it Tryed. In a Sermon Preach'd before the Worshipful Society of Merchants, in the City of Bristol* (London, 1728), 20.

Daniel Defoe called 'Expensive living ... a kind of slow fever ... fatal and sure to kill'.[131] London Magazine in 1758 diagnosed luxury as a 'pestilence' which had spread throughout the nation.[132]

Another metaphor frequently employed in religious and secular publications to highlight the dangers of business are the risks presented by deep water. Authors drew on Psalms 69.2 – 'I am come into deep waters, where the floods overflow me' – to liken taking risks in business to drowning.[133] Ambrose Rigge warned that

> There are some amongst us ... [who] have launched from the Rock which is firm and sure, into the Great Sea of Troubles and Uncertainty, where some have been drowned, others hardly escaping, and many yet labouring for the Shore, with little hopes of coming at it; who have not only brought themselves in Danger of suffering shipwreck, but have drawn in others, and have endangered them also.[134]

Similarly, Steele's *Religious Tradesman* of 1747 recommended 'That you launch out no farther than you can feel ground under you'.[135] Defoe compared a tradesman's overtrading to 'a young swimmer going out of his depth; when help does not come immediately, 'tis a thousand to one but he sinks, and is drown'd'.[136] The reverend William Scott found that the contemporary proneness to extravagance and luxury led men to 'plunge headlong into engagements immense, distant and dangerous'.[137]

The above discussion shows that Friends' epistles, pamphlets and books address the same themes as the non-Quaker merchant manuals and sermons. Their main concerns are covetousness and the vices related to it, as well as its negative implications for society as a whole. These reflected an increased consumerism, a core social development of the period. All sets of sources reference the same scripture verses, such as 1 Tim. 6.9–10 and Romans 13.8. Finally, all sets of sources use the same metaphors: the image of deep water for dangerous business ventures, and epidemic disease for pride and luxury.

---

131 Defoe, *Complete English Tradesman*, 111, also Richard Steele, *The Religious Tradesman, or, Plain and Serious Hints of Advice for the Tradesman's Prudent and Pious Conduct, from his Entrance into Business, to his Leaving it Off* (London, 1747).
132 *London Magazine* 27, 233, May 1758, cited in Sekora, *Luxury*, 65.
133 John Ayto and Judith Siefring, *From the Horse's Mouth: Oxford Dictionary of English Idioms* (Oxford: Oxford University Press, 2009).
134 Rigge, *Commerce and Trading*.
135 Steele, *Religious Tradesman*, 39.
136 Defoe, *Complete English Tradesman*, 47; see also a similar quote on 48; also Supplement to *Tradesman*: 'Ocean of Business', 3.
137 William Scott, *A Sermon on Bankruptcy, Stopping Payment, Debts, Preached at Various Churches in the City* (London, 1773).

The basic elements of Quaker business ethics were similar, if not identical to mainstream business ethics. There is no sign that Friends possessed a distinctive ethic.

It is possible that Friends followed the same business ethics with more vigour than others. Especially the first two generations who were faced with persecution joined the Society at potentially great personal cost. They may have been particularly concerned not to give anyone reason for complaint about them and protecting their communities' reputation, or simply more committed to maintaining and expressing their faith throughout all sides of their lives. Equally, Friends may have adhered to business ethics more stringently than others because their religious organization formally enforced these.[138] This possibility will be explored in the next chapter.

---

138 Zahedieh, *Capital*, 109.

5

Quaker Discipline in Practice

Early Friends aimed to minimize contact with church and state. As a substitute, they developed their own structures to supply those services that the parish usually provided. During the 1650s and 1660s, the Society began to set up the monthly meetings, whose purpose it was to administer the community. As such they were also known as 'meetings for business'. In charge of organizing poor relief and conducting marriage ceremonies, the monthly meetings became the administrative unit most closely involved in individual Friends' lives. Upon arrival in Pennsylvania, the Quaker colonists of Philadelphia immediately set up a monthly meeting there. This was followed in 1686 by a separate monthly meeting of women Friends. In London, women's monthly meetings were set up only in the second half of the eighteenth century, when each of the six men's meetings received a 'twin' meeting for women. Until then, it appears that at least some of the London monthly meetings were attended by both men and women, and had both male and female officers.

Extensive records of the monthly meetings in London and Philadelphia survive. They include monthly meetings' accounts, records of disciplinary measures, records pertaining to apprentice placements organized by the meetings, marriage, birth and death certificates of members, and papers pertaining to poor relief. Importantly, the complete minutes of five out of the six London monthly meetings are extant. Missing are the minutes of Gracechurch Street meeting, which were lost in a fire. The London monthly meetings' minutes commence in the later seventeenth century, and continue well into the nineteenth century. The minutes reflect the tasks the monthly meetings undertook, and what they considered their primary duties. As such, they are evidence of the relationship between the Society of Friends' formal organs and its members.

The women's monthly meetings of both Philadelphia and London were in charge of administering poor relief and preparing marriage ceremonies. They investigated brides' circumstances and issued certificates confirming 'clearness for marriage'. These explained that neither bride nor groom were already engaged to somebody else. They also oversaw female community members' behaviour. This involved investigating reports of 'disorderly walking'.[1] If

---

[1] Pullin, *Female Friends*, 96, 109, 121, 126.

they found a female Friend had broken the discipline and was not sufficiently repentant, they proposed the culprit's disownment to the men's meeting. The men's meetings routinely confirmed the women's meetings' decisions in these matters, and then drew up testimonies of denial.[2] The women Friends did not execute disownments themselves, which is why this study focuses on the men's meetings minutes as sources.

The Society's organization in the American colonies resembled that in England. Therefore, the types of records its meetings have left are also similar. When the first Friends arrived in Philadelphia in 1682, they immediately set up a men's monthly meeting. This was located on the corner of 4th and Arch Streets, where a meeting house still stands today. After 1772 two additional men's monthly meetings were created, one in the Southern District and one in the Northern Liberties. For the three men's meetings uninterrupted minutes survive covering the period from their founding to the year 1800 and beyond.

Over the course of the seventeenth and eighteenth centuries, both extent and content of the monthly meetings' minutes changed significantly. Their transformation reflects changes in the meetings' priorities, as well as their relationship with their congregations. First, the London monthly meetings' minutes grew from an average of 150.6 entries per meeting in 1700 to an average of 211.8 entries in 1750 and 311.2 entries in 1800. As discussed above, the London Quaker community's membership peaked during the 1680s and 1690s, and dropped in the eighteenth century. The minutes' growth can therefore not be explained with the requirements of a larger Quaker population. Instead, they show an increase in the monthly meetings' monitoring of their congregations. Over the course of the period, London's monthly meetings came to take a greater interest in individual Friends' lives, monitoring the community ever more closely.

Second, the minutes' content changed. While the tasks which the meetings recorded remained the same, their focus shifted into a new direction. I coded the minutes' content and divided them into categories. Table 4 shows which areas became more or less represented in the minutes.

The category 'discipline' includes actual sanctions the monthly meetings administered, as well as readings of the Yearly Meeting epistles, which contain large sections of advice on how to behave. The category 'unclear' includes mostly minutes relating to individuals' cases being continued. These usually mean disciplinary actions, or enquiries into whether somebody required poor relief. Hence, the majority of unclear cases belong in either of those categories. 'Poor relief' includes decisions to give cash to individuals in need, as well as delivery of coal for poor families, and entries regarding the admittance of adults or children into the Friends' workhouse or school in Clerkenwell. The

---

2 Jean R. Soderlund, 'Women's Authority in Pennsylvania and New Jersey Quaker meetings, 1680–1760', *William and Mary* (1987), 736, 742, 744.

Table 4. Contents of London Monthly Meeting Minutes

Category	N			%		
	1700	1750	1800	1700	1750	1800
Finances	210	341	186	27.9	32.2	12
Certificates of removal	43	89	426	5.7	8.4	27.4
Births and burials	21	20	56	2.8	1.9	3.6
Discipline	101	197	239	13.4	18.6	15.4
Administration	92	109	244	12.2	10.3	15.7
Appointments	56	43	42	7.4	4.1	2.7
Apprentices	42	16	55	5.6	1.5	3.5
Poor Relief	67	126	86	8.9	11.9	5.5
Marriages	68	25	38	9	2.4	2.4
Unclear	53	93	184	7.04	8.8	11.8
Total	753	1059	1556	100	100	100

Sources: Minutes of Horsleydown, Westminster, Devonshire House, Peel and Ratcliff Monthly Meetings for the years 1700, 1750 and 1800.

category 'Apprentices' includes information on apprentice indentures being agreed, as well as ongoing searches for placements for young people. The category 'Finances' includes accounts and notes on expenses incurred by the meetings in various ways. For example, Ratcliff monthly meeting in 1750 recorded settling a 'bill for Publick Friends Horses amounting to five pounds six shillings'.[3] The minutes also include references to subscriptions being raised to pay off the debts of the London Six Weeks Meeting.[4] The large category 'Administration' includes general administrative issues, such as the maintenance of meeting houses and burial grounds, and the writing up of answers to yearly and quarterly meeting queries. 'Appointments' includes the appointing of representatives of the monthly meeting to quarterly and yearly meetings, offices within the meeting such as clerk, as well as, and primarily, door keepers during the meetings for worship.

3   Rattcliff MM minutes, v/1750, 279.
4   Consisting of representatives of the London monthly meetings, the Six Weeks Meeting was in charge of maintaining the Society's buildings and burial grounds, circulating testimonies of denial and mediating disputes between the monthly meetings in the capital. See Beck et al., *London Friends' Meetings*, 91–100.

Several categories, including discipline, poor relief and marriages, include references to ongoing processes, i.e. a matter of discipline was investigated over several months, every month containing an entry that the 'matter is continued'. I counted each of these entries individually. The same is true for 'marriages'. A couple had to announce their intention to become married three times. Hence, each marriage appears repeatedly in the minutes. The category 'Certificates' refers to documents Friends were supposed to apply for from their home meeting when moving to a new town and submit to their new meeting there. They certified that the Friend was in good standing with the community.[5] Finally, 'Discipline' includes references to enquiries made about individuals in order to issue them with certificates or sanction them rather than total numbers of certificates or sanctions. This makes the count a measure of the intensity of meetings' attention to issues rather than a measure of the scale of particular tasks. In other words, the count shows the frequency with which the meeting would attend to issues of each category.

The by far most important category in 1700 was finances, as table 4 shows. This had grown further by 1750. By the year 1800, however, it appeared far less frequently. It was surpassed by 'discipline' and 'certificates of removal'. 'Certificates of removal' was the strongest growing category, with an increase from 5.7 per cent in 1700 to 27.4 per cent in 1800 of total entries in the minutes. This was followed by 'discipline' and 'administration' with 15.4 and 15.7 per cent of total entries each.

The minutes show that the London monthly meetings actively enforced the Quaker discipline from their inception in the 1660s. Over the course of the period, the attention they paid to this aspect grew, as represented in both the categories of 'discipline' and 'certificates of removal'. Especially in the second half of the eighteenth century, entries in the minutes referring to disciplinary matters increased dramatically.

The minutes of the Philadelphia monthly meetings follow a similar trend that we observed for the London meetings. They became more extensive, and the focus of their contents shifted, too. During the seventeenth century, Philadelphia monthly meeting's minutes usually consisted of less than a page per month. By 1800, a monthly gathering produced an average of 26.4 pages of minutes. This constitutes approximately a twenty-six-fold increase in the meetings' record keeping. As the number of Friends in Philadelphia roughly doubled between 1690 and 1760, the growth of the meetings' minutes is evidence of an intense

---

5 See chapter 8 for further details on certificates of removal. This policy closely followed the contemporary Settlement Acts which, as part of the Old Poor Law, regulated in which parishes English paupers were entitled to settle and receive poor relief. See for instance James Taylor, 'The Impact of Pauper Settlement 1691–1834', *Past & Present* 73 (1976). Certificates were also issued and required by Independents, see for instance Lime Street Independent Meeting House, 1692–1764.

Table 5. Contents of Philadelphia Monthly Meeting Minutes

	N			%		
Years	1690	1750	1790	1690	1750	1790
Marriages	9	16	15	14	7	5
Certificates	6	48	94	10	20	32
Mediation	19	3	1	30	1	0
Administration	21	94	58	33	40	20
Discipline	8	76	125	13	32	43
Total	63	237	293	100	100	100

Sources: Haverford Quaker Collections, Philadelphia MM minutes.

increase in the meetings' efforts of administration per capita. In addition, the contents of the minutes changed. Table 5 shows the frequency with which the minutes addressed different topics.

In the Philadelphia monthly meeting records, the category 'discipline' includes concerns about drinking, 'extravagancies of wedding dinners', sanctions, and public readings of the epistles of the London Yearly Meeting. The category 'administration' includes looking after meeting houses and other properties, as well as poor relief.

The changing relative importance of different categories in the Philadelphia monthly meeting minutes bears resemblances to those of London meetings. As in London, Philadelphia meetings were interested in discipline from the beginning. Equally as in London, the relative importance of this category grew, as did that of the related category of certificates of removal. Over the course of the period, the monitoring of the community and enforcement of the discipline became central tasks of the meetings. Put differently, the meetings put ever more efforts into controlling their members.

Monthly meetings and discipline

Within the Society of Friends' formal structure, different meetings had different responsibilities. These evolved over time. London and Philadelphia Yearly Meetings formally assigned to the monthly meetings the task of enforcing the Quaker discipline among their congregations in 1719. London Yearly Meeting's epistle of that year called upon monthly meetings to 'severely reprehend and testify against such offenders, and their unwarrantable, clandestine and unlawful actions'.⁶ At the same time, Philadelphia Yearly Meeting compiled the Society of Friends' first Book of Discipline. In manuscript form, this was circulated among meetings in the Delaware Valley. The Discipline instructed that

> Where any professing Truth are guilty of any gross, or notorious crimes or such other disorderly and indecent practices as shall give or occasion public scandal ... [they] ought to appear, as soon as possible at the monthly meeting whereunto he or she belongs.

The Discipline provided detailed instructions on how the monthly meetings were to handle offenders. Upon appearing at their monthly meeting, a delinquent was to

> acknowledge the offences, and condemn the same in writing, under his or her hand, to the satisfaction of the said meeting, and let such acknowledgement & condemnation be published by the sd meeting in such manner as that it may probably reach as far, and become as publick as the offence hath been.

It directed that 'where any such offender, refuseth to acknoweldge and condemn the fault, then the said monthly meeting ought speedily to testifie upon record, against him or her, and the fact'.⁷ The minutes of the London and Philadelphia monthly meetings show how the meetings implemented these instructions.

The monthly meetings' involvement usually began when they received reports of a member's misconduct. Sometimes, a Friend approached the meeting out of their own initiative to confess a transgression. At other times, members of the congregation informed the monthly meeting about the culprit. The monthly meeting thereupon appointed a committee to make inquiries. The committee members visited the accused at their home and questioned them. In addition, they questioned witnesses to the transgression. Then, they reported back to the monthly meeting. This process could take several months.

If the investigation led the monthly meeting to find an accused guilty of misconduct, it gave them a chance to repent and submit a paper of self-condemnation. This contained the offender's admission of guilt and declaration of their repentance. The monthly meeting would evaluate the paper. London Yearly Meeting warned monthly meetings to 'be careful not to admit such persons into fellowship ... before the meeting or meetings are satisfied of their repentance or amendment'.⁸

---

6 Friends, *Epistles* 1719, 124.
7 Yearly Meeting of Philadelphia, Book of Discipline, 1719, 39–41.
8 Friends, *Epistles* 1708, 96. For examples of London meetings following these guidelines see: Ratcliff MM, Minutes, x/1750, 294; 7/i/1749; xii/1750, 295.

Monthly meetings considered papers of self-condemnation carefully before deciding whether to accept them. For instance, in 1750 London's Ratcliff monthly meeting recorded that 'Zachariah Cockfield and Joseph Taylor brought in from Dinah Dury, a paper of condemnation of her practices in Marrying from Friends, said paper continued to be considered, said Friends continued to visit her again'.[9] They noted about another case that 'The paper brought in from Samuel Lawrence is continued to be considered.'[10] The next step was to have the paper of self-condemnation read to the congregation at Friends' meetings for worship. Philadelphia monthly meeting in 1724 recorded that 'William Fishbourn having been duly dealt with for his scandalous conduct and behaviour with women did send in a paper to the said meeting wherein he acknowledges & condemned the same, which paper by the direction of the said meeting was read in or first days meeting of worship.'[11] If the monthly meeting was convinced of a delinquent's contrition, this would be the end of the matter, and the Friend was received back into the fold of the community. There is also evidence that the meetings sometimes rejected the papers and returned them to the delinquents in order to be revised, as demonstrated by the instance when Ratcliff monthly meeting noted that 'William Smith and Josiah Hoskins are desired to visit Susannah Brewster and Hannah Renton, and let them know, wherein their papers are dissatisfactory to the meeting.'[12] Similarly, when Horsleydown monthly meeting in 1754 testified against Jonathan Hobson, it explained that 'he did not manifest to the friends who visited him, nor to the monthly meeting, where he appeared to be sensible of his past evil conduct, nor seemed to have any remorse on his mind for the same'.[13]

If a monthly meeting did consider a Friend's self-condemnation insufficient, they would prepare to 'disown' the Friend. A disownment was a form of ostracism, in which the Society publicly and in writing declared its disunity with the offender. The monthly meeting would compose a paper detailing the cause for the disownment. This paper was called a 'testimony of denial'.[14] Testimonies of denial could include detailed explanations of the delinquent's offence, and the efforts the monthly meeting had made to reclaim her or him. The Peel meeting for example explained in 1786 how it came to ostracize the delinquent Thomas Wright. It noted:

---

9 Ratcliff MM minutes, x/1750, 294.
10 Ibid., 7/i/1749.
11 Philadelphia MM minutes, 1715–1744, 128, report on the case of William Fishbourn, and ToD, 8th month 1725.
12 Ratcliff MM minutes xii/1750, 295.
13 Horsleydown MM, Book of Disorderly Walkers, 1728–1783, 1784–1805, vol. 1, ToD Jonathan Hobson, 1754.
14 Simon Dixon, 'The Life and Times of Peter Briggins', *Quaker Studies* 10, no. 2 (2006).

Thomas Wright a member of this meeting having lately attended Lectures in the episcopal way of worship conforming thereto (although many years has he had left that profession & joined himself to our Society by convincement) was visited thereupon by appointment of this meeting. At several opportunities which Friends had with him, they endeavoured in Gospel Love to make him sensible of the Inconsistency of such conduct, but in stead of yealding to their reasons he justified himself, pleaded for a liberty to attend what Places of worship he pleased, and expressed a great preference for the above mentioned, yet without disclaiming his pretensions to our Society.[15]

The meetings did not always go into so much detail. Instead, they sometimes merely attested that a delinquent had committed 'gross crimes of a scandalous nature' or 'evil conduct'. The reasons for the disownment were always followed by a declaration that the meeting no longer considered the offender a member of the Society of Friends.

The case of Peel meeting member James Jackson illuminates the procedure leading to the production of a testimony from different perspectives. In 1707, the monthly meeting initiated an investigation into his suspected disorderly conduct. After talking with the appointed Friends, James Jackson wrote a letter to the meeting, which survives among the Peel's records. In this he furiously complains about the treatment he received by the meeting's officers:

> my crude treatment from friends is even as when a combined party of usurping husbandmen seize, bind, strip & hang up alive one of their fellow tenants to affright others for disseisin from there Detenure, & cease not sending messengers to see if he will recant & rejoyn them, Give this in answer to them yt sent you from yr dispised persecuted & faithfull frd James Jackson.[16]

Shortly after, Peel meeting member Peter Briggins noted in his diary: 'In ye evening wt wth Jno Staple, I Butr, W. Widow & Jn Stringelo to Rd Millers about drawing up a papr about I.I.'[17] The minutes of the following monthly meeting at the Peel contain a description of the meeting's investigation into James Jackson's disorderly conduct for preaching ideas the monthly meeting did not agree with. It is followed by a copy of the testimony against Jackson:

> We whose names are under written being desired by ye Peel Mo meeting ye 24 of 7 mo 1707 to visit J. Jackson & signify their dissatisfaction with his appearing in publick as also his late printed book entitled ye Greate Question answered in Defence of ye Camisers wherein he passes a severe sentence against all yt will not own yem & c.

15 ToD Thomas Wright, Ratcliff MM, Testimonies of Denial, 1697–1797.
16 Peel MM minutes, 31/x/1707.
17 Peter Briggins, Diary, 1711–1713, 24/vii/1707.

Did repeatedly visit ye sd J.Jackson and laid before him our sense of his present state & errors in Judgment & did as much as in us lay endeavour to bring him to a sense thereof in much love & tenderness with him yet he roughly & absurdly treated us & sd if you reject me & those lines inserted in ye above sd book god will reject you & ym yt sent you & farther sd yt if he was deceived God had deceived him.[18]

Copies of these testimonies were kept with the monthly meeting's records, and also shared with other meetings. For example, Westminster monthly meeting in 1700 'Agreed that the paper given forth agst Hannah Shophoards disorderly walking be entd in ye book & a copy of it to be sent to ye six weeks meeting in London.'[19] Additionally, the meeting distributed copies of the disownment among nearby monthly meetings. The circulated copies were read out in the receiving monthly meetings. There is moreover some evidence indicating that copies were distributed among the public. Horsleydown monthly meeting in 1720 noted that 'John Padley reports that John Gleed & himself have delivered to Thomas Steen a coppy of this Meeting's Testimony agt him, and have also dispersed coppys & brought in the original.'[20] They also ordered that 'Richard Crofton continued to Deliver Steven Coachman a copy of this Meetings Testimony against him, and to disperse Coppys also to bring a copy to this meeting.'[21]

From the Society's London and Philadelphia records, it appears that few of those who demonstrated repentance in this form were later disowned. In other words, repentance was a way of avoiding further punishment. If a disownment did take place, it constituted a form of ostracism. However, monthly meetings did not cut disowned Friends off completely. They merely banned them from preaching, attending monthly meetings and receiving poor relief. Disowned Friends could continue to attend meetings for worship, and be buried in Friends' cemeteries. What is more, a disownment did not have to be permanent. Disowned Friends always had the option of submitting a self-condemnation at a later point, and rejoining the Society. The case of Gilbert Hagen illustrates this. In 1750, Horsleydown monthly meeting found him guilty of 'divers scandalous and evil practices'. In its testimony against Hagen, the meeting explained that they felt obliged to disown him, 'until he clear himself of this charge, and shew marks of a sincere repentance by publick confession & future amendment of [his] life'.[22]

---

18 Peel MM minutes, 29/viii/1707.
19 Westminster MM minutes, 4/i/1700, 119.
20 Horsleydown MM minutes, iv/1720.
21 Horsleydown MM minutes, ii/1720; another reference to dispersing copies is at iv/1720, Benjamin Reeve, ToD.
22 Horsleydown MM, Disorderly Walkers, vol. 1, ToD Gilbert Hagen, 1750, 75.

With their extensive enquiries, the monthly meetings invested a lot of time and effort before deciding to disown a Friend. Moreover, as we have seen, a disowned Friend's ostracism was not complete, and disowned Friends could apply for re-entry into the Society at any time. The precise nature of disownment as a punishment is important. The minutes show that a disownment's threat lay not in an absolute or permanent exclusion from the community. Instead, its power lay in the offender's exposure, their public embarrassment, and the harm the public testimonies did to their reputation. In this, the Quakers' sanctions are reminiscent of those of other Christian communities, where exclusion from communion was a common punishment for transgression.

With the actual punishment of 'disorderly walkers' apparently being so lax, what purpose did the monthly meetings pursue with their disciplinary measures? Both the London Yearly Meeting's 1719 epistle and the Philadelphia Yearly Meeting's Book of Discipline explain the aim of their sanctions. They specify that this was to protect the Society of Friends' reputation. The Philadelphia Book of Discipline explains that Friends hoped that through disownments, 'scandal may be removed, and our Holy Profession clear'd'.[23] The London Yearly Meeting's epistle instructed all monthly meetings to not only disown offenders, but also 'publish such testimony, so far as shall appear requisite for the clearing of Truth'.[24] The meetings were concerned that the misconduct of individual Friends would reflect badly on the Society as a whole. In order to protect the Quaker community from repercussions, they decided it was necessary to clearly disassociate themselves from individuals whose behaviour in some respect or other might blemish Friends' collective reputation. The testimonies of denial confirm that monthly meetings followed these directions. The vast majority of testimonies from both London and Philadelphia monthly meetings explain that the meeting regretted having to disown the Friend, but saw no other way to protect the Society's name. For example, the Peel monthly meeting explained that it had to disown the insolvent Leonard Snowden because his conduct had 'brought great sufferings upon many persons and families, as well as heavy reproach upon our Christian profession'.[25] It testified against Hercules Williams because he had been 'falsely charging men in high reputation, not of our persuasion', as well as publicly insulting a 'man of eminence ... in the street, in order to obtain money from him under pretence of a just

---

23 Philadelphia MM, Book of Discipline.
24 Society of Friends, *Collection of the Epistles from the Yearly Meeting of Friends in London to the Quarterly and Monthly meetings in Great Britain, Ireland and Elsewhere, from 1675 to 1805; being from the First Establishment of that Meeting to the Present Time* (Baltimore: Cole and Hewes, 1806), 1719.
25 Peel MM, Book of Sufferings 1753–1773 (containing condemnations and sanctions 1676–1773), Library of the Religious Society of Friends, London, Leonard Snowden, ToD, 1799.

demand'.[26] This was a serious matter, as rumours of an inability to pay one's debts severely harmed one's reputation, and thereby the ability to obtain credit and do business.[27] Equally, Horsleydown monthly meeting testified against Thomas Merrick after mishandling bills of exchange, as 'much reproach & scandal has been brought on our Society'.[28] Philadelphia monthly meeting in 1735 testified against William Masters for living with a woman 'to whom it is generally supposed he is not married'. The monthly meeting declared that 'for the clearing of truth, and avoiding that reproach which such actions might otherwise justly occasion to our Society, we find ourselves under a concern to Testify against all such vicious practices, and to disown him from being of our Religious community'.[29]

Prosecuting Quaker crimes

London monthly meetings preserved records of the sanctions they executed against delinquent Friends. As shown in table 6, the individual monthly meetings' sanctioning collections cover the period from the 1670s to 1800. They include both self-condemnations and testimonies of denial.[30]

---

26   Ratcliff MM, Testimonies of Denial, 1697–1797. ToD Hercules William, 1761.
27   Carlos, Kosack and Castro Penarrieta, 'Bankruptcy, Discharge, and the Emergence of Debtor Rights', 13.
28   Horsleydown MM, Disorderly Walkers, vol. 1, ToD Thomas Merrick, 1760. For further examples see Ratcliff MM's testimony against Ralph Thorne, recorded in Peel MM, Sufferings, 1759; Devonshire House MM, ToD Robert Williamson 1773, Ratcliff MM, Testimonies of Denial, 1697–1797; Horsleydown MM, ToD Thomas Summerfield, 1757, Horsleydown MM, Disorderly Walkers, vol. 1.
29   Philadelphia MM minutes, 1715-1744, ToD William Masters, 1735, 260. For further examples from Philadelphia see ToD Jacob Jones 1740, Ibid, 318, ToD Hannah Brientnall 1730, Ibid, 189.
30   London's Six Weeks Meeting also collected copies of testimonies of denial. Using its minutes, Beck et al. counted 818 Testimonies of Denial for the period 1734-1794. Relying on my sources, the records of the individual monthly meetings, I collected 750 testimonies of denial for the same period. My collection therefore misses 68 testimonies of denial registered by the Six Weeks Meeting. However, the sanctioning collections have the advantage that they also include self-condemnations, which the Six Weeks Meeting minutes omit. As self-condemnations formed an important part of the sanctioning process, omitting them would distort the picture of monthly meetings' sanctioning practices. Furthermore, the individual meetings' sanction collections cover a longer period than the Six Weeks Meeting minutes. They date back at least to the 1670s and continue up to 1800 and beyond, i.e. at least 70 years more than the Six Weeks Meeting minutes, and include 107 sanctions more. They therefore provide a better basis for an analysis of the institutional changes that the Society underwent in this period. See Beck et al., *London Friends' meetings*, 122-124.

Table 6. Sources for London Monthly Meeting Sanctions

Meeting	Period covered	Sanctions included
Horsleydown	1728–1805 (included up to 1800)	245 (included up to 1800)
Peel	1676 (or earlier)–1773	223
Westminster	1666–1777	30
Devonshire House	1688–1740	46
Ratcliff	1697–1794	670

Sources: Horsleydown MM, Book of Disorderly Walkers, 2 volumes, 1728–1805; Peel monthly meeting, Book of Sufferings 1753–1776 (containing sanctions c. 1676–1773); Westminster monthly meeting, Condemnations, 1666–1777; Devonshire House monthly meeting, Testimonies, 1688–1740; Ratcliff monthly meeting, Testimonies of Denial, 1697–1794.

There is a large overlap between the cases the different monthly meetings recorded in these collections, suggesting that they are quite complete. Philadelphia meetings did not keep such separate collections. Therefore, this study relies on samples of one year in five of these minutes.[31] There is a certain overlap between self-condemnations and testimonies of denial in the Philadelphia meetings' minutes. This creates the risk of counting cases twice. For Philadelphia I therefore included testimonies of denial only.[32]

Philadelphia and London monthly meetings punished a wide range of offences. The causes for these sanctions ranged widely, from violent crimes such as rape, to playing the lottery, public drunkenness and bankruptcy.[33] The most common cause throughout the entire period in both locations were offences related to the Quaker marriage discipline.

London's first disownment took place in 1689, when Devonshire House monthly meeting testified against Jane Hynd for having had a 'child with

---

[31] An earlier study of Pennsylvania Quaker meetings' sanctions by Jack Marietta analyzed the minutes in total. However, he included cases of dispute mediation as delinquencies, even if they did not lead to a disownment or self-condemnation. He thereby lumped together activities of the meetings which I argue were distinct from each other. Dispute mediation was a key activity of Philadelphia monthly meeting until about 1720. Counting these as delinquencies skews the image of the development of sanctioning. See Marietta, *Reformation*.
[32] See Appendix II for statistics of Philadelphia monthly meetings' self-condemnations.
[33] My sample of Philadelphia MM sanctions contains all cases for one year in five, 1685–1900. These are 383 Testimonies of Denial. The London numbers are derived from the collections of sanctioning papers of the different London meetings, rather than the minutes. This has the advantage that it includes cases of Gracechurch Street meeting, the minutes of which are lost.

another woman's husband'.³⁴ The first disownment in the Philadelphia monthly meeting minutes stems from fourth month 1720. In this instance, the meeting disowned 'John Locke of this city' for having 'wickedly and scandalously behaved himself, by running away with an infamous lewd woman, leaving his wife & children to the charity of others, or greatly to suffer, endeavouring to cheat divers persons by getting into their debt'.³⁵

The testimonies of denial often list more than one reason for a Friend's disownment. Jonathan Hitchcock in 1777 had become 'married by a priest', had his 'children sprinkled & absented himself from the due attendance of our meetings'.³⁶ In this instance 'sprinkling' refers to baptism, a practice of the church which Quakers rejected. John Heydon in 1761 accumulated debts before going 'aboard in the East India Company's Service as a Soldier', an action that clashed with the Society's rejection of violence.³⁷ Samuel Arnold had been 'guilty of Dishonest, Fraudulent and unlawfull actions, having use of his master's money wherewith he was intrusted, without his privity or consent and embezzled the same for his own private purposes, and is not able to repay the same'.³⁸

The monthly meetings' records tell only one side of the story. What is missing is the perspective of those Friends who found themselves disowned. What did being disowned mean for them? The sheer ubiquity of self-condemnations for both Philadelphia and London monthly meetings suggests that many of the Friends who violated some of the Society's rules still valued their membership in the organiaation. Putting an admission of one's guilt into writing and having the paper read out publicly cannot have been pleasant. The self-condemnations are highly formulaic, yielding little information on individuals' motives for their transgressions. However, the mere fact that many Friends were willing to submit to this procedure hints at the importance belonging to the Society held for them. From the later eighteenth century, letters of about sixty delinquent Friends survive among the London meeting records. In these, the writers resign their membership and offer explanations for their choices. A common reason to leave the Society was that former Friends had joined other religious groups, sometimes decades ago, and did not consider themselves members of the Society.³⁹ Many of these were women, who had married non-Friends. Elizabeth Broom is exemplary for these cases. She informed Gracechurch Street monthly

---

34   ToD Jane Hynd 1669, Devonshire House MM, Testimonies.
35   ToD John Lock, Philadelphia MM minutes, vol. 1715–1744, 63.
36   ToD Jonathan Hitchcock, 1777, Ratcliff MM, Testimonies.
37   ToD John Heydon,1761, Peel MM, Sufferings.
38   ToD Samuel Arnold, 1753, Peel MM, Sufferings.
39   John Clapp, Devonshire House MM, 1780; other examples include Joseph Nelms 1779, Devonshire House; George Clerk 1783, Gracechurch Street; Sarah Bishop 1784, Peel, – all in Ratcliff MM, Testimonies of Denial.

meeting in 1778: 'As I am married out of the Society, I must tender to go the way that is the most pleasing to my husband, but I should be glad to be accepted, when it shall please God to put it into our minds to change.'[40]

Others recognized irreconcilable differences between themselves and the Friends running their monthly meetings. Thomas Wakefield wrote to Gracechurch Street meeting that he had

> not at present, the least Idea of altering my present Situation as Commander of one of the East India Company's ships. I am sorry that that Situation is so incompatible with the principles of the Society in which I have been educated, and for which I have great respect.[41]

The limited surviving papers of individual London Friends shed further light on how contemporaries responded to disownments. The journal of Quaker merchant James Jenkins reveals him to have been a perceptive witness who not only noted down what he heard, but also reflected on individual cases of disownments and on their increase during the 1780s and 1790s. He was highly critical of this development, as illustrated by this entry from first month 1784:

> When a society, or body of men conceal the motives for their actions, & adduce reasons for their conduct different from the real one, they exercise a [illegible] of low cunning & depart from that dignity which a Religious Community should ever be careful to maintain.[42]

He expressed the same sentiment again more than a decade later. This entry also shows that news of disownments travelled beyond the immediate compass of the sanctioning monthly meeting. In 1797 Jenkins wrote of four Friends

> all lately disowned by the monthly meeting in Reading for 'opposing the Rules of Discipline'. As far as relates to their conduct at the time this is wrong. It was only one Rule they opposed, which was, that of dealing with a delinquent for paying Tithes. I know this case exceedingly well, & the termination of it, has proved, that in the application of our Discipline by ignorant men, it often happens that it is done left-handedly.[43]

---

40 Letter by Elizabeth Broom to Gracechurch Street MM 1778. For similar cases see Dorothy Briggs and Elizabeth Cooper, both 1777 to Gracechurch Street MM; Rebecca Spriggins 1781 to Devonshire House MM – all in Ratcliff MM, Testimonies of Denial.
41 Thomas Wakefield to Gracechurch Street MM, 1782, Ratcliff MM, Testimonies of Denial.
42 James Jenkins, Diary, 1763–1830, 17/i/1784.
43 Ibid., 1/xii/1797.

Jenkins elaborated that the disownment was not a one-sided act in which the meeting penalized the delinquents. He explained how the disownment came about:

> These men having by withdrawing themselves from all meetings of Business virtually disowned the Society. The Society in turn have disowned them for non-attendance of Meetings, instead of bringing forward a general charge very ambiguously worded & for the punishment of which, our Book of Extracts does not contain any rule.[44]

In addition to being sceptical of the monthly meeting's honesty in reporting reasons for disownment, Jenkins also criticized their judgement. In 1784 he recorded that he

> Heard that Wm Mathews of Bath was disowned for holding heterodox opinions. These opinions are that no member of our Society should be disowned for offences not immoral or of scandal to the body at large.

He pondered the consequences of the monthly meetings' strictness with perceived delinquents: 'In case of error, undeserved severity instead of reclaiming will widen the breach.' He himself was more liberal-minded, expressing the opinion that 'surely it is hard to disown a man for having a particular opinion of his own about non-essential matters. It is not always in the power of one man to adopt the sentiments of others & what is not in our power surely cannot be our duty.'

Jenkins expressed further criticism of the Society's sanctioning practices in 1786, when he observed that:

> A great many have been lately disowned by our Society in London. Were causes of evil removed, effects would cease. I wish our Friends of London were more concerned in promoting the social virtues than they are. Many delinquents have said, that they have never had any converse with the Friends appointed to visit them, previous to their being dealt with.[45]

That those disowned 'have never had any converse with the Friends appointed to visit them' implies a lack of pastoral care by the monthly meetings. The meetings showed an interest in their members only after their delinquency, but made no effort to guide or support them beforehand.

London Quaker merchant John Eliot shared Jenkins's concern over monthly meetings' lack of pastoral care and hasty sanctioning. Devonshire House monthly meeting had assigned Eliot the task of informing a member of an

---

44 Jenkins, Diary, Book of Extracts contains the Quaker Discipline.
45 Jenkins, Diary, 4/v/1786.

Oxfordshire meeting, who had removed to London some time ago, of his disownment. Oustwick monthly meeting's testimony against Thomas Soundy survives among the London records. This explains that Soundy was disowned for an:

> inordinate pursuit of concerns in trade too hazardous & extensive for his circumstances to support, and without due regard to the answering his engagements therein, he has thereby become a Bankrupt, greatly to the injury of some individuals & his effects fallen very short of the discharge of his debts, after borrowing & endeavouring to borrow monies immediately before his absconding from his creditors, and he also continuing to afford us no due satisfaction respecting those his proceedings.[46]

In a letter to a Friend in Oxfordshire, Eliot wrote of his encounter with Soundy:

> In order that I might have a good opporty of discourse with Thos Soundy, I got him to come last night to my house, when I delivered him the Testimony of Denial given forth by your Monthly meeting against him. I cannot say he reced it in the manner I wished, but shed resentment reflecting on the conduct of Friends in your Parts towards him, with which I was grieved & told him it would do him hurt. He said diverse things had been reported of him by Friends that were not true and that he wondered you never dealt with him for his failure whilst he was in the Country & thought upon what he said to thee & John Mathews when you visited him, that the monthly meeting wd have born with him longer.

> I did not shew my sentiments to him, but indeed I thought the Testimony deficient, no mention being made of any dealing in it, which I believe is very unusual neither do I think it is common to proceed to a Denial on the first Visit. The Distance of the way might be your reason for not repeating it, but in this case you might have put the affair into the Hands of our monthly meeting to manage for you & thereby obviated the complaint of an hasty proceeding. He complaind likewise of a want of love & tenderness for Friends towards him whilst he lived in Oxfordshire, wch I hope is without Foundations.

Eliot felt sorry for Soundy. He thought that it might as easily have been him who became bankrupt and hoped that Friends would treat him with more kindness in such a case:

> I felt my Bowells roll compassionately towards him, as one that had fallen from a good state being sensible of the like danger attend me, which might

---

46   ToD Thomas Soundy 1780, Ratcliff MM, Testimonies of Denial.

overtake me also throu unwatchfulness. In this feeling sense I was enabled to drop some Advice on his present condition, & am not without hopes it may have some weight with him in his cooler moments. I gave him an invitation to come another time, which he was very willing to embrace and I shall use my endeavours with Divine assistance to restore him if possible, as I apprehend there are some sparks of light & life left in him, altho Darkness seems in great measure to have overspread it.[47]

The limited evidence we have on individual Friends' responses to the Society's sanctions suggests that they did not reject the monthly meetings' policing of the community per se. Jenkins's diary and Eliot's letters suggest that the monthly meetings' increased sanctioning in the later eighteenth century was to at least some degree controversial. These Friends expressed concern that the persecution of delinquencies outweighed the pastoral care meetings gave their members.

Crisis

Both London and Philadelphia monthly meetings' records show that sanctions were not distributed evenly across time. As figures 3 and 4 illustrate, both London and Philadelphia monthly meetings sanctioned delinquents only rarely before 1750. In London, only seventy-seven cases or 9.3 per cent of the total fell into this period. Philadelphia monthly meetings disowned twenty-eight Friends, that is 7.3 per cent in the sample years before 1750.

In contrast, after 1750 both cities' monthly meetings increased their sanctioning of offences against the discipline dramatically: 90.7 per cent (752 cases) of London sanctions occurred between 1750 and 1800. In Philadelphia, 92.7 per cent (354 cases) of disownments took place in the second half of the eighteenth century.

Not just the overall number of sanctions changed. The offences for which the monthly meetings ostracized Friends changed as well. After 1750, types of offences that appeared only occasionally before 1750 became major concerns. For instance, London meetings disowned only three Friends for 'drinking to excess' before mid-century.[48] Afterwards, sanctions related to alcoholism become commonplace. What is more, after 1750, entirely new offences begin to appear in the minutes. While the monthly meetings prosecuted nobody for bankruptcy before 1750, in the later eighteenth century this cause came to be of considerable importance.

---

47 Philip Eliot, Letter Book, 30/vii/1763.
48 Horsleydown MM, Disorderly Walkers, vol. 1: ToD by Horsleydown MM, Benjamin Kemp, 1746; ToD by Horsleydown MM, John Bentley, 1748; ToD by Horsleydown MM, Nathan Tillotson, 1749. In all three cases drinking was one offence among others.

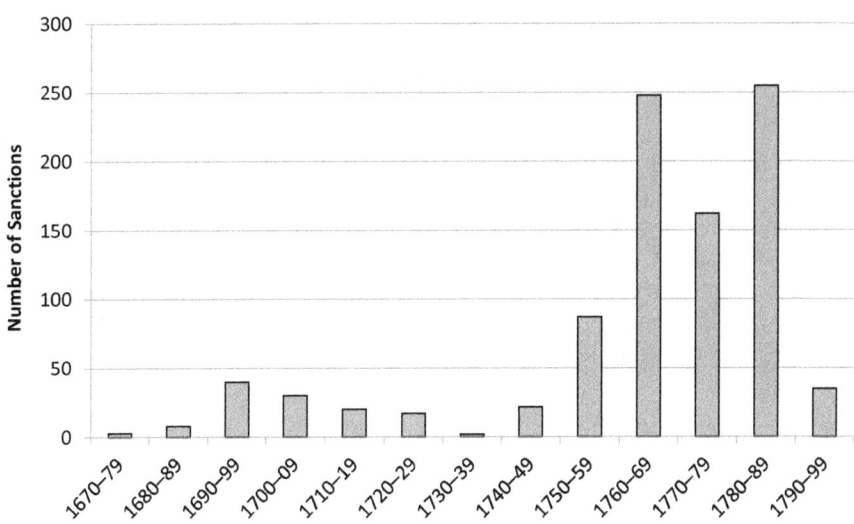

Figure 3. Disownments by London Monthly Meetings

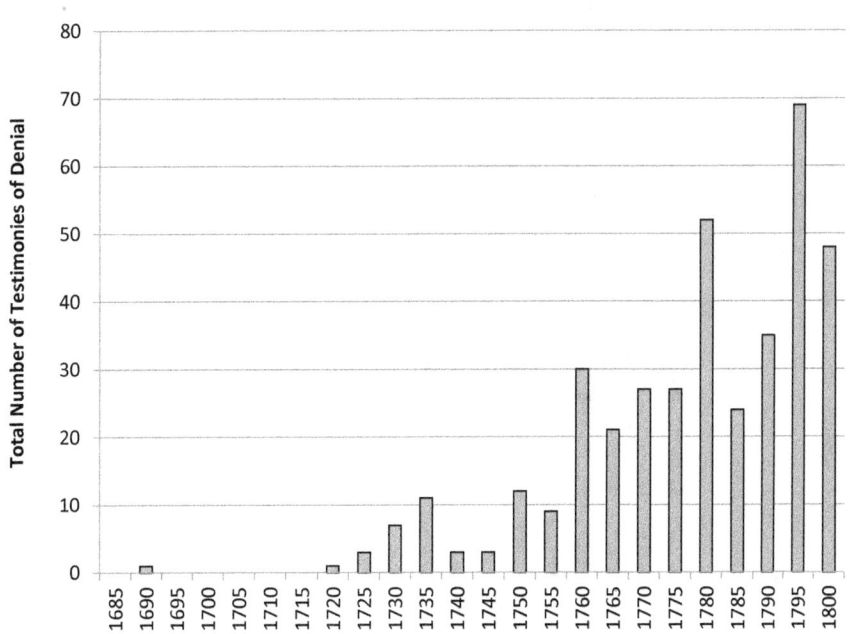

Figure 4. Disownments by Philadelphia Monthly Meetings

After 1750, London monthly meetings' sanctions are concentrated in four areas. As in the earlier period, offences against the Quaker marriage doctrine remained the most important cause for self-condemnations and disownments during the second half of the eighteenth century. From 1750 to 1800, they constitute the main cause behind 47.3 per cent of London monthly meetings' sanctions. The second-largest category consists of offences related to the conduct of business. Crimes such as fraud or irregularities in one's repayment of debts caused 18.7 per cent of London meetings' prosecutions in this period. Besides marriage offences, cases related to business constitute the most frequently sanctioned category of delinquencies. A third category that appears regularly after 1750 is alcoholism. 'Drinking to excess' and related disorderly conduct make up 9.3 per cent of total London sanctions. The remaining 20.4 per cent of sanctions were for miscellaneous other causes, ranging from having a child out of wedlock to being found guilty of a crime in a court of justice, to unspecified 'evil conduct'.

The patterns we find in the Philadelphia minutes contains both similarities and differences to those of London meetings. In the Quaker City, irregular marriage also constituted the most frequent cause for sanctions throughout the period. As in London, business offences also appeared increasingly after 1750. However, the Philadelphia meetings also investigated offences that played only a minor role in the London meetings' minutes. Striking is the importance Philadelphia Friends attributed to offences related to violence and warfare. While pacifism appeared in Quaker records occasionally from the movement's beginning, the monthly meetings only began to prosecute involvement in warfare from the 1750s onwards. Before the mid-century, the sample reveals only two instances of Philadelphia monthly meeting testifying against a Friend for an offence related to pacifism: William Brookes and Joseph House were both disowned in 1745 for their involvement in privateering.[49] Later in the century, participating in local riots and joining the American army became ubiquitous causes for disownment by Philadelphia monthly meetings.[50] Moreover, the first disownment relating to slavery in the Philadelphia meetings sample took place in 1770, when it testified against Henry Lisle for first purchasing, then selling on, a 'negro-woman for a small consideration to a Person, who declared he is not able to pay for her, and she becoming destitute of Support and liable to the Parish, if the Overseers of the Poor of the City had not taken care to provide for her'.[51] This reflects Philadelphia Friends' growing interest in the abolition

---

49 Philadelphia MM minutes, viii/1745, ToDs William Brookes and Joseph House, both p. 9, volume for years 1740–1755, accessed via ancestry.com.
50 Bauman, *Reputation*, 165. At the end of the War of Independence there were 908 such cases.
51 Philadelphia MM minutes, iii/1771, ToD Henry Lisle, vol. 1765–1771, 382, accessed via ancestry.com.

of slavery. While there had been instances of individual Friends taking a stand against slavery since the seventeenth century, it was only in the later eighteenth century that abolition became a key Quaker doctrine. It evolved as such in response to an increased presence of enslaved Africans in Philadelphia during the Seven Years' War. Warfare required troops, and in Europe, men joined the armies who would otherwise have gone to America as indentured servants. In the colonies, indentured servants left their masters to join the army. As a consequence, labour in the colonies became even more scarce than it had been before. In response to the massive labour shortage, Pennsylvanians began purchasing enslaved Africans at a much higher rate than before. During the 1750s, the number of slaves imported to Philadelphia tripled, to peak at almost 500 in 1762. Against this backdrop, Philadelphia Friends developed the Quaker doctrine against slavery.[52] Broader studies of Quakerism in the Delaware Valley at the time show that this shift in the themes the monthly meetings focused on is representative for the whole region.[53]

In contrast, the London meetings showed little concern over their members' involvement in military activities even in the later period. There were no disownments or self-condemnations for offences related to military activities before 1750, and only thirty-four such cases appear in the minutes after 1750. These make up 4.3 per cent of the total cases in the later period. The Friends whom monthly meetings did ostracize for violence-related offences included several cases of men who went to sea, such as Edmund Durston who in 1763 became a 'soldier in the service of ye East India Company', or the apprentice Benjamin Holmes, who in 1783 'Absconded from his master and entered a ship of war'.[54] Finally, in spite of London Friends' strong ties to the plantation economies of the Caribbean, offences related to slavery are completely absent from the capital's meetings' minutes.

The growth of the monthly meetings' policing of their communities from the mid-eighteenth century onwards was dramatic. Together with the increase in the extent of the meetings' minutes for each gathering over the course of the seventeenth and eighteenth centuries discussed above, they are evidence of a deep-reaching institutional change. What caused this transformation? And did it affect individual Friends' behaviour, and thereby potentially Quaker merchants' success in trade?

---

52 Marietta, *Reformation*, 115.
53 Ibid.; Bauman, *Reputation*.
54 Horsleydown MM, Disorderly Walkers, vol. 1, ToD by Horsleydown MM, Edmund Durston, 1763; Ratcliff MM, Testimonies, ToD by Gracechurch Street MM, Benjamin Holmes 1783.

6

The Quaker Reformation

The drastic increase of sanctions in the mid-eighteenth century reflects a religious crisis: at this time, a spirit of renewal took hold of the Society of Friends. Since the 1730s, voices criticizing the spiritual condition of the Society had begun to grow louder on both sides of the Atlantic.[1] This is reflected in the London Yearly Meeting's annual epistles, which from this decade onwards display an increasing uneasiness over the conduct of Friends and the state of 'Truth'. In 1732 the London Yearly Meeting's epistle lamented that the old way 'of our holy profession is too much lost among us'.[2] In 1735 the meeting commissioned the first Book of Extracts, consisting of a collection of such passages from its annual epistles as were concerned with Friends' conduct. This was first published in 1738 and has been updated and republished as the Society of Friends' Book of Discipline ever since.[3] The London Yearly Meeting's epistles reflect a sense of religious crisis throughout the 1740s and 1750s. As it sent these to quarterly and monthly meetings in the colonies, American Friends became aware of the English Quakers' concerns, as well. In addition, the London Yearly Meeting sent personalized letters to all American Yearly Meetings, including that of Philadelphia. From the later 1740s onwards, several of these contain appeals to 'stir up their members so that renewal and reform might take place'.[4]

The most vocal agents for renewal were a set of prominent Friends from Pennsylvania and London. As travelling ministers, they spent years on their respective opposite sides of the Atlantic, visiting over 1000 meetings and connecting with great numbers of Friends throughout the 1740s and 1750s.[5] They reported extravagance, payment of tithes, drunkenness, exogamous marriages and deism. American ministers were shocked at endemic 'corruption' among their English brethren.[6] English ministers thought the discipline in

---

1 Beck et al., *London Friends' meetings*, 188.
2 Friends, *Epistles 1737*.
3 Kenneth L. Carroll, 'A Look at the "Quaker Revival of 1756"', *Quaker History* 65, no. 2 (1976), 64.
4 Carroll, 'Quaker Revival', 71.
5 Marietta, *Reformation*, 40–41.
6 Marietta, *Reformation*, 35.

Pennsylvania was 'weak & almost ruined'.[7] Clearly, the Quaker community as a whole was in need of reform. Everywhere they went, these ministers preached discipline, right conduct and the better education of Friends' children in the ways of Truth.[8] They aimed to return the community to the 'pure' state they thought it had enjoyed in its early years.

Quaker ministers convinced London and Philadelphia Yearly Meetings to introduce a hands-on approach to community reform. The monthly meetings' increased policing reflected in the growth of the meetings' minutes over the course of the eighteenth century took place at this higher administrative level within the Society, as well. From the 1720s onwards, London Yearly Meeting had regularly made amendments to the queries the quarterly meetings had to answer annually. These concerned the administration of the meetings' poor relief and also asked how the Yearly Meeting's advice was being implemented. In 1742, London Yearly Meeting revised the existing queries and added six new ones. The new queries' focus was still on the overall 'state' of the meetings, but they also included questions regarding individual Friends' behaviour. For instance, Yearly Meeting now sought reassurance that all Friends 'stand clear in our Testimony against Defrauding the King of his Customs, Duties or Excise, or in Dealing in Goods suspected to be Run'. Pacifism made a first appearance in the Yearly Meeting's epistles since 1693, as London Yearly Meeting asked whether all Friends abided by the rule 'against bearing Arms and paying Trophy money or being in any manner concerned in Privateers, Letters of Marque or in dealing in Prize Goods as such?'.[9] In 1755, London Yearly Meeting directed all quarterly meetings to ask the monthly meetings under their jurisdiction to reply to a standardized set of eight questions four times a year.[10] These resembled the Yearly Meeting's queries to the quarterly meetings, but also included a few innovations. For instance, monthly meetings were to report whether their members avoided the 'unnecessary frequenting of ale houses'.[11] In 1757 the Yearly Meeting referred to monthly meetings' responsibilities to sanction offences against the discipline by adding an amendment to the queries, which asked: 'Are Friends faithful in Admonishing such as are remiss therein?'[12]

---

7   John Fothergill, cited in Marietta, *Reformation*, 41.
8   Marietta, *Reformation*, 38.
9   Stagg, 'Queries', 230. The 1693 Epistle had called upon monthly and quarterly meetings 'to deal with' Quaker shipmasters who carried 'guns on their ships, supposing thereby to defend and secure themselves and their ships, contrary to their former principle and practice, and to the endangering their own and others' lives thereby'. Friends, *Epistles*, 77.
10 Stagg, 'Queries', 214.
11 Ibid., 231. For Philadelphia Yearly Meeting, see Marietta, *Reformation*, 54; Rufus M. Jones, *The Later Periods of Quakerism* (Macmillan, 1921), 137–43; Milligan, *Dictionary*, 566.
12 See Appendix I for a full list of queries.

Quaker meetings throughout the Atlantic world regularly responded to these queries in writing. The aim of these efforts was that Yearly Meetings had a better understanding of the state of the Quaker community as a whole. The queries were part of increased efforts by the Society to monitor the community. They reflect the same effort we saw in the growth of the monthly meetings' minutes, which increasingly policed their congregations. London and Philadelphia Yearly Meetings appointed committees to travel across their jurisdictions and inspect quarterly and monthly meetings to ensure that they carried out the Yearly Meeting's admonitions and implemented a reform of the discipline.[13] These committees visited monthly meetings, using the Yearly Meetings' queries as 'a means to cross-examination'.[14] The consequence was a tightening of oversight of Friends by the Society's institutions overall.

Contemporary Friends were convinced that they were witnessing a decline of Friends' conduct, and thereby of the Society as a whole. Later historians took their verdict at face value. John Stephenson Rowntree, for example, attributed this decline to a mixture of causes, including 'the withdrawal of the stimulus of persecution, increasing opulence, the declining number of ministers ... and the traditional, unadaptive character given by birthright membership'.[15] Given the context of persecution, imprisonment and even death, first-generation Quakers joined the Society at great risk to their safety, their property and their lives. Later generations of Friends mostly grew up in the community. They did not experience the fear and repercussions the first Quakers faced, neither did they make an active choice to join the community. Perhaps this younger generation took it for granted, and made less of an effort to follow its rules. At first sight, the increase of sanctions for delinquencies of all kinds, which we find in the monthly meetings' records, seems to confirm this suspicion. But had individual Friends' behaviour actually worsened? Were eighteenth-century Friends really so much less disciplined than their seventeenth-century forebears?

It is equally possible that rather than individual Quakers behaving worse, it was the Society of Friends as a body that changed its attitude towards discipline. It is possible that yearly and monthly meetings grew more sensitive about individual Friends' conduct. This change in attitude could have incentivized the meetings to increase their efforts of policing the community, in turn leading them to notice and register more delinquencies, which would in earlier times have not triggered a response in the form of an investigation and sanction. This could explain the growth of sanctions we find in the monthly meeting records from the 1750s onwards.

---

13 Marietta, *Reformation*, 54; Jones, *Later Periods*, 136.
14 Stagg, 'Queries', 217.
15 John Stephenson Rowntree, *Quakerism, Past and Present: Being an Inquiry into the Causes of Its Decline in Great Britain and Ireland* (London, 1859), 122–23.

The minutes of Devonshire House, one of London's largest monthly meetings, provide support for this hypothesis. In 1751 it appointed a committee of Friends to 'prepare and bring to this Meeting an Acct or List of such of our members as have either married by the Priest, Fail'd of paying their just Debts, been guilty of drinking to excess, or any notorious Immorality, that they may be dealt with in Order to remove the reproach by them brought on our holy Profession'.[16] Over the following months, the committee reported back to the meeting regularly. It transpired that the list included names of individuals who, upon being questioned, had not considered themselves members of the Society for many years and even decades. A typical case of this is John Clapp, who, upon being questioned by the committee, informed them that 'when young he sometimes attended our meetings, but knew nothing of our Principles, since he had grown up, had attended the public worship & did not deem himself a member of our society'.[17] The meeting had apparently not noticed his absence before. This reflects a second process that was taking place among London Quaker meetings in this period: the establishment of boundaries between their own members and those of other faith communities. Membership in the Society of Friends up to this point had been fluid. It was not unusual for individuals to worship with different religious denominations at the same time, or drift from one sect or church to another. During the eighteenth century, London Quaker meetings at least began to define their boundaries more clearly. In 1737, Horsleydown monthly meeting compiled the first list of members we have for a London meeting. Devonshire House monthly meeting ordered its list of 'disorderly walkers' on the same day as it asked 'the same Friends ... to endeavour to make out a list of all the members of this meeting digested in alphabetical order, with their places of abode'.[18] The investigation of delinquencies was part of an effort to establish membership of the meeting. That the meeting began these two efforts now indicates that perhaps it was the meeting that experienced a change of spirit, rather than increasing corruption among Friends.

In order to better understand the mid-eighteenth-century growth of sanctions, the following chapters investigate these in more detail. They focus on delinquencies related to the conduct of business, and marriage, as these were the key concerns of the London meetings, and have the greatest potential of affecting Quaker merchants' commercial success. First, London meetings' policing of dishonesty in business is examined. A glimpse over the Atlantic at Philadelphia meetings' sanctioning of business offences provides context for

16 Devonshire House MM minutes, vii/1751, 303.
17 John Clapp, Devonshire House MM 1780; other examples include Joseph Nelms 1779, Devonshire House; George Clerk 1783, Gracechurch Street; Sarah Bishop 1784, Peel – all in Ratcliff MM, Testimonies, 1697–1797.
18 Devonshire House MM minutes, fourth day of seventh month, vol. 7, 303.

the London developments, as befits the history of a transatlantic community. Second, a closer look is taken at what kinds of behaviour exactly London meetings prosecuted as part of their efforts to enforce the Quaker marriage doctrine. The study focuses on both the development of ideas about business and marriage within the Society, and the comprehensiveness with which monthly meetings sanctioned delinquencies in these areas – in other words, whether it was indeed Friends' conduct that deteriorated after 1750, or if an ideological shift led the meetings to monitor their congregations more strictly.

7

London Friends and Honesty in Business

In the context of trade, the most striking innovation of the eighteenth-century crisis is the monthly meetings' increased sanctioning of Friends' misconduct in business. The testimonies of denial after 1750 display a strong interest in Friends' conduct of business, and particularly their payment of debts. In order to understand Friends' relationship to debt, we need to be aware of contemporary attitudes towards credit, as well as the existing legislation on insolvency and bankruptcy. Debt and bankruptcy in the beginning of our period were generally regarded as moral failures. Over the course of the eighteenth century, this moral understanding was replaced by an economic one, as increasing commercialization generalized debt across a wider spectrum of society. However, it also became more controversial.

One of the most important factors shifting English attitudes to debt and bankruptcy came from changes led by the state in the management and distribution of public debt. Successive seventeenth-century governments struggled to finance England's many wars. The reign of Charles II saw the stop of the exchequer and subsequent financial crisis due to the government's inability to repay the loans it had taken out in order to finance war with the Dutch Republic. After the Glorious Revolution, William of Orange struggled to continue financing the Nine Years' War against Louis XIV. The development of a new system of credit 'became an interest of state'.[1] In order to obtain new funds, the government tried a new strategy: it founded the Bank of England. The Bank lent the government money to continue the war. It raised these funds by issuing shares, with interest on income and profits then being paid out as dividends.

At the same time, up to 100 new joint stock companies sprang up between 1685 and 1695.[2] Together, the Bank of England, the East India Company and the South Sea Company came to hold about a third of the government's public

---

1 Carl Wennerlind, *Casualties of Credit: The English Financial Revolution, 1620–1720* (Cambridge, MA, and London: Harvard University Press, 2011), 5.
2 Anne L. Murphy, *The Origins of English Financial Markets: Investment and Speculation before the South Sea Bubble* (Cambridge: Cambridge University Press, 2009), 37.

debt.³ The subscriptions to the Bank of England shares were open to all, 'Native and foreigners, bodies politick and corporate'. The same was true for the joint stock trading companies. This constituted an important step: it turned credit into a commodity, which could be bought and sold. In consequence, new groups, i.e. anyone with money to purchase shares, could purchase government debt. Accordingly, subscribers to the Bank of England and the joint stock companies came from across the social spectrum. About one-third of subscribers consisted of aristocrats, gentlemen and esquires. The largest groups represented were merchants, retailers and manufacturers.⁴ The rest came from working people. During the South Sea Bubble subscribers came from in and around London, with most traders participating in the market only twice at most.⁵ Thus, a connection was established between the moneyed men of the city and the government. The founding of the Bank of England and the stock companies therefore presents a shift in power away from the aristocracy and monarchy, and towards the bourgeoisie. It also presented a move away from an agrarian society, in which power was vested in owning land, into a commercial one. The 'creation of a direct link between the country's government and the moneyed men through the establishment of the public funds' caused concern among the public. A debate arose which represented investment in equity and debt instruments as dangerous and dishonest.⁶ It was thought that those who speculated in financial instruments sought to profit from the misfortune of others.

Within this sensitive climate, a series of innovations were made to English bankruptcy legislation.⁷ Acts 4 and 5 Anne 1 c4 (1706) and 6 Anne 1 c 22 (1707) represented a fundamental change.⁸ English bankruptcy legislation had begun under Henry VIII with a law aimed at preventing bankruptcies. A bankrupt at this point was anyone who became insolvent due to her or his own misconduct.⁹ The term 'bankruptcy' thus signified culpability, and bankrupts were regarded as defrauding their creditors of their property. The new laws, in contrast, recognized that bankruptcy could arise out of misfortune rather than

---

3   The trading companies received monopolies on trades with certain regions in exchange for payments to the government.
4   Murphy, *Origins*, 152.
5   Ann Carlos and Larry Neal, 'The Micro-Foundations of the Early London Capital Market: Bank of England Shareholders during and after the South Sea Bubble, 1720–25', *Economic History Review* 59, no. 3 (2006).
6   Murphy, *Origins*, 66.
7   Emily Kadens, 'The Last Bankrupt Hanged: Balancing Incentives in the Development of Bankruptcy law', *Duke Law Journal* 59, no. 7 (2010).
8   Ann Carlos and Jessica Lamping, 'Conformity and the Certificate of Discharge: Bankruptcy in Eighteenth Century England' (Economic History Association Working Papers, 2010).
9   Hoppit, *Risk and Failure*, 19.

misconduct. They introduced the concept of 'innocent bankruptcy' in addition to the traditional culpable one.[10]

In order to be declared bankrupt, three requirements had to be met: one had to be a trader, i.e. make one's living through buying and selling; one had to owe debts of at least £100 to one creditor, £150 to two or £200 to three creditors or more; and one had to have committed an act of bankruptcy, i.e. the 'unreasonable evasion of one's creditors' just demands for repayment'.[11] The law did not allow for voluntary bankruptcy. In order to start the bankruptcy procedure, the debtor had to be sued for bankruptcy by his creditors.

What is more, the new laws allowed for discharge from bankruptcy. A bankrupt could receive a certificate of discharge, allowing her or him to walk away from unpaid debts, while keeping a certain amount of her or his assets.[12] Once discharged, a bankrupt was no longer liable for previously incurred debts. The new laws thereby also allowed entrepreneurs a second chance, and saved the human capital of businesspeople active in the economy.[13]

Those who did not make their living through trade were not subject to the bankruptcy law. Instead, they fell under the jurisdiction of the standard law on debt. This allowed creditors to file a law suit against debtors to have them arrested and jailed until the debt was paid. The idea underlying this legislation was that debtors were scheming and hiding assets. Imprisonment would pressure them or their families to settle. In preceding centuries, litigation, including for debt, had been ubiquitous in England. It peaked in the seventeenth century, when litigation between traders and customers occurred at an extraordinarily high level. Litigation subsided thereafter. By the early eighteenth century, however, conflict over debts became viewed as negative and was no longer normalized.[14] The general rejection of debt mediation coincided with a massive growth in imprisonment for debt. Large numbers of insolvents stayed in jail for long periods of time. In the eighteenth century about 90 per cent of English and Welsh prisoners were debtors.[15] Parliament passed twenty

---

10   Ibid., 20. The same distinction was made in laws of the Holy Roman Empire since the sixteenth century: see Paul Fischer, 'Bankruptcy in Early Modern German Territories', in *The History of Bankruptcy: Economic, Social and Cultural Implications in Early Modern Europe*, ed. Max Thomas Safley (New York: Routledge, 2013).
11   Hoppit, *Risk and Failure*, 36; Kadens, 'The Last Bankrupt Hanged'.
12   This required the agreement of four-fifths of their creditors.
13   Ann Carlos, Luis C. Penarietta, and Edward Kosack, 'Bankruptcy in Early Modern England: Discharge and Debtors Rights' (LSE Economic History Seminar Papers, 2013), 3–4.
14   Craig Muldrew, *The Economy of Obligation: The Culture of Credit and Social Relations in Early Modern England* (Basingstoke: Macmillan, 1998).
15   Ian P. H. Duffy, *Bankruptcy and Insolvency in London during the Industrial Revolution* (New York and London: Garland, 1985), 372.

temporary insolvent debtors' relief acts in the eighteenth century, in order to empty the crowded gaols.[16]

London Quaker meetings and the misconduct of business

As shown in figure 5, London monthly meetings' sanctions include 168 cases relating to business. This constitutes 17.9 per cent of total sanctions. Among these are four self-condemnations; the remainder are testimonies of denial. In the years before 1750, the number of sanctions related to honesty was tiny. This period saw only nineteen cases related to dishonesty, constituting 11.3 per cent of the total of this category. These nineteen cases included two self-condemnations, neither followed by disownment.[17] The monthly meetings' pre-1750s disownments for business offences reflect no particular interest in debts. The nineteen cases related to business include many instances of fraud. Debt was not a primary concern even among business-related offences. Bankruptcy was not mentioned once.

The first testimony of denial referring to dishonesty was issued in 1694 by Devonshire House monthly meeting against Elizabeth Nichols, who

> under ye pretence of having visions, & hearing voices yt speak locally to her, has presumed through dreams & imaginations to charge divers notorious forgerys, falsehoods & reproaches upon several honest people ... also works in her to report by fire & sword the destruction of this nation, such false predictions of hers we doe reject.[18]

The first sanction specifically for fraud in business was the disownment of Joshua Stephens of Broad Street. The Peel monthly meeting disowned him in 1699 after it found that he had

> been prevailed upon through ye subtility of ye devil to fall into many snares in matters relating to conversation and trade of which he was timely caution'd and advis'd, but not regarding ye counsel of his friends, he persisted and run into many irregularities.[19]

---

16 Paul Haagen, 'Eighteenth-Century English Society and the Debt Law', in *Social Control and the State*, ed. Stanley Cohen and Andrew Scull (Oxford: Palgrave Macmillan, 1983), 227–28.
17 SC William Clark 1712, Peel MM, Sufferings, No. 32; SC William Roper 1739, Peel MM, Sufferings, No. 56.
18 ToD Elizabeth Nichols 1694, Devonshire House MM, Testimonies, vol. 1.
19 ToD Joshua Stephens 1699, Peel MM, Sufferings, No. 37.

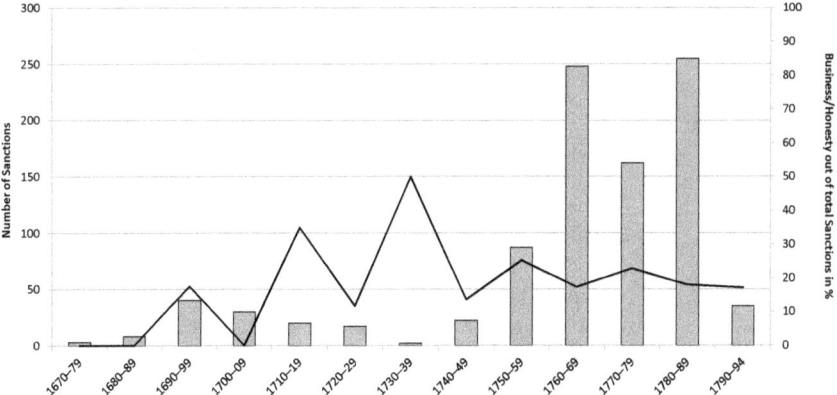

Figure 5. Sanctions of Offences Related to Honesty in London

It is noteworthy that among the pre-1750 sanctions related to business and financial matters, debts played a minor role. Instead, meetings reacted primarily to anti-social behaviour such as fraud and drinking to excess. Debts appeared merely as a contributing factor. Nathan Tillotson in 1749, for instance, had been guilty of

> drinking to excess, gaming and other evils, and late absconded from his family and creditors with great part of his effects, and left his wife and child in a very miserable condition destitute of subsistence.[20]

Similarly, the Peel meeting in 1722 disowned James Hoskins for absconding from his creditors and 'wickedness'.[21] More elaborate information is given on a fraud committed by George Roberts in 1729. Ratcliff monthly meeting disowned him after

> the Testimonies & Evidence of several credible Persons were given in against him, face to face, importing that he the said George Roberts, pretending skill in Alchymistry, or the act of transmuting & working metals to great advantage, did by false & deceitfull speeches, covered with a pretence of Charity & Religion, delude, ensnare, & draw in the said Persons, to erect a large & costly Laboratory or Workhouse, and to make vain & costly experiments, to their very great loss and detriment.[22]

---

20 ToD Nathan Tillotson 1749, Horsleydown MM, Disorderly Walkers, 72.
21 ToD James Hoskins 1722, Peel MM, Sufferings, No. 47.
22 ToD George Roberts 1729, Ratcliff MM, Testimonies.

In the course of the eighteenth century the belief in transmuting metals was increasingly rejected.[23] Before then, attempts of transmutation were not only informed by the desire for profit, but also by the scarcity of money in a rapidly expanding market economy.[24] Roberts had used this argument in a petition for a patent in 1720. This stated that

> George Roberts of the City of London, Chymist, one of the people called Quakers upon his solemn affirmation saith that he, this affirmant by long study, the experience of many years & numerous tryals hath found out and discovered an art or method by which he can and hath graduated, ameliorated or produced from lead and lead oar a considerable quantity of bullion, more than can be or is produced or extracted by the common & usual methods of smelting or refining the same.[25]

This, he argued, would

> be of general use and profit to the Kingdom not only in regard that ye Majesty's silver coin, and thereby the riches of the nation will be much increased, but many lead mines will on this accot be wrought and made to yield considerable profit which at present [?] neglected by reason of their poverty.[26]

This indicates that Roberts may have acted in good faith when he recruited investors for his 'laboratory'. It was however not the first time Roberts had gotten into serious trouble over business matters. In 1720 he had petitioned the Court of Chancery for help in a debt case: he claimed that he had been hired by one Francis Richardson of the parish of St Margaret Westminster as a manager for his lead mine in Northumberland. Roberts claimed he never received his payment of £100, nor reimbursement for wages for workmen and other expenses. He sought Richardson out in London, but Richardson hid from him. When Roberts eventually managed to locate Richardson, the latter became 'so enraged that he threatened to stab ye Orat.' and continued to force him into a 'house with his drawn sword and carried the Orat. into a chamber up two pairs of stairs where he kept the Orat. for one day and two nights without fire or candle or water or drink not suffering ye Orat. to see or speak to anyone during all that time'. He only let him go after Roberts handed him 'a bond for payment of one hundred pounds' as well as linen worth £20. After finally being

---

23 Lawrence M. Principe and William R. Newman, 'Some Problems with the History of Alchemy in Early Modern Europe', in *Secrets of Nature: Astrology and Alchemy in Early Modern Europe*, ed. William R. Newman and Anthony Grafton (Cambridge, MA: MIT Press, 2001).
24 Wennerlind, *Casualties of Credit*, ch. 2.
25 George Roberts, Petition, TNA, microfilm, SP 36 20-22, 2.
26 Ibid.

set free, Roberts explained, he was not able to pursue the case immediately, as his 'wife being taken sick soon afterwards ... and at the point of death ye Orat. was obliged to go into the country to take care of her'. After his return to London, however, he found that 'the said Richardson [had] died having ye Orat said Bond and note in his custody and without making ye Orat any satisfaction for the money owed to him upon the amount before mentioned of the said cloth which he extorted from ye Orat'. As if this weren't enough misfortune, Richardson's widow, executrix of his estate, then sued Roberts for the amount of the bond. Unfortunately, we do not know how the case ended. It seems that either Roberts was exceptionally unlucky, or a very daring conman, making up elaborate stories in order to escape his obligations. The monthly meeting may have been aware of the history and may have used Roberts's alchemical project as an opportunity to rid itself of a Friend who continuously attracted scandal.

With the onset of the Society's reform efforts after 1750, the number of disownments for business offences increased dramatically: 148 instances, constituting 88.7 per cent of all the honesty-related sanctions monthly meetings imposed during the seventeenth and eighteenth centuries, fall into the period 1750–1800. Moreover, in the second half of the century, debts began to appear as the main and even sole reason for a disownment. William Smith's 1760 disownment constitutes the first instance of this. He had

> launched into Trade & Business beyond his own Capital & ability to manage, with reputation, whereby he hath frequently been tempted to break his word & fair promises & at last hath failed & fell short of paying his just debts, to the loss & damage of many honest & industrious persons.[27]

This period also witnessed the first ever disownment for bankruptcy. In 1754 Horsleydown monthly meeting learned

> that Jonathan Hobson is become a Bankrupt ... found his conduct hath been very blameable & scandalous, having contracted Debts when he was not able to pay; Also his conversation hath been at times very disorderly in being overcharged with strong Liquor, to the great Scandal and Reproach of himself, and the Society,

and decided to testify against him.[28] Similarly, in 1759 Gracechurch Street meeting disowned Benjamin Titley, who

> did embark in and pursue divers hazardous and unwarrantable schemes of Trade, whereby he became greatly embarrassed in his circumstances and was guilty of many fraudulent practices to support his credit, which at length

27 ToD William Smith 1760, Peel MM, Sufferings.
28 ToD Jonathan Hobson 1754, Horsleydown MM, Disorderly Walkers.

being discovered, he clandestinely absconded from his family & creditors, and has not appeared to a commission of bankruptcy taken out against him.[29]

Bankruptcy became an increasingly common cause of disownment in the 1780s.[30] William Crawley was disowned by Peel monthly meeting in 1782, for having fallen

> into ambitious pursuits, and engaged in trade beyond his capital, and ability, to manage, ... he proceeded therein till he became a bankrupt, to the great loss of his relations, other creditors, and reproach of our self-denying profession.[31]

The same year Devonshire House monthly meeting testified against John Fincham, who 'fell into disorderly conduct, by means of which he became embarrassed in his circumstances, and at length declared a Bankrupt'.[32] John Bangs, 'through imprudent & extravagant conduct involved himself in Debt, considerably beyond his ability to discharge, and in consequence thereof has been declared a bankrupt'; he was disowned by Westminster monthly meeting in 1783.[33]

These findings show a shift towards a greater importance of business offences among the monthly meetings' sanctions. Moreover, within this category, the importance of debts grew relative to other offences, such as fraud. This increasing sensitivity towards debts is furthermore evidenced in the introduction of bankruptcy as a delinquency meriting disownment. These developments coincided with contemporary trends in the impact of debt and bankruptcy. In the second half of the eighteenth century, financial crises began to affect private investors more than before. In England, bankruptcy numbers rose steadily from about 1760 onwards.[34] The average number of bankrupts, which stood at only 44.9 per year in the decade from 1691 to 1700, increased to 210.2 annually by 1751–60, and to 762.7 per year in 1791–1800.[35] Moreover, the numbers of imprisoned debtors doubled between 1759 and 1779.[36] By the mid-eighteenth century moreover, the public had become used to the innovations of public debt and credit, and the debate surrounding them calmed down. Instead, public concern now shifted towards private debt and credit.

---

29 ToD Benjamin Titley 1759, Ratcliff MM, Testimonies.
30 Number of testimonies mentioning bankruptcy per decade: 1750s: 4; 1760s: 6; 1770s: 2; 1780s: 9.
31 ToD William Crawley 1782, Ratcliff MM, Testimonies.
32 ToD John Fincham 1782, Ratcliff MM, Testimonies.
33 ToD John Bangs 1783, Ratcliff MM, Testimonies.
34 Hoppit, 'Attitudes to Credit in Britain, 1680–1790'.
35 Hoppit, *Risk and Failure*, 46.
36 1759: 3814 debtors, 1779: 8238 debtors. Duffy, *Bankruptcy and Insolvency*, 372. See also Margot C. Finn, *The Character of Credit: Personal Debt in English Culture, 1740–1914* (Cambridge and New York: Cambridge University Press, 2003), 109.

Debtors' conduct and financial instruments

The London monthly meetings' disownments do more than reflect Friends' reform efforts of the mid-eighteenth century. The aspects of debt that they discuss enable us to map the Society's sense of what types of debt were more or less unacceptable. We can also explore who was subject to discipline and their relationship to the community. London Quaker meetings expected their members to be risk-averse in business in order to avoid insolvency and bankruptcy. In this context, the Society condemned some financial instruments and strategies which, however legal, it judged unethical. For instance, William Clark's self-condemnation at the Bull & Mouth meeting in 1711 explained that he had been 'going into bonds for others & contracting of debts beyond my power to answer' and furthermore gone 'into a privilege'd place contrary to ye known order of friends'.[37] The term 'bonds for others' refers to joint securities, which at the time were considered risky and hence controversial. Defoe expressed concern about these in 1726, when he advised tradesmen 'Never [to] be bound to another tradesman for a debt' as this was 'reason for a tradesman's frequent ruin'.[38] Going 'into a privelege'd place' refers to one of London's debtors' sanctuaries. Until 1723 several areas in London, such as the Mint in Southwark, granted fugitive debtors indefinite protection from their creditors.[39]

Debtors' conduct remained a concern throughout the eighteenth century, as illustrated by the 1762 disownment of Jane Clark, who had had herself 'arrested in a friendly action and took the benefit of the compulsive clause in the late act of parliament for the relief of Insolvent Debtors, by which means her Creditors were deprived of their just Debts'.[40] Debt law allowed creditors to pursue either the person or the property of a debtor. As soon as any creditor had a debtor arrested, all of that debtor's creditors lost their right to proceed against his or her property. Debtors could, therefore, protect their property and gain leverage in negotiations with their creditors by having themselves arrested in 'friendly actions', and await release through one of Parliament's regularly occurring acts for the relief of insolvent debtors.[41] The Society judged Clark's conduct as dishonest and fraudulent, in spite of it being legally sound. A related instance is the case of James MacDonald in 1757.[42] He was disowned

---

37   SC William Clark, Peel MM, Sufferings, No. 32.
38   Defoe, *The Complete Tradesman*.
39   Nigel Stirk, 'Arresting Ambiguity: The Shifting Geographies of a London Debtors' Sanctuary in the Eighteenth Century', *Social History* 25, no. 3 (2000), 175; Defoe, *The Complete Tradesman*, 58.
40   ToD Jane Clark 1762, Horsleydown MM, Disorderly Walkers.
41   John Sainsbury, 'John Wilkes, Debt, and Patriotism,' *Journal of British Studies* 34, no. 2 (1995); Hoppit, 'Attitudes to Credit in Britain, 1680–1790'.
42   ToD James MacDonald 1757, Peel MM, Sufferings.

for fraud, absconding from creditors and, interestingly, using a composition. The use of a composition refers to the freeing from one's debts by paying a portion to one or several of one's creditors, but not the full amount of what was owed. Apparently, the meeting disapproved of these practices, although they were legally sound.

Towards the end of the eighteenth century, disownments repeatedly include references to accommodation bills. Accommodation notes were a form of bill of exchange, which was signed by a guarantor, as discussed in chapter three. This is probably what the 1788 disownment of John Thackall refers to, which explained that:

> his failure appears to have arisen from engaging in Trade more extensively than he had property to manage, which led him to unite with others in circulating a fictitious paper currency & thereby involved himself in difficulties he was unable to extricate himself from.[43]

Another case is that of William Kaye, who was not only guilty of using accommodation notes, but also of a lifestyle inappropriate for a bankrupt. Gracechurch Street monthly meeting disowned him in 1775, after, having fallen 'short of paying his debts', he 'became a bankrupt, to the great injury of his creditors'. Moreover:

> since he obtained his certificate, he has engaged in an extravagant way of living, highly inconsistent with his situation, and has been concerned in very unjustifiable methods of supporting it, by raising a fallacious credit, which being discerned, the same friends have again endeavoured to deal with him, but have not been able to much with him.[44]

Similarly, in 1783, Westminster monthly meeting testified against John Bangs, who became a bankrupt due to his 'wasteful lifestyle'.[45] From this it appears that spending more on a livelihood than could be supported by one's own income as a cause for insolvency was unacceptable. It was especially unacceptable in the case of debtors who had been discharged of bankruptcy, who the meeting regarded to be living at the expense of their unsatisfied creditors.[46]

Aside from their offences, we know little about those who were disowned. In seventy-four cases some indication of profession could be identified, either from the testimonies of denial themselves, or from the meetings' vital records. They include several apprentices and servants, merchants and factors, as well as

---

43 ToD John Thackall 1788, Ratcliff MM, Testimonies.
44 ToD William Kaye 1775, Ratcliff MM, Testimonies.
45 ToD John Bangs 1783, Ratcliff MM, Testimonies.
46 Friends, *Epistles* 1759, 257.

drapers, tailors, two watchmakers and one surveyor of ships. For others we have some indication of how they made their living because they were disowned for bankruptcy, which only applied to traders, or for 'trading beyond their means'. As they were disowned for debts, bankruptcy and fraud, there is a bias towards businesspeople in this group. Descriptions of professions in this period were not clear cut, as many people pursued a variety of occupations simultaneously. Moreover, we have no information on their incomes. However, the information we do have indicates a predominantly middling sorts background for this group.

Furthermore, the disownments include cases of individuals both from the core and periphery of the Society. Some were officers of meetings, such as Joseph Lovell, officer of Peel monthly meeting, disowned in 1757 after becoming a bankrupt.[47] Benjamin Rickman, merchant, and officer of his monthly meeting, was disowned by Horsleydown for bankruptcy in 1771, and John Wallis, who was disowned by Peel in 1787 and 'who from his station in the church ought to have set a better example'.[48] Contemporary Quaker merchant and diarist James Jenkins commented on the failure of John Wallis in his journal:

> This is an extraordinary affair. A very much esteemed Publick Friend, has been found guilty of losing his money in the lottery & afterwards borrowing from several Friends at a time, when he knew himself to be insolvent. I understand that his affairs are compromised at 10s in the £. Jn Wallis was for many years a woollen Draper in Cornhill & retired from Trade a few years ago, supposed <u>then</u> to be rich.[49]

Others had lost touch with the Society, such as John Haylor, whom Horsleydown monthly meeting disowned in 1762, after he had been 'absent from meetings for some years', which was also true of James Richardson and his wife in 1786.[50]

What unites those disciplined is that the monthly meetings identified their insolvencies and bankruptcies as the consequences of a failure to adhere by the discipline. All those who were sanctioned were considered to have acted dishonestly. They broke the promises they made to their creditors, either by taking undue risks in their businesses, or taking advantage of legal loopholes such as debtors' sanctuaries or debtors' relief acts in order to avoid repaying their creditors. The limited number of cases before 1750 emphasized dishonest behaviour independent from insolvency and bankruptcy. Dishonesty was

---

47 ToD Joseph Lovell 1757, Peel MM, Sufferings.
48 ToD Benjamin Rickman 1771; ToD John Wallis 1798, both Ratcliff MM, Testimonies.
49 Jenkins, Diary, 21/v/1787, emphasis in original; ToD John Wallis 1787, Ratcliff MM, Testimonies.
50 ToD John Haylor 1765, Horsleydown MM, Disorderly Walkers; equally ToD Joseph Pearce 1760, Horsleydown MM, Disorderly Walkers; ToD George Rand 1768, Ratcliff MM, Testimonies; ToD Thomas Benwell 1786, Ratcliff MM, Testimonies.

admonished in the same breath as alcoholism, vanity and extravagance. These weaknesses led individuals to violate the discipline and thereby caused their disownments. Bankruptcy emerged in the Quaker mind as a symptom of dishonesty only in the later decades of the eighteenth century.

Eight bankrupt London Quaker merchants

The sanctions for offences related to honesty in business reflect the overall trend observed in the records: Quaker monthly meetings disowned more Friends for business offences, especially debt and bankruptcy, in the second half of the eighteenth century. Were Friends in this period more prone to insolvency and bankruptcy than in the preceding hundred years? Or did the Society change its attitude towards financial failure?

We can find out by comparing Quaker records to public records of insolvency and bankruptcy. If the Society of Friends effectively sanctioned business misbehaviour throughout this period, we would expect to find that bankrupts were among those sanctioned – and that few Quakers ever became bankrupt.

The *London Gazette* began to list bankruptcies in the 1680s.[51] It included the name and town or county of residence of the bankrupt. The docket books of the Court of Chancery survive for the period 1710 to 1764. They contain the names, occupations and residences of bankrupts as well as the names and sometimes occupations and abodes of the creditors suing them for the period 1710–64.

Comparing Quaker merchants found in Quaker birth, marriage and burial records with the names of individuals who appeared as bankrupts or insolvents in the Gazette and the docket books revealed eight Quaker merchants who became insolvent and bankrupt in the period 1697–1761.[52] They are a diverse group in every respect. The vast majority went bankrupt in the earlier half of the century. Some were established members of London's business community. Joseph Strutt, the earliest case, was a Barbados merchant, trader in coffee and chocolate, and freeman of the City of London. He was incarcerated in the Fleet prison for debts in 1697. After his release he quit trading and became a

---

51 How thoroughly this was implemented is unclear. However, the *Gazette* published several cases per week. As it is also the only source for the seventeenth century and first decade of the eighteenth century, it has to suffice.
52 The source used here is a database developed by the Quaker Family History Society (hereafter QFHSDB) using Quaker digest registers of births, marriages and burials held at the Library of the Religious Society of friends (LSF). The QFHSDB was also used to identify the merchants' monthly meetings.

Table 7. Insolvent/Bankrupt London Quaker Merchants

Merchant	Date of Failure	Monthly Meeting
Strutt, Joseph	1697	Ratcliff
Coysgarne, Joseph the Elder	1707	Ratcliff
Ormston, Joseph	1720	Bull & Mouth
Hitchcock, John	1721	Bull & Mouth
Lovell, William	1727	Bull & Mouth
Coysgarne, Joseph the Younger	1752	Devonshire House
Farmer, James	1755	Devonshire House
Barclay, David	1761	Devonshire House

Sources: London Gazette, Docket Books, QFHSDB.

ship builder instead.[53] Joseph Ormston and John Hitchcock appear in the 1695 census of the inhabitants of London. This lists them as owning wealth of £600 or more, which is the highest income category in the census.[54]

The bankrupt merchants belonged to different generations, and had different local origins. Ormston stemmed from a Scottish merchant family, the Coysgarnes from Bristol. From their papers it appears that some of them were religious, others were not. There is no relationship between their social standing, their closeness to the Society or any other aspect of their personal or business lives to the way the Society dealt with their failures.

If the monthly meetings' sensitivity towards malpractice was comprehensive, as well as constant over time, we would expect these merchants to have faced investigations and sanctioning. However, the meeting minutes show that none of these Friends faced recrimination from the Society.[55] Friends conformed to contemporary understandings, and distinguished between culpable and innocent bankruptcy and insolvency. It is possible that none of them were culpable. Still, we would expect to at least find evidence in the minutes that their cases were investigated and the merchants found innocent. Yet there is no evidence that the monthly meetings made any enquiries at the time. This suggests that the Society was not actively enforcing this aspect of its discipline against its members.

53   Fleet Prison Committment Books, July 1697; Gauci, *The Politics of Trade*, 45.
54   D. Glass, *Inhabitants of London within the Walls, 1695* (London: London Record Society, 1966).
55   The search included the year the bankruptcy appeared in the *Gazette* or docket books, as well as the year immediately before and after. In addition, I searched the meetings' collections of disownment records.

The meetings' lack of action was not due to their ignorance of these traders' insolvencies. Joseph Coysgarne the Older removed from Barking into the city some years after his failure. The certificate of removal his meeting invested him with makes no mention of his bankruptcy, and instead attests that 'his conversation for aught we know appears to us agreeable to his profession, so we heartily recommend him and his family to your meeting'.[56] Given that Barking was a small place at the time, it is highly unlikely that Coysgarne's meeting was not aware of his failure. In other cases, there is direct evidence of meetings' knowledge of their members' bankruptcies. Devonshire House monthly meeting knew about James Farmer's bankruptcy, as his brother-in-law was one of its officers.[57] William Lovell in 1721 was sued by 'Richard How of Gracechurch Street, linen draper, and John Eccleston', his partner.[58] Eccleston had been an officer of the Society's Six Weeks Meeting since 1713, a role in which he regularly interacted with officers of Lovell's Gracechurch Street meeting.[59] In 1721, he was still a member of the Six Weeks Meeting, being present at three of its sessions that year. His relative, Theodore Eccleston, was present at five sessions. There they would have interacted with representatives of Lovell's Gracechurch Street Meeting.[60] The creditors suing Joseph Coysgarne the Younger for bankruptcy in 1752 were John and Capel Hanbury. Not only were they among the richest London merchants of the time – John was one of England's leading tobacco importers – the brothers were also members of Coysgarne's Devonshire House monthly meeting.[61] Their names appear throughout the minutes, mostly as the meeting approached them for money and employment possibilities for poor Friends.[62] Finally, David Barclay of Cateaton Street, merchant and insurer, was sued by his Quaker relatives, John Barclay, David Barclay the Elder and David Barclay the Younger.[63]

Of course, eight bankrupts are a small sample. It is possible that the knowledge of the threat of disownment was enough to deter most Friends from risky business engagements and sufficed as motivation to avoid taking risks and becoming insolvent. If this was the case, we would expect Quaker

---

56 Ratcliff MM, Certificates of removal, received, 1720.
57 Robert Plumsted, brother of Farmer's wife Priscilla. See QFHSDB for kin relationship, and Devonshire House MM minutes of that year for officer status.
58 Bankruptcy Commission Docket Books vol. 5, 18.5.1727.
59 Devonshire House MM minutes vol. 6, 9.12.1713, 232; London Six Weeks Meeting, minutes vol. 6, 9.12.1713, 232.
60 London Quarterly Meeting, minutes vol. 3, 1713–24, 178. Richard How appears in the minutes of the Quarterly Meeting of 30/vii/1717 in respect to his proposed marriage.
61 Price, *Credit*, 72.
62 Devonshire House MM minutes vol. 7, 2.iii.1750, 211; vol. 7, xii.1749/1750, 188, 211, 342, 500.
63 Bankruptcy Commission Docket Books vol. 16, 217, 21.4.1761.

merchants to discuss the threat of disownment in their papers, especially if they struggled financially.

Personal records relating to several of our bankrupt Quaker merchants survive. They include papers by Farmer, as well as correspondence of Joseph Ormston's son Charles. James Farmer was partner and London agent for the Birmingham gun manufacturers Farmer & Galton. They were one of the biggest gun manufacturers of the time and main supplier to the African company.[64] We are lucky to have correspondence written by James Farmer to his business partner Samuel Galton as well as Samuel Galton's letters to Farmer. Their business correspondence uses Latin dates instead of Quaker ones and also otherwise contains no indicators of faith. They address each other as well as their other correspondents with 'you' instead of 'thee', suggesting that they were not among the most devout of Friends.

Debt and bankruptcy figured prominently in Farmer's correspondence. Farmer told Galton that he feared having lost a lot of property in the Lisbon earthquake of 1755 that destroyed much of the city.[65] A little while later, Samuel Galton's letters to James Farmer reflect increasing financial difficulties, urging Farmer to remit as promised, which it appears he had failed to do for several months.[66] Farmer reported that a commission of bankruptcy had been set up against him, and his wife summoned to give evidence to the commission. He reassured Galton that they would not be able to prove him bankrupt.[67] The two Quaker businessmen's extensive discussion of the bankruptcy procedures stands in stark contrast to the complete lack of references to possible responses from the Society to Farmer's failure. We learn from the certificate issued to Farmer years later for his removal back to Birmingham 'that by the late dreadful Earthquake at Lisbon, He sustained so great a Loss, as to Involve his Estate, which otherwise would have been equal to the payment of all his Debts, and a large Surplus remaining'.[68] Yet the records hold no indication of questions being asked by the monthly meeting at the time. Upon his bankruptcy, the partnership with Galton was dissolved. However, he managed to return to business and rejoin the partnership later.[69]

The letter book of Joseph Ormston's son Charles survives for the period 1720–30. Charles Ormston was a merchant and family father resident in Kelso

---

64 Richards, 'The Birmingham Gun Manufactory of Farmer & Galton and the Slave Trade'.
65 Letters from James Farmer 1748–60, MS3101/C/D/15/1–52, Birmingham City Library.
66 Letter book of Samuel Galton 1755–57, MS3101/C/D/15/1/2, Birmingham City Library. 15/1/1.15.12.1755.
67 Devonshire House MM, Certificates Issued, 1765.
68 Papers relating to the financial affairs of Farmer & Galton 1754–70, MS3101/D/1, Birmingham City Library.
69 Letter Book of Charles Ormston of Kelso, National Library of Scotland.

in the Scottish borders. He engaged foremost in trade in clothing, and his letter book suggests that purple silk stockings were the height of fashion in Kelso at the time. Ormston Jr. corresponded with business associates and family members all over England as well as in Ireland.[70] A frequent correspondent was his father Joseph in London. They discussed the financial difficulties the South Sea Crisis had caused for many merchants in London and the lack of availability of bills of exchange in Newcastle that followed the crisis.[71] Their letters do not, however, discuss Joseph's bankruptcy. Charles's letters are filled with references to his faith and his involvement in the Society. In the vast majority of letters he addresses his correspondence Quaker-style using 'thou' and 'thee' and Quaker dates instead of Latin ones.[72] Of his father he enquired about details of the London Yearly Meeting, explaining that he himself was planning to attend the Scottish Yearly Meeting in Aberdeen soon as a representative of his quarterly meeting, and desired to attend the London one as well.[73] He also reported of his travels as a minister to several meetings in the region.[74]

The collection of debts, either for himself or on behalf of correspondents, constitutes a dominant theme in Ormston's correspondence.[75] The letters show him resorting to the full range of usual legal mechanisms. In 1723 there are several letters in which he related the problems he was having collecting outstanding debts from one James Kerr, against whom all available legal measures had been taken, 'and all that remains is to have him thrown into prison to make him pay'.[76] Moreover, he threatened William Norton, Ironmonger of Birmingham, in 1720 with a law suit, threatening 'I have good evidence against you'.[77] The correspondence, however, includes no evidence that this pious Friend feared repercussions from the Society of Friends against his father.

These Quaker merchants' papers betray no awareness of the possibility that the Society might react to bankruptcy. Neither James Farmer, his Quaker correspondents, nor Joseph Ormston's obviously religious son Charles expressed any such concern.

---

70   There is evidence of one correspondent from the North American colonies, who judging from the address Ormston uses for him is not a Quaker: Ormston, Letter book of Charles Ormston of Kelso, to J. Honeyman, 6 April 1720, 87. More references to his business: 371, 30/v/1727; 368–69, 28/v/27, 370 28/v/1727, 371, 30/v/1727 and following letters.
71   Ibid., 67 (19 November 1720), and 69 (undated).
72   In xi/1720 he wrote to an aunt thanking her for an epistle she had sent him. Ibid., 71.
73   Ibid., 73, 4/xii/1720/21.
74   Ibid., 82,3, 6/ii/1721.
75   On 24 November 1723 he asked Wm Seller, 'Writer' in Edinburgh, for assistance in an unspecified legal matter. Ibid., 201.
76   Ibid., 198, 30/viii/1723; also 200, Nov/20th/1723. Debt problems with James Kerr continue; dealings with other debtors are described. For more correspondence about problems enforcing debts see 326, 12th/8br/1726; 99, 15/6/21; 87, 6 April 1720.
77   Ibid., first letter in book, undated, must be early 1720; Charles Ormston 54, 26/v/1720.

Certificates of Removal

The increase in sanctions for business offences in the mid-eighteenth century may have reflected a broader change in the Society's attitude towards debt. If this was the case, we would expect to find increasing references to members' solvency in its records. The problem of debt should then be discussed outside the context of misdemeanour. Fortunately, another set of records from the vaults of London's Friends House allows us to examine how Quakers viewed the significance of debt to individual character in cases that did not involve misdemeanour.

Since the seventeenth century, Quakers who moved from the compass of one meeting into that of another were required to obtain certificates of removal from their home meetings. Upon arrival at their new residence, Friends would hand in this certificate to their new monthly meeting, and be received into the community.[78] 676 certificates received by four of the London monthly meetings, Devonshire House, Ratcliff, Horsleydown and Westminster, survive for the years from 1680–1809. Figure 6 shows the distribution of certificates of removal over time. Certificates in these collections stem from all over England, Scotland, Wales, Ireland and North America.

In the early decades of the eighteenth century certificates rarely mentioned debts, and only if an individual had failed to pay them. Such was the case of Miles Walker and his wife, members of Devonshire House monthly meeting, who obtained a certificate upon their removal to Nunington in Kent. Devonshire House Friends certified

> that after due inquiry made we do not find but that he & his wife have been of a sober conversation though he hath met with disappointments in the world under which circumstances he advised with Friends in accommodating his Affairs and their removal is with our consent and in unity with us and as such we recommend them to you.[79]

Later, confirmation of clearness of debts became commonplace, as in this certificate sent from Brighouse monthly meeting in Leeds to Horsleydown monthly meeting in 1771, on behalf of Ann Kellet:

> This may certifie that two Friends were appointed to make the necessary enquiry who report that they find nothing but her conduct has been orderly, that she left us free from Debts & Marriage engagements.

---

78 This policy closely followed the contemporary Settlement Acts which, as part of the Old Poor Law, regulated in which parishes English paupers were entitled to settle and receive poor relief. See for instance Taylor, 'The Impact of Pauper Settlement 1691–1834'. Certificates were also issued and required by Independents: see for instance Lime Street Independent Meeting House.

79 Miles Walker, Certificate 1734, Devonshire House MM, Certificates of Public Friends.

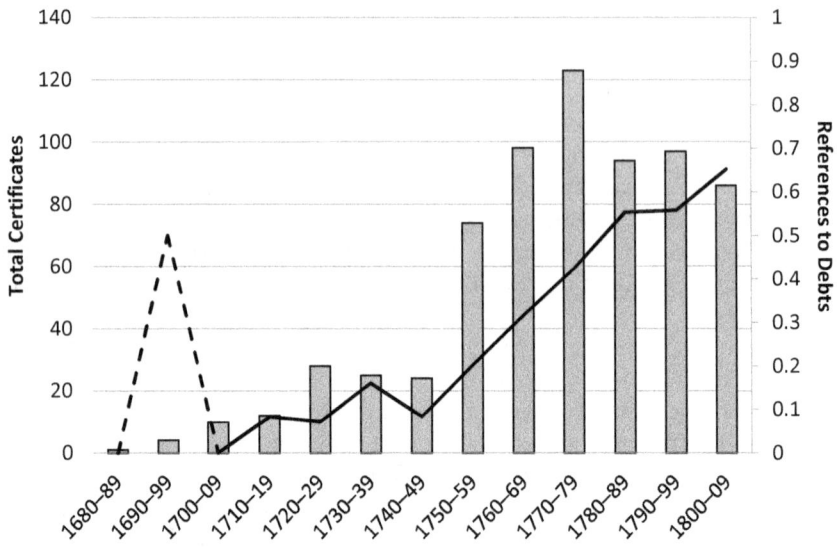

Figure 6. Certificates of Removal Received by London Monthly Meetings

By the end of the century, the majority of certificates confirmed the bearer's solvency. It became one of three attributes certificates mentioned regularly. Information about an individual's marital status and the confirmation of the orderliness of their conversation were included from the earliest days. From the mid-eighteenth century, intelligence about their solvency came to be considered part of the essential information a monthly meeting required about a new member. Thus, the certificates reflect the same increased interest in debts as do the sanctions. This evidence further supports the findings from the sanctions, that the Society of Friends' attitude towards debt underwent a significant transformation in the second half of the eighteenth century.

The analysis of these London records shows that the Society increasingly noted Friends' financial situations, irrespective of misconduct. This suggests that it was in fact not individual Friends' conduct which deteriorated after 1750, as lamented by contemporaries. Rather, the evidence suggests a transformation in the Society of Friends' attitude towards its members behaviour. In particular, we saw an increased sensitivity towards debt and bankruptcy. The fact that the certificates of removal that newly arrived Friends submitted to London monthly meetings came from meetings near and far suggests that this change was not restricted to the metropolis. In order to understand whether this phenomenon affected the transatlantic Quaker community as a whole, the next chapter discusses the development of sanctions, in particular for debt, in the second-largest community of the time: the Quaker city of Philadelphia.

8

Trade and Debt in Philadelphia

Debt and credit were the life blood of trade, and trade was central to Philadelphia's economy. Under mercantilist trade policy the colonies were restricted to exchange within the British Empire. Being able to trade only with the motherland or other colonies made Pennsylvania closely dependent on British economic trends. Periods of boom and recession in England were manifested in the extension of credit or the recall of loans to colonial merchants. During most of the eighteenth century, the British demand for colonial goods grew. As a consequence, the terms of credit granted in London to colonial merchants who were funding imports increased as well. In some cases, they grew from less than a year in the seventeenth century to an average of at least two years in the eighteenth century.[1] Britain and her Quaker colony also experienced periods of economic decline, however. When the British economy went into recession, demand for colonial goods dropped, and merchants in England recalled loans from their American counterparts. On several occasions during the eighteenth century, this led to mass insolvencies in the colonies.

Philadelphia's economic development in this period can be divided roughly into three phases. The first phase stretches from the beginning of colonization in 1682 to the 1720s, and is marked by modest but stable bilateral trade with the other colonies. Philadelphia exported provisions mainly to the West Indies. These included tobacco, skins, furs, lumber and, of particular importance, flour. The annual exports of flour were as valuable as all other exports combined. In return, Philadelphia's merchants received bills of exchange. While Pennsylvania itself was not primarily a plantation colony, as Bryccan Carey pointed out, the central role of the Caribbean trade meant that 'Philadelphia's economy nevertheless depended in large measure on the wealth generated by slaves'.[2] Philadelphia merchants used the bills they received from their Caribbean trading partners to purchase manufactured goods. While these goods were produced in England, Philadelphia merchants did not buy them there. Instead, they received them from middlemen in the New England colonies. Direct trade with England was minimal, regarding both the export of primary products

---

1 Jacob Price, 'What did Merchants Do?,' *Journal of Economic History* 49, no. 2 (1989).
2 Carey, *Peace*, 12.

there and the imports of manufactured goods from thence. The port's connections were therefore primarily colonial. This regional pattern of trade, as Jacob Price observed, 'encouraged the development of a large community of small merchants in Philadelphia, big enough to trade to the West Indies but not very venturesome outside those familiar waters'.[3]

The second phase, from about 1720 to the Seven Years' War (1756–63), saw an expansion of Philadelphia's external trade. The export sector became more lively. The West Indian trade declined in relative importance, while more wheat and flour were sold to Southern Europe and Ireland. The coastal trade with the other colonies grew as well. These developments allowed Philadelphia's external trade to almost triple by 1740.

The third phase began with the Seven Years' War and lasted into the nineteenth century. The Seven Years' War marked a turning point in the port town's fortunes. Philadelphia benefited greatly from the war, as troops had to be supplied and expenditures for army supplies were particularly great in Pennsylvania.[4] This period saw a significant shift in both destinations and volume of shipping. Philadelphia's trade grew rapidly and shifted its orientation more dramatically than any other colonial port. The war provided Philadelphia merchants with a windfall of bills of exchange on London. Many used these to enter into direct trade with England. This window of opportunity was sustained through an upswing in cereal prices in Europe at the same time. Populations in Europe grew, and together with a series of bad harvests this conspired to raise grain prices. As Philadelphia was specialized in exporting grain, this combination of factors allowed its merchants to expand their small, pre-existing trade with the Iberian peninsula, and enter new markets in Europe, France and Britain. Philadelphia's direct trade to Southern Europe and Great Britain grew rapidly. The grain exported from Philadelphia was drawn not only from its immediate hinterland, but also consisted of re-exports of grain imports from other colonies. Philadelphia merchants were 'taking greater control of their own trade and were sending their cargos to places where they had not previously sailed'. In the early 1750s, only about 20 per cent of the port's shipping was directed to Europe. Twenty years later, it was more than 30 per cent. By the early 1770s, three-quarters of Philadelphia's transatlantic shipping was owned in the colony, which was a similar increase to that of overall shipping to Europe. The port's new dynamism is reflected in the fact that between the 1750s and the Revolution, Philadelphia's export trade tripled. In comparison, that of the next largest port, New York, only doubled. The Philadelphia merchant community

---

3 Jacob M. Price and G. E. Clemens Paul, 'A Revolution of Scale in Overseas Trade: British Firms in the Chesapeake Trade, 1675–1775', *Journal of Economic History* 47, no. 1 (1987).
4 John J. McCusker and Russell R. Menard, *The Economy of British America, 1607–1789*, 2nd edn (Chapel Hill: University of North Carolina Press, 1986), 194.

in this period became 'much wealthier, more sophisticated, better connected, and more aggressive'.[5]

War-induced boom periods were regularly followed by periods of post-war depression.[6] The aftermath of the Seven Years' War saw a grave economic crisis. A severe shortage of specie made it extremely difficult for colonists to settle debts. This contributed to the post-war recession turning into a period of full-blown economic depression. An increase in insolvencies accompanied the crisis, which lasted until the late 1760s. During that decade, growth in the parent country stalled and 'transatlantic commerce was filled with insistent requests for repayment, and pleas from the colonies for leniency', leading to a scarcity of money and a wave of insolvencies in the colonies.[7] The crisis was intensified further by a series of British attempts to reform the colonial economy and to tighten the imperial administrative system.[8] The Declaration of Independence for the first time completely broke the navigation laws and opened American commerce to the world.[9] However, after the Revolutionary War there was another nationwide economic depression.[10]

After struggling for several years after the end of the War of Independence, Philadelphia's commerce recovered by late 1779 and the city received much-needed stores. 1780 saw a generally prosperous situation in Philadelphia. New trade began to take place largely with Northern European countries, as well as with France and the Netherlands. Still, the colony as a whole experienced mass insolvencies throughout the 1780s. The struggle continued in the 1790s, as the young republic's first financial crisis led to an epidemic of business failures. In Philadelphia in 1796, contemporaries reported 150 failures within a six-week period, and sixty-seven individuals were imprisoned for debt in 1796 within just one two-week period.[11]

---

5   McCusker and Menard, *British America*, 194–95.
6   Terry Bouton, 'Moneyless in Pennsylvania: Privatisation and the Depression of the 1780s', in *The Economy of Early America: Historical Perspectives and New Directions*, ed. Cathy Matson (University Park: Pennsylvania State University Press, 2006), 233.
7   Marc Egnal, *New World Economies: The Growth of the Thirteen Colonies and Early Canada* (New York and Oxford: Oxford University Press, 1998), 74, 76. See also McCusker and Menard, *British America*, 352; Bouton, 'Moneyless in Pennsylvania'.
8   McCusker and Menard, *British America*, 65.
9   Robert Abraham East, *Business Enterprise in the American Revolutionary Era* (New York: AMS Press, 1969), 37.
10 Ibid., 239, 243.
11 Bruce H. Mann, *Republic of Debtors: Bankruptcy in the Age of American Independence* (Cambridge, MA, and London: Harvard University Press, 2002), 202.

Debt and bankruptcy in Philadelphia

In the seventeenth and early eighteenth centuries, attitudes towards debt and credit in the North American colonies resembled those in England. As we saw in the discussion of the English and British sermons above, seventeenth- and early eighteenth-century people regarded debt as a moral problem, rather than an economic one. As their compatriots in England, the colonists considered paying debts in full, no matter at what personal costs, if their business failed. Accordingly, there was no legislation relieving a debtor from their obligations if their business failed. If a debtor became unable to pay, their creditors could have them arrested and claim their belongings.

A debt suit commonly began with a writ of attachment. Upon being served, a debtor had to supply security for the money they owed, or they were arrested. Release from debtors' prison occurred either upon payment or supply of security. For the poorest of debtors, there was the possibility of a poor debtors' oath. This was intended for those too poor to maintain themselves in prison. After thirty days in gaol, they could swear an oath that they were unable to pay, and were free to go. This did not absolve them from their debts, however – it merely protected them from being arrested for the same debt again.[12]

Several colonies had a parallel procedure through which debtors might try to escape the worst consequences of their failures. They could send a petition to the colonial assembly and plea for relief. In these petitions, the debtors explained their situation, and how they had done everything in their power to pay their creditors, arriving in their lamentable situation through external circumstances outside their control. There was no way to predict how assemblies would decide these requests. The outcome depended entirely on the individual, their situation, and the assemblymen's preferences. If successful, a petition liberated the debtor from prison, but not from the obligation to repay their debts. Any future earnings could be claimed by the creditors. There was no provision for discharge from debt. The Pennsylvania Assembly passed eighty-one such laws during the eighteenth century. Among the beneficiaries were several Pennsylvania Quakers.

Over the course of the eighteenth century, in the colonies as in England, the attitude towards debt changed from a moral towards an economic understanding. This transformation went hand in hand with the experience of increased commercialization. The economic situation in the colonies in this period, while it saw starts and fits, was overall one of growth.[13] The increase of trade, especially long-distance trade across the Atlantic, was based entirely on credit. It was also greatly impacted by war. While wars provided great

---

12 Ibid., 51.
13 Ibid., 36.

opportunities for business, they also increased risks, losses and the possibilities for insolvency. Through these experiences, the colonists gained a greater understanding of commercial debt and credit. They realised that insolvency was not necessarily caused by a debtor's wasteful lifestyle, bad habits or malpractice. People became more aware of the difficulty of foreseeing losses in an increasingly global market.

The Seven Years' War played a key role in this development. While British war expenses provided unprecedented business opportunities, they also caused uncountable insolvencies. In addition, the international financial crisis of the 1760s and 1770s compelled British merchants to call in debts, which colonists perceived as crushing. In Philadelphia, respected, wealthy and influential merchants became prone to insolvency. At the same time, debt and credit were discussed widely in both religious and secular literature, as well as in the press.[14]

As a consequence of this experience, the colonies introduced their first bankruptcy legislations. Between 1755 and 1763, New York, Rhode Island, Massachusetts and Connecticut passed bankruptcy statutes which distributed insolvents' property evenly among creditors, and allowed debtors to walk away from their remaining obligations to start anew.[15] Pennsylvania introduced a bankruptcy law in 1785. This was modelled upon the British one and allowed discharge from debts. It expired in 1793 and was not renewed. While the law was in place 172 petitions were filed against 184 debtors, 145 of them doing business in Philadelphia.[16] In all other colonies, the bankruptcy statutes lapsed or were repealed as well. Thus, the legal situation of debtors and creditors by the end of the eighteenth century was little different from what it had been a hundred years earlier. However, the mentality around debt and credit had changed significantly.

Philadelphia Quaker meetings and debt

Interestingly, the Philadelphia Quaker monthly meetings' sanctions for debt-related offences do not mirror the overall social and intellectual trend regarding debt and credit in the colonies. Rather than relaxing in their condemnation of debt, Philadelphia Friends punished debt with increasing frequency over the course of the period.

Figure 7 shows the development of the Philadelphia monthly meetings' sanctions for offences related to honesty in business. We see very few sanctions during the seventeenth and early eighteenth centuries. From 1750, the overall

---

14 Finn, *The Character of Credit*, 25. For the colonies see Mann, *Republic*.
15 Mann, *Republic*, 55.
16 Ibid., 177–78.

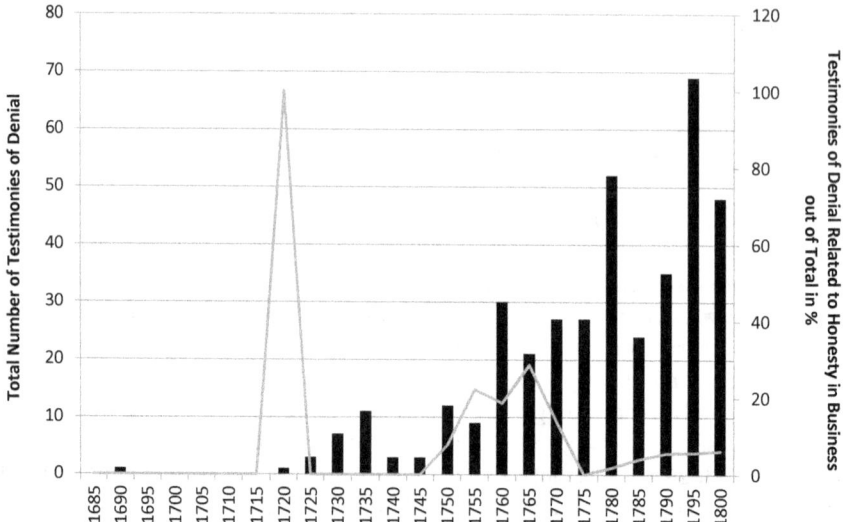

Figure 7. Philadelphia Monthly Meetings' Testimonies of Denial Related to Honesty

number of disownments grew. The proportion of business-related offences among the sanctions increased dramatically as well. This trend indicates a sudden increase in interest in the honest conduct of business in this period.

Sanctions for debts in Philadelphia peaked in the 1760s. The two sample years 1760 and 1765 saw six disownments for debt-related offences each.[17] They include the case of Peter Widdowfield, who was disowned after having been reported by the overseers for 'his idle course of life, neglect of attending meetings for publick worship, breach of promises, running in debt & neglecting the necessary care of his family'.[18] A 1765 case is that of Timothy Matlack, who was disowned for absence from meetings, neglecting his business and having requested to be left alone and not be 'treated with' any more.[19] Equally, Philadelphia monthly meeting found William Parker guilty of neglecting his business, keeping loose company, pursuing disreputable schemes in business and, finally, debts.[20] Finally, Nathanial Goforth was disowned for 'imprudent conduct in involving himself in debt', neglecting attending meetings of worship and joining the military.[21] The interest in business-related offences dropped off again in the 1770s.

17 Philadelphia MM minutes, 14/viii/60, 30/xii/60.
18 Philadelphia MM minutes, 31/v/65; 28/vi/65; 26/vii/65.
19 Philadelphia MM minutes, ToD Timothy Matlack 1765.
20 Philadelphia MM minutes, ToD William Parker 1743.
21 Philadelphia, MM minutes, ToD Nathanial Goforth 1759.

Resemblances and differences between Philadelphia and London

The development of sanctions for business-related offences in the Philadelphia community bears both resemblances and differences to their development in London. The increased sensitivity about debt reflected in an increase of sanctions related to debt in Philadelphia resembles the development in the London community. While significant, this is where the commonalities end. The increase we see in Philadelphia is less intense than that in London. After the 1760s, the numbers of business-related sanctions plateau in London. In Philadelphia they decline. What is more, unlike their London brethren, Philadelphia Friends' meetings disowned nobody for debts alone. Rather, testimonies of denial always listed several offences, among which indebtedness often played a minor role. Moreover, after the 1760s, sanctions for debt dropped to four cases in 1770 and no cases at all in 1775. Disownments for business offences remained low until another 'peak' of four cases in 1795, which roughly coincided with the United States' first financial crisis and mass insolvencies in Philadelphia.

However, disownments for business offences did not mirror economic cycles. The strongest illustration of this is that sanctions for business offences did not soar during the South Sea Crisis. In the wake of this event, in Philadelphia

> over two hundred houses stood empty, ... labouring people were daily forced to leave the city, shopkeepers had no money with which to replenish their stocks, and the prices of wheat, flour, bread, and other farm products fell to a point at which it was scarcely worthwhile for farmers to bring them to market.[22]

Yet the year 1720 saw only one testimony of denial, that of John Locke, who 'ran away with an infamous lewd woman, thereby abandoning his family' and absconding from his creditors.[23] This inclusion of business misbehaviour as part of a condemnation for a range of more general moral failures is seen elsewhere in the sanctions, just as in London. Almost thirty years later, John Cresson was reported to Philadelphia monthly meeting for excessive drinking. Eventually the meeting disowned him for embezzling funds of 'some orphan children under his care'.[24] Similarly, Jonathan Lewis was disowned for the 'frequenting of taverns, keeping idle company' and, finally, 'engaging in business beyond his means' and not paying his debts.[25] In each case, the meeting's primary concern was not the Friend's lack of honesty or risk-aversity in business. Instead, they

---

22 Tolles, *Meeting House*, 100.
23 Philadelphia MM minutes, ToD John Locke 24/iv/1720.
24 Philadelphia MM minutes, ToD John Cresson 25/v/1749.
25 Philadelphia MM minutes, ToD Jonathan Lewis 28/xi/1755; ToD Robert Owens 20/xi/55, 26/xii/55.

focused on other offences, and dishonesty and debts were added to the list of delinquencies later.

Instead of reflecting economic trends, the Philadelphia meetings' disownment records show that, as in London, business offences were sanctioned regularly from about 1750 onwards. However, unlike in London, Philadelphia monthly meetings did not sanction Friends for debt offences alone even after 1750. Nor did bankruptcy ever appear as a cause for disownment – likely because the lack of such legislation during most of the period made this a practical impossibility.

Bankrupt, insolvent, fraudulent Philadelphia Quaker merchants

Did Philadelphia monthly meetings capture all delinquents? Or was their sanctioning, as that of London, incomplete? Pennsylvania archives hold records on insolvency, bankruptcy and laws issued by the Pennsylvania Assembly for the relief of individual debtors. Among these, I identified eight certain Philadelphia Friends. Most of these were merchants. Abraham Howell was a saddler; he may have traded in leather.[26] Allen Ridgeway was a lumber merchant, and Joshua Pusey a merchant and miller.[27] Both lumber and flower were important export products of Pennsylvania. William Fishbourne was an attorney, as well as a public servant.[28] The bankrupts are listed in table 8.

Table 8. Insolvent/Bankrupt/Fraudulent Philadelphia Quaker merchants

Name	First Name	Failure	Sanction	Type of Failure	Sanctioned
Sykes	William	1788	1789	bankrupt	yes
Pusey	Joshua	1787	–	bankrupt	no
Garrigues	Samuel	1786	1786	bankrupt	yes
Meng	John	1786–87	1787	bankrupt	yes
Ridgeway	Allen	1788	–	bankrupt	no
Fishbourne	William	1731	1731	law	yes
Howell	Abraham	1769	1769	law	yes
Griffitts	William	1761	1761	law	yes

Sources: See text.

26 ToD Abraham Howell, Philadelphia MM minutes, vii/1768.
27 Petitions, 1781–1815, RG033/A/R85, Supreme Court of Pennsylvania.
28 'The Statutes at Large of Pennsylvania'; Philadelphia MM minutes, 1/iii/1717, 28. Note that Fishbourne's law was not about debts. He is included as a Friend who was convicted for dishonesty in relation to money.

In contrast to the sample of failed Quaker merchants in London, only one of the Philadelphia cases fell into the period before 1750. Moreover, unlike their London brethren, the majority of these Philadelphia Friends were disowned. The only two not sanctioned were Allen Ridgway and Joshua Pusey.[29] Four of the others were disowned swiftly after their bankruptcy suits or private laws were issued.

The degrees to which these Friends were involved with the Society varied. Abraham Howell and Samuel Garrigues appear in the Quaker records only in connection with the offences they were eventually disowned for.[30] Sykes's and Griffitts's marriages were recorded in the meeting minutes.[31] John Meng and William Fishbourne were officers of their meetings.[32]

The greatest amount of information is available for the cases of Fishbourne and Griffitts, as the laws passed for and against them describe their circumstances in detail. The cases took place thirty years apart, and Philadelphia monthly meetings' response to both differed significantly.

On 6 February 1731 the Assembly of Pennsylvania passed 'An act to disable William Fishbourne from holding any office of trust or profit within this province and to secure the payment of a provincial debt due from the said William Fishbourne'.[33] Fishbourne was a prominent figure among Friends as well as greater Philadelphia society. He was an officer of the Quaker monthly meeting and trustee of the general loan office of Pennsylvania. The law stated that 'it had become manifest' that during his eight years as a trustee, from 1722 to 1730, 'he had fraudulently concealed and applied to his own use a considerable sum of the said bills of credit in high violation of his trust and in open breach of the duty of his office'. At that point, he owed the province almost £2000. Philadelphia monthly meeting disowned Fishbourne the same year.[34] The testimony against him explains elaborately how he had come to be disowned and reinstated repeatedly since 1724. In previous years the meeting had testified against him for his 'scandalous conduct towards women'. Interestingly, however, the new testimony referred to his latest misconduct only as 'some late reports concerning his continued unchaste practices and other unrighteous proceedings'. This sounds as if the fraud he committed was not the meetings' main concern. On the other hand, we do not know the details

---

29 Monthly Meeting of the Northern Liberties, minutes, x/87. Pusey had been disowned for irregular marriage in 1784, but appears to have been reinstated by the time of his failure.
30 Sykes, Philadelphia MM minutes, xi/81; Griffitts, Philadelphia MM minutes, iv/61.
31 Sykes, Philadelphia MM minutes ii/86, iii/86, and membership list 1782; Griffitts, Philadelphia MM minutes iv/1752.
32 Meng, iii/84 Liberties, Northern Liberties MM minutes. Fishbourne for instance, Philadelphia MM minutes, 27/viii/27, ix/22, xi/23.
33 'The Statutes at Large of Pennsylvania', chapter CCCXXVI, 1730–31.
34 Philadelphia MM minutes, x/1732.

of his 'unchaste practices', perhaps these were even more scandalous than the committed fraud. After submitting another self-condemnation, he was readmitted as a member in 1739.[35]

In stark contrast to Fishbourne's case stands that of William Griffitts, whom the Philadelphia monthly meeting disowned for malpractice in business in 1761. His disownment closely followed the adoption of a law introduced upon a petition by him. This law explained that Griffitts had become unable to pay his debts. Upon realizing this, he came to an agreement with the majority of his creditors, to divide what money and assets he had among all of them. What was more, Griffitts's wife 'also added all her estate, amounting to several thousand pounds, on condition that the said William Griffitts' body should be free from arrest and imprisonment'. A minority of his creditors, however, refused to agree to this arrangement, 'thereby obliging the trustees of the said estates to suspend making the intended dividend thereof amongst all his creditors' and threatening Griffitts such that he expected 'himself daily to be closely confined in gaol'.[36] His petition was signed by a long list of his supportive creditors. It includes prominent Quaker merchants and politicians, such as Jacob Schoemaker Jr, Israel Pemberton and Isaac Greenleafe. All of these were active on behalf of Philadelphia monthly meeting, appearing throughout its records. Yet the meeting proceeded to disown Griffitts after thirteen months of enquiries. For reasons that do not become clear from the minutes, the meeting in the course of its dialogue with Griffitts decided that 'no condemnation of his misconduct can be acceptable', unless he included that his failure was caused by his 'having been addicted to excess in the use of strong Drink'.[37] Griffitts refused this last demand. The meeting thereupon proceeded to issue a testimony of denial against him. This did not refer to his alleged drinking. Instead, it explained that Griffitts

> hath conducted with so much imprudence as to involve himself in great difficulties in his temporal affairs, whereupon it became the concern of Friends to visit & advise him to an adjustment thereof for the satisfaction of his creditors, which he neglected to do, & hath been so unjust, as to satisfy some of his creditors to the prejudice of the rest, on which it became the further care of Friends to visit him, in order to bring him to a just sense of his reproachful conduct, but he not appearing convinced of the evil tendency thereof, so fully, as to condemn the same to the satisfaction of this meeting.[38]

---

35 Philadelphia MM minutes, vi/1739.
36 'The Statutes at Large of Pennsylvania', 1761, No. 0471, Relief of William Griffitts.
37 Philadelphia MM minutes, ii/1761.
38 Philadelphia MM minutes, iv/1761.

While the Assembly believed Griffitts and his petitioning creditors that he was working at settling his affairs and discharging his debts as quickly and justly as possible, the meeting reached a different verdict. It is not clear why this was the case, and it is also odd that the charge of alcoholism appeared so suddenly, its recognition being made a requirement for his being forgiven, but then was not included in the testimony of denial. The minutes contain no evidence of a later reinstatement of Griffitts into the Society. Neither Griffitts's nor Fishbourne's testimonies of denial referred explicitly to the laws passed about them.

With the exception of William Fishbourne, all the Friends in this study failed in their businesses in the later part of the eighteenth century, i.e. during a period in which Philadelphia monthly meetings' sanctions had already increased substantially. Six of the eight bankrupt or fraudulent Philadelphia Quaker merchants were disowned. These include two cases of Friends for whom laws were passed, William Fishbourne and William Griffitts (see above). The two who were not reprimanded, Joshua Pusey and Allen Ridgeway, were also not investigated by their meetings.

These cases suggest that the Philadelphia monthly meetings' enforcement of the discipline, just as in London, even after 1750, was not comprehensive. The fact that the Pennsylvania Assembly, the colony's chief legislative body, discussed William Fishbourne's and William Griffitts's cases strongly suggests that they were widely known about. If it was the monthly meetings' aim to clear the Society's name of scandal, as they repeatedly stated, they had to respond to cases with that much publicity.

The case of William Fishbourne may be unusual, but it still contains some interesting implications. Not only was the Society willing to readmit repeated offenders, who presumably had caused great scandal, it was also in the interest of such offenders to be included in the organization again. Membership at least in this early period, when Quakers still dominated the political and economic life of the colony, likely brought benefits great enough for Fishbourne to go through the presumably embarrassing process of applying for re-entry and condemning his behaviour. Over thirty years later, when the situation for Friends in Pennsylvania was much changed, William Griffitts still did not accept his disownment easily. From the minutes it appears that he cooperated with the meeting, discussed his accounts with its officers and assured them of his regret for his failure. His desire to remain a member of the Society was, however, not great enough to make him admit to the charge that he had brought his failure about by excessive drinking. Possibly such an admission would have done more harm to his reputation and credit than ostracism from the Society of Friends. Griffitts's case also shows us that knowing important people within the Society, such as those of his creditors supporting his petition to the assembly, did not necessarily protect individual Friends from sanctions. Notable in both cases is that the meeting invested a great amount of time in investigating the cases and maintained a dialogue with the offenders. The Philadelphia monthly meetings were clearly interested in keeping their members. Even in the second half of the eighteenth century, disownments did not come easily.

Certificates of Removal

Philadelphia monthly meetings received 4,316 certificates of removal between 1681 and 1800. Their numbers increased in the 1710s, and dropped off during the 1770s. The latter mirrors the pattern of Pennsylvanian archival records in general. They are scarcer for the years around the Revolutionary War, which may also have curbed migration flows. After the war, the number of certificates increased again steadily until the end of the century. Friends arrived in Philadelphia from the immediate vicinity, other colonies, as well as from England, Scotland and Ireland. In 1797, a Friend arrived from France.[39] Moreover, it appears that it was not uncommon for Friends to move to a different monthly meeting, either in Pennsylvania or another colony, for a few months and then return. Sometimes self-condemnations occurred just before somebody requested a certificate, implying that the offenders felt these were useful or necessary.[40] Indeed, William Nichols wrote back to Horsleydown monthly meeting in London, requesting a certificate, in spite of having left in debt.[41] He explained that he thought 'it would be a great help to my settling myself in business'.[42] Philadelphia monthly meetings occasionally prosecuted non-deliverance of certificates. For instance, Philadelphia monthly meeting in 1750 testified against Joseph Harvey Jr for having 'liv'd some years in this city, and never produced any certificate from Darby monthly meeting from whence he came'.[43]

As shown in figure 8, Philadelphia monthly meeting received far fewer certificates before than after 1750. Among the certificates arriving Friends submitted to Philadelphia meetings before 1750, seventy-four mentioned debts. Among these, five referred to actual solvency problems. Elizabeth Thomas, who moved to Philadelphia from nearby Radnor, was actually free from debt, but her certificate specified that her husband had been disowned for indebtedness some years before.[44] About John Crew, his former meeting in Dunn Creek, North Carolina wrote that 'unpaid debts remain'.[45] It is worth noting

39 Philadelphia MM, Certificates of removal received. From Congenie, France.
40 Ibid., Cert. No. 1492.
41 Ibid., Cert. No. 834, 1748.
42 Horsleydown MM minutes, 1748, 211.
43 Philadelphia MM minutes, ix/1750.
44 Philadelphia MM, Certificates of removal received, Cert. No. 458, 1722.
45 Ibid., Cert. No. 806, 1748.

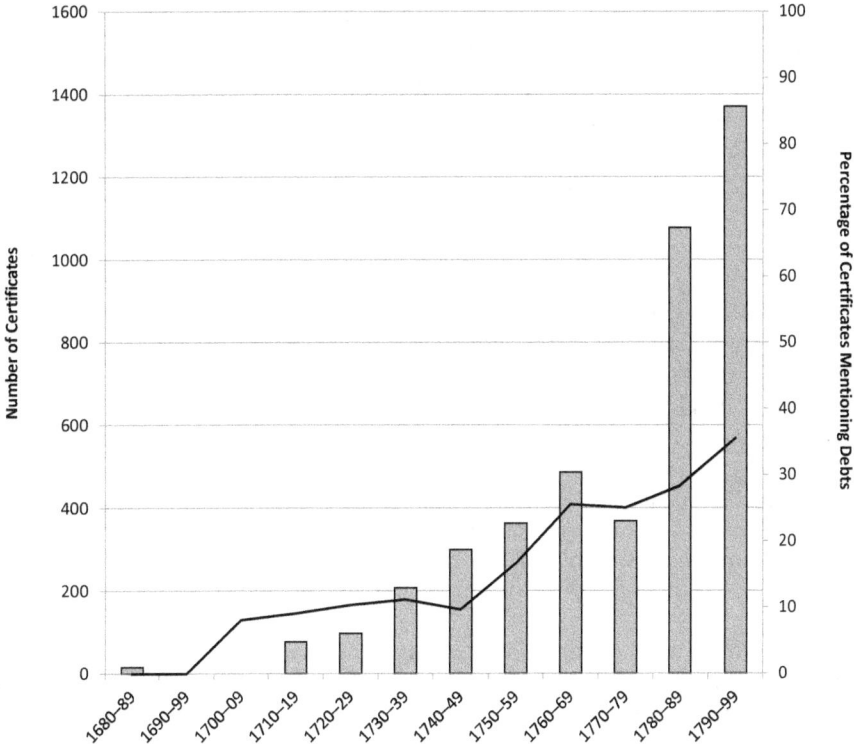

Figure 8. Certificates of removal received by Philadelphia Monthly Meetings
Sources: see text.

that the settling of debts did not necessarily mean their full payment. Rather, it implied that debtor and creditor had reached an agreement, and that the departing Friend was not absconding and trying to avoid payment.[46] Friends whose certificates mentioned unpaid debts may therefore still have been honest people who arranged later payments with their creditors. The mentioning of unpaid debts, if not otherwise specified, did not have to constitute a negative verdict on the person's character. Perhaps the fact that they remained in the Society, and could therefore easily be tracked down and confronted, worked as a form of insurance, or at least assurance, for creditors.

After 1750 the total number of certificates Philadelphia monthly meetings received increased significantly. The frequency with which the certificates mentioned debts grew substantially. Of 3,664 certificates, almost 30 per cent

46 Mann, *Republic*, 22.

included references to debts. The vast majority of these stated that the bearer was either clear of debt or had settled her affairs to satisfaction. Only six of the certificates in this later period included reference to actual solvency problems. Thus, the number of certificates containing 'negative' references remained almost unchanged, in spite of the overall number increasing dramatically. The six certificates with negative solvency information resemble the pre-1750 certificates. John Bezer received a certificate from his meeting in Middleton, Bucks County in 1757, stating that he left in debt.[47] Benjamin Hough left Newark in 1760. His certificate stated that 'after enquiry made we do not find but he hath been to a good degree of an orderly conversation, except his going away in debt, for which his acknowledgement hath since been received & his affairs are now settled to satisfaction…'[48] A similar case was that of John Nancarrow, who arrived in Philadelphia in 1774. His home monthly meeting recommended him as

> a valuable member of our Society … At the same time we have to inform you that by his connexions in some unsuccessful mining partnerships he has been somewhat embarrassed, through which he has conducted himself to the general satisfaction of Friends of this Meeting.[49]

In spite of having made amends, the legacy of past insolvency followed these Friends to the New World. Finally, John Stall and his family moved from the Southern District in Philadelphia into the compass of the monthly meeting for the Northern District. Southern District meeting described them as having been

> in a good degree orderly in life & conversation, frequently attended our religious meetings, yet we may further observe that for want of due & timely care respecting the situation of their outward affairs have been under necessity of making composition with their creditors and transferrance of their property.[50]

The Philadelphia monthly meetings' records include a further source. In addition to copies of certificates they received from arriving Friends, the city's monthly meetings from the 1740s onwards kept copies of all certificates they themselves wrote for departing Friends. The certificates Philadelphia monthly meetings received display a cross-section of the significance monthly meetings across the Atlantic world placed on debts. The certificates the Philadelphia monthly meetings themselves issued departing Friends with, in contrast, provide

---

47 Philadelphia MM, Certificates received, Cert. Nos 1203, 1250. (Also Thomas Cooper, from Brighouse MM, Yorkshire, 1795.)
48 Ibid., Cert. No. 1324, Benjamin How, 1760.
49 Ibid., John Nancarrow the Younger, 1774, no certificate number.
50 Ibid., John Stall & family, i/1792, 282.

insight into the attitudes towards debts among meetings in the Quaker city. The archives contain 396 copies of certificates; their distribution is shown in figure 9.

Certificates are extant from the mid-eighteenth century onwards. Their number increased during the 1750s and 1760s to peak in the 1770s. After a brief slump in the 1780s, their number returned to roughly the same as in the 1770s. The dip in the 1780s may be caused by the survival of records. The overall trend remains clear: an increase in issuing certificates, which fits with the overall increase in recordkeeping we witnessed in the Philadelphia meetings' sources discussed in chapter four.

The certificates of removal Philadelphia monthly meetings issued between 1745 and 1800 mentioned clearness of debts with increasing frequency from the 1750s to the 1770s. In fact, the growth of references to debts is exponential. The vast majority of these confirm clearness from debts. This development peaked in 1770 at just over 30 per cent of cases, dropped to about 20 per cent in 1795 and rose again sharply thereafter. From the 1780s, this frequency became less pronounced and decreased continuously until the year 1800.

The increased volume of references to debts, or clearness thereof, in the certificates issued by Philadelphia meetings resembles those we saw in the certificates which London and Philadelphia meetings received. However, as in the certificates received by Philadelphia, references to debts in the Philadelphia meetings' own certificates never become as common as in those certificates received by London meetings.

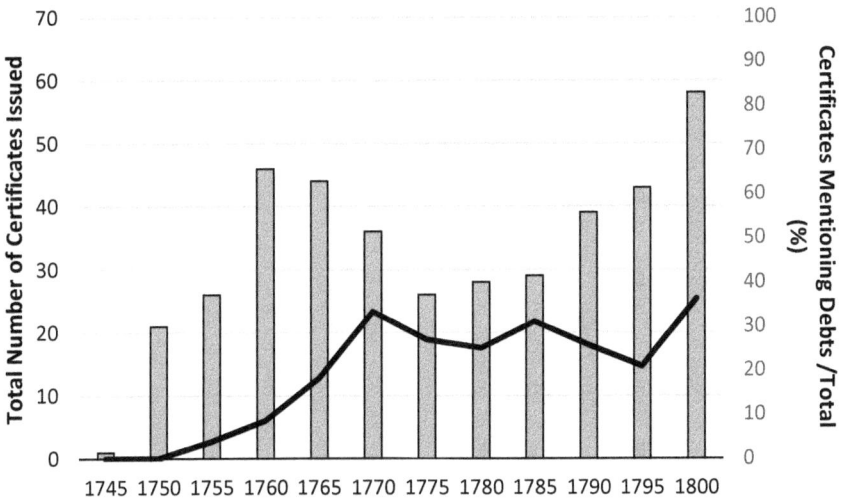

Figure 9. Certificates of Removal Issued by Philadelphia Monthly Meetings
Sources: Records of Philadelphia Monthly Meetings

Conclusion

Philadelphia monthly meetings' interest in debt, as evidenced in the number of sanctions for debt-related offences, emerged in the mid-eighteenth century. It was not a practice evident in the records from the meetings' beginnings in 1682. Rather, it took almost forty years before Philadelphia's monthly meeting first disowned a Friend for crimes that included debt. What is more, the fact that insolvent and bankrupt Philadelphia Quaker merchants were not investigated by their meetings strongly suggests that these American meetings did not sanction insolvency and bankruptcy comprehensively.

The surveys of both the collection of certificates addressed to Philadelphia monthly meetings as well as that of certificates it issued for departing Friends confirm an overall increase of sensitivity about debts among Friends in the second half of the eighteenth century. What distinguishes these certificates from the ones London monthly meetings received is that references to clearness of debts never became quite as ubiquitous. The certificates Philadelphia meetings issued include fewer references to debts than those received by Philadelphia or London meetings. Apparently, Philadelphia Friends were somewhat less concerned about debt then their metropolitan brethren.

Thus, the emergence of monthly meetings' interest in their members' debts, as well as their policing of their congregations' conduct in general, that we observed in the London records was an Atlantic-wide phenomenon.

9

Marital Endogamy

In both Philadelphia and London, the greatest cause for sanctions was marriage delinquency.[1] For London, a unique source on Quaker marriages exists: the Quaker Family History Society has compiled a database of all London Quaker marriages from the meetings' records. This allows a detailed examination of how the Society's mid-eighteenth-century reform efforts influenced metropolitan Friends' marriage patterns, as well as monthly meetings' prosecution of marriage offences.

Quaker marriage was distinctive in several ways. First of all, the Society held a doctrine of religious marital endogamy. Both George Fox and Robert Barclay argued that marriage to non-Quakers would have a negative spiritual impact on Friends.[2] At least in theory, therefore, seventeenth- and eighteenth-century Friends were allowed to marry co-religionists only.[3] As Quakers rejected church weddings as part of their doctrine against professional clergy, the Society required Friends to marry in its monthly meetings.[4] A marriage by a priest or a magistrate was considered irregular and might lead to reprimands by the Society.

While in Pennsylvania Quaker marriages were considered legal from day one, in England the law did not formally recognize them until the Marriage Act of 1836. However, they were 'repeatedly held valid in the courts (when, for instance, the legitimacy of children was questioned)'.[5] This was important not only for inheritance, but also as illegitimate children were excluded from important aspects of civil life, such as joining livery companies or claiming urban citizenship. A series of court cases during the early decades of the

---

1   For Pennsylvania, see Marietta, *Reformation*, 51.
2   Robert the Elder Barclay and William Works, with prefaces etc. by William Penn, *Truth Triumphant through the Spiritual Warfare, Christian Labours and Writings of ... R. Barclay [Collected Works. With a preface by William Penn]* (London: Thomas Northcott, 1692). George Fox in Swarthmore Women's MM, vol. II, 2.i 1701, cited in Lloyd, *Social History*, 58.
3   Lloyd, *Social History*, 58; Vann, *Social Development*, 186; Moore, 'Beginnings', 25.
4   Thomas Hamm, '"Chipping at the Landmarks of our Fathers": The Decline of the Testimony against Hireling Ministry in the Nineteenth Century', *Quaker Studies* 13, no. 2 (2009).
5   Vann and Eversley, *Friends*, 15.

movement were decided in favour of Quaker marriages. These included cases of inheritance. In 1658 a Lincoln man argued his deceased brother's Quaker wedding was invalid, making the deceased's child illegitimate and therefore unable to inherit. Instead, the surviving brother himself ought to be considered the heir. The court decided against him. A manor lord in Carlisle in 1681 tried to end the tenancy of a Quaker widow and her daughter of their deceased husband and father's land, arguing that the child was illegitimate and could not inherit. This too was overturned by the court. In 1679, the Meeting of Sufferings consulted the attorney Thomas Corbett of Grey's Inn on the matter. He argued that marriages, though in catholic tradition understood to require presence of a priest for validity, in fact only required the mutual consent of both parties. Neither a priest nor a church was necessary.[6] Hence, over time the validity of Quaker marriages in practice, as well as the legitimacy of children born into Quaker marriages, was established.

At the time the understanding was that a marriage was valid if the partners declared that they 'took each other in marriage'. A priest acted merely as a witness. Quakers instead celebrated weddings in their meetings, following much the same procedures and rules as did parish churches. In order to qualify for a Quaker wedding, a couple had to attend the bride's monthly meeting on three First Days (Sundays) to announce its intention of marriage. This allowed members of the community to raise objections, for instance because one partner was already engaged to someone else, or the couple were too closely related to each other. In this the Quaker practice of marriage closely followed the practice of parish churches. Under canon law as codified in 1604 Anglican weddings were to take place in the parish church of one or both of the parties, during divine service, between 8 a.m. and 12 p.m. There were two possible procedures. The first of these was following the publication of banns on three Sundays or holidays. The calling of the banns gave members of the public the opportunity to object to the marriage taking place.[7] Banns were unpopular and considered embarrassing. This motivated some couples to choose the second marriage procedure: marriage by licence, which allowed for the banns to be dispensed of. Licences offered greater privacy, sped up the process, and allowed the couple to marry in a different parish. They also, however, cost money.[8]

One aspect in which Quaker marriage differed from Anglican practices was in the lack of any equivalent to the clandestine marriages that were becoming

---

6 Craig W. Horle, *The Quakers and the English Legal System, 1660–1688* (Philadelphia: University of Pennsylvania Press, 1988), 234–38.
7 Roger Lee Brown, 'The Rise and Fall of the Fleet Marriages', in *Marriage and Society: Studies in the Social History of Marriage*, ed. R. B. Outwaite (New York: St Martin's Press, 1981).
8 Dandelion and Collins, *Condition*; Moore, 'Beginnings', 25; Price, *Overseas Trade*; Milligan, *Dictionary*, 588.

so popular in this period. Clandestine was the term applied to Anglican marriages breaking any of the restrictions applied to marriages by cannon law as discussed above.⁹ The Restoration saw the emergence of clandestine marriage as a social custom of huge popularity in the London suburbs.¹⁰ Their exact extent is unclear, but they may have accounted for more than 40 per cent of total marriages.¹¹

Clandestine marriages were conducted in various parts of town, which, for historical legal reasons – or perhaps just tradition – were exempt from certain ecclesiastical laws. Due to a change in legislation in the 1690s, they were later restricted to the area around the Fleet prison.¹² Here a couple could get married in a chapel – or even in some taverns – without any advance planning, calling of banns or other bureaucratic hurdles. Fleet marriages were extremely popular. The couples marrying there were representative of the London population as a whole, coming from all socio-economic backgrounds.¹³

The motivations for clandestine marriages are disputed. They may have been financial. While the cost of the ceremony was often similar to those of the city churches, the couple could avoid taxes, the fees for the calling of the banns and costs of entertainment.¹⁴ The increasing popularity of clandestine marriages may also have been due to their becoming a consumer good. Private marriages had been popular with the upper classes for a long time. Now, middling people followed their social superiors and made them popular. Their main attraction lay in the privacy they afforded. They allowed the couple to avoid a public ceremony during regular Sunday service.¹⁵ There is evidence that at least some Friends envied the possibility of private marriages. Seventeen-year-old Betty Fothergill described a wedding ceremony she attended in London in 1769. Fothergill was a niece of the prominent Quaker physician John Fothergill, and visited her uncle and his family for several months in London in 1769–70.¹⁶ Her

---

9   Jeremy Boulton, 'Clandestine Marriages in London: An Examination of a Neglected Urban Variable', *Urban History* 20, no. 2 (1993); Martin Ingram, 'Spousal Litigation in the English Ecclesiastical Courts, c. 1350–1640', in *Marriage and Society: Studies in the Social History of Marriage*, ed. R. B. Outhwaite (New York: St Martin's Press, 1981), 40.
10 Boulton, 'Clandestine Marriages', 192–97.
11 Ibid., 203; Gill Newton, '*Clandestine Marriage in Early Modern London: When, Where and Why?*', *Continuity and Change* 29, no. 2 (2014).
12 Boulton, 'Clandestine Marriages', 192, 201; Brown, 'The Rise and Fall of the Fleet Marriages'.
13 Jacob F. Field, '*Clandestine Weddings at the Fleet Prison, c. 1710–1750: Who Married There?*', *Continuity and Change* 32, no. 3 (2017).
14 Brown, 'Rise', 124.
15 Boulton, 'Clandestine Marriages', 197.
16 H. C. G. Matthew and Brian Harrison, *Oxford Dictionary of National Biography*, new edn (Oxford: Oxford University Press, 2004), entry for John Fothergill, physician and naturalist, 1712–1780.

extensive journal survives. Recently engaged to be married herself, her distaste for the ceremony she witnessed at the Savoy meeting house is revealed in her diary.[17] The crowd, she wrote,

> was as large as the confined walls of that little meeting house will permit. Was I often to attend these occasions I almost think it would deter me from the thoughts of matrimony ... what must be the poor brides situation to sit and be stared at and endure the remarks and criticisms of every impertinent observer, the tremor that attacks when she is going to speak gives me some little idea what I should feel were it my own case...surely Friends marriages in this Respect are exceptionable for I cannot see one substantial reason for their being so public and most people can five reasons against it ...[18]

Clandestine marriages were outlawed by Hardwicke's Marriage Act of 1753. This made marriage in a church in the parish of residence of one of the parties mandatory, and thus also necessary to establish property and hereditary rights.[19] Quakers and Jews were exempted from the new legislation and Quaker marriages continued to be recognized de facto.[20]

As well as its unavoidable public character, a wedding in a Quaker meeting required the consent of both partners' parents. The meeting furthermore required assurance that neither of the parties was previously engaged.[21] The degree to which entry to marriage was subject to investigation offers a further difference between Quaker and Anglican marriage. Monthly meetings – in Philadelphia these were early on the women's meetings; in London, in the later eighteenth century, women's meetings took over these responsibilities from the men's – undertook enquiries into the parties' circumstances before giving their permission for the wedding. If the partners belonged to different monthly meetings, the wedding usually took place in the bride's meeting. The groom had to produce a certificate from his own monthly meeting permitting the marriage. At times the meeting objected, as illustrated by the case of James Hoskins. His request for permission to marry was declined by Horsleydown monthly meeting, which advised him 'to see how his business will succeed before he marrys'.[22] During the actual Quaker wedding ceremony the bride and groom exchanged the promise of 'taking each other in marriage'. Then

---

17 Fothergill married Alexander Chorley on 18 October 1770: see first page of her diary. Betty Fothergill, Diary, 'Transcript', 1769–70.
18 Fothergill, Diary, 82.
19 Kathleen Davies, 'Continuity and Change in Literary Advice on Marriage', in *Marriage and Society: Studies in the Social History of Marriage*, ed. R. B. Outhwaite (New York: St Martin's Press, 1981), 67.
20 Vann and Eversley, *Friends*, 16.
21 Ibid., 84; Vann, *Social Development*, 184.
22 Horsleydown MM minutes, iv/1720.

the couple and several witnesses present signed a marriage certificate. Couples could present these certificates to the authorities in case evidence of their married status was required.

Friends' expectations of marriage

The surviving correspondence and diaries of four eighteenth-century London Quakers provide insight into metropolitan Friends' expectations of marriage. In addition to the journal of Betty Fothergill, whom we met above, the diary of London merchant James Jenkins survives. This he kept at intermittent intervals throughout his life. It contains reflections on acquaintances and events in his life, as well as those of others. Philip Eliot and John Eliot III were both members of a London Quaker merchant family, which was active in trade for several generations throughout the eighteenth century. All of these authors were upper middling sorts, urban Quakers, which limits the scope of our understanding of other parts of the Quaker community. Nonetheless, they offer a view of attitudes that are otherwise lost to us.

Historians have argued that Quakerism placed an unusual emphasis on love as the basis of marital relationships.[23] The sources confirm that London Friends shared in this sentiment. Love appears as an important factor for the choice of a partner throughout. James Jenkins married out of affection, as he wrote of his proposal to his future wife: 'staid there [in London] a few days during which I made an offer of Marriage to my dear, little, innocent Betsy Lamb'.[24] The marriage lasted almost thirty years, until Elizabeth's death, whom he then described as 'my entirely beloved, & ever dear Eliza'.[25] Betty Fothergill also married for love, describing her fiancé in her diary as 'that person who is dearest to me and in whom all my earthly happiness is centred'.[26]

Both Fothergill and Jenkins moreover display a sharp awareness that their fellow Friends sometimes married out of financial interest rather than affection. Fothergill's time in London was filled almost entirely with social engagements with the upper echelons of London Quaker society, especially other young Friends. Among themselves they frequently discussed their peers' marriages and marriage prospects. One evening Betty pondered the prospects of two of her friends, both daughters of the Barclay banking family:

> Friend Barclay along with her Sisr Prissy and the two lovely cousins Agatha and Lucy drank tea with us. A critic in beauty would find employ in deciding

23 Pullin, *Female Friends*, 45.
24 Jenkins, Diary, iii/1778.
25 Jenkins, Diary, 23/xii/1806.
26 Fothergill, Diary, 1, n.d. See also John Eliot, Letter to Sister Mariabella, 1763.

which of these amiable girls deserved the palm – nature and fortune have conspired to render them two of the greatest prizes in our Society ... I hope the men they favour with their hands will consider themselves independent of their large fortunes, as the most valuable it would be a pity indeed if such merit as theirs should be less dazzling then a certain shining metal.[27]

Fothergill identified three factors as important for the girls' marriage prospects: their beauty, their personalities and their wealth. While she seems to have believed that the first two should be the most important, she worried that the last might crowd out the others in the minds of potential suitors. Interestingly, her observation that they were 'two of the greatest prizes in our Society' suggests that she did not consider non-Quakers as potential future husbands for the girls. About another acquaintance she wrote: 'Prissy seems to be good natured and obliging though no ways else particularly agreeable. But she possesses a power of attraction which few men pretend to resist that is a fortune of 8 or 9 000£.'[28] About yet another visitor to the house she wrote: 'Frd Bourn was raised from a low situation by marrying a man of considerable fortune. Tho what attracted him I can't tell, for she has not the least remains of anything more than tolerable either in her person or manners.'[29] This comment smacks of disapproval and her own opinion of strategic marriages becomes even clearer when she describes the courtship of her cousin Elizabeth:

> If cos Elsy accepts of him I shall always attribute her motives to interest and convenience. The idea of raising herself into ease and affluence may for the present have charms ... but these will soon grow familiar and tasteless without a union of minds the most exalted station may become wretched ... and within the lowest station may in part become happy. It is not external circumstances on which our satisfaction depends, the mind is the source of both happiness and misery.[30]

For Quaker women's marriages, their financial security played a role, too. William Somerton struggled to obtain his future father-in-law's consent to his marriage, due to William's perceived lack of income. Parental consent was crucial to Friends' marriages, and no marriage could take place in a Quaker meeting without either the couple's parents being present or their written permission for the marriage being presented. Somerton had apparently asked Philip Eliot to speak to his potential father-in-law on his behalf, after having been rejected himself. Eliot replied:

---

27 Fothergill, Diary, 114, n.d.
28 Fothergill, Diary, 1st Day, 14 January.
29 Fothergill, Diary, 22, 4th day (November).
30 Fothergill, Diary, 68.

If your affections are engaged to each other I should be pleased if it were the will of Providence that you came together and accordingly I have spoke to her uncle since the receipe of thy letter together with [illegible] & Jn Townsend and we laboured to persuade him to obtain his Brother's consent. He assured us that his Brother's objection to thee was that he thought thee not in a capacity at present to maintain a wife & family, having all along declared this as his mind to thee, upon thy informing him of thy circumstances. I know that delays in such cases as these are disagreeable, but if thou could jst wait till the objection was removed as I hope by the blessing of providence on thy industry it may before long, it might end in thy satisfaction. I just think to remind thee of good Jacob, how long he was willing to wait for his beloved Rachel.[31]

How Somerton received this advice we do not know. He and Rachel Powell, 'daughter of Thomas Powell, late of Battersea in the county of Surrey, Schoolmaster & Maria his wife, him surviving' were married two years later.[32] Whether he had made enough money or their path was merely cleared by the late Thomas Powell's death is unclear.

Upon the occasion of his father, Zephaniah Fry's death, James Jenkins in later years reflected on how the former came to be married. He judged that the wife he chose, 'Abigal Hiscocks was (however qualified in some respects) an unsuitable partner for Zephan. Fry.' This was because 'her personal charms were below mediocrity & she was many years older than him'. Jenkins explained this apparent mismatch with the fact that, 'if she was older, she was also considerably richer & it therefore seems reasonable to suppose that neither the dictates of prudence or the natural bias of youth, had upon this occasion their usual influence'.[33]

As Fry's illegitimate son by a servant, Jenkins take on his father's marriage may have been biased.[34] He emphasized the age difference between the two, which he thought required explanation. However, he was equally critical of age differences in other Friends' marriages, as evidenced in his diary entries about their weddings: 'Obed Cocke married to a young woman abt half as old as himself. A strange mixture of Dotage, & Folly in this affair.'[35] In another entry he noted that age differences were also regarded critically by others. In this

31 Eliot, Letter Book, 1757, 2/vi/1764.
32 January 1766, Piece 1108: Kingston MM: Marriages (1672–1776), accessed via ancestry.co.uk.
33 Jenkins, Diary, vii/1791.
34 Gil Skidmore, *Strength in Weakness: Writings of Eighteenth-Century Quaker Women* (Walnut Creek, CA: Altamira Press, 2003).
35 Jenkins, Diary, 4/iv/1784.

they conformed to a growing contemporary criticisms of unequal marriages, including difference of age.[36]

Quakers faced – and recognized – much the same risks through marriage as other members of English society. First among these was the restriction that common law placed on early modern English women's property rights. Upon marriage, women entered into the legal status of coverture. This meant that wives were included into the legal person of their husbands. Their property and their debts, as well as any inheritance made while married, became that of their husbands. As Davidoff and Hall put it, 'on marriage a woman died a kind of civil death'.[37] The limitations extended beyond husbands' deaths. Married women were not able to make wills. If they inherited property from their husbands, this was often limited either until male heirs reached adulthood or the widow remarried.[38] In essence, as wives, women served as mediums for the transfer of property between families, and as mothers between generations, but they rarely controlled property themselves. Contemporaries were aware of the disadvantages this brought for women, and *femmes coverts* were often 'likened to slaves'.[39]

A letter Philip Eliot wrote to his father in 1749 reflects the concern women's families had over potential husbands' motives. Philip attacked the marriage his father had arranged for Philip's sister. He warned: 'the offer thou hast accepted off bears no proportion with such who are esteemed in any degree answerable to what she has.' He supported his argument by analysing his future brother-in-law's supposed income, claiming that it was exaggerated:

> I notice thou says he has improved five hundred pounds to seven thousand pounds & has been at it only thirteen years, & that this trade produces him now six hundred pounds per annum, which certainly must be considerably increased then what it was in ye beginning. Now pray take notice that six hundred pounds for thirteen years produces no more than seven thousand eight hundred pounds. So then by this calculation for House Keeping, Servants Wages & other incident charges his expenses had not exceeded to more than & 61.10.9 per annum [illegible] unless calculations set off for that (a Fine trade indeed) which gives me just cause to call the truth of the whole in question & to believe his fortune to be only an imaginary one.[40]

James Jenkins, at the time apprenticed to 'Hannah Joseph, grocer, near two years', upon her death expressed a similar concern as Eliot: 'I have often

---

36 Todd, 'Demographic Determinism'.
37 Davidoff and Hall, *Family Fortunes*, 200; Maxine Berg, 'Women's Property and the Industrial Revolution', *Journal of Interdisciplinary History* 34, no. 2 (1993).
38 Davidoff and Hall, *Family Fortunes*, 276.
39 Paul Langford, *Polite and Commercial People*, 110.
40 Eliot, Letter Book, 'Honoured Father', London, 8/vii/1749.

thought it a pity that an elderly woman with a large fortune acquired by industry should have married a man with 5 children, & leave her near Friends & native country.'⁴¹ Her 'fortune acquired by industry' should have enabled her to remain independent. He regarded her marriage as a loss for her. Surely his concern was partly caused by the fact that the marriage meant a move of his mistress, away from her home and friends to her new husband's native Ireland. It appears that his mistress's friends had also been opposed to the union. Some time before the marriage, Jenkins wrote in his diary:

> My mistress has received a letter from Geo Boon … of Birmingham who is often here in the course of his services in trade, annexed to a bill of parcel, he advises against an union with RD & cautions her to guard against [crossed out] … I hinted that it was indelicate to put such advice at the bottom of a Bill of parcels. She replied 'Yes, but let him advise as he <u>will</u>, I <u>must</u> attend to my own sense of Duty' – from this I have learned two things – that she inclines to have RD & <u>thinks</u> it is her duty & that almost everyone else thinks it her duty not to have him.⁴²

There were ways to limit the impact of coverture. Women, or their families, could arrange prenuptial contracts to regulate the use of property during the marriage.⁴³ Brides' families could use these to protect their daughters' portions from being spent by sons-in-law. They could ensure that a woman's property would pass onto her children, rather than her husband's children from past or future marriages. When remarrying, widows could negotiate the entitlements of their children from previous marriages, and the control over assets they had inherited from deceased husbands, and their own right to make a will if they died in coverture. At least 10 per cent of married men's probate accounts in Lincolnshire and Northamptonshire included marriage settlements for their wives' benefit. The vast majority of settlements were made by wealthy middling sort couples below the status of gentry.⁴⁴ The women who did have settlements included a disproportionate number of widows – i.e. women with previous experience of coverture, who knew the risks they were taking on their own and their children's behalf upon entering into a new marriage.⁴⁵ Furthermore, eighteenth-century marriage settlement commonly included the provision of

---

41 Jenkins, Diary, 23/i/1773.
42 Jenkins, Diary. 8/xi/1770. Emphasis in original.
43 Amy Louise Erickson, 'Common Law versus Common Practice: The Use of Marriage Settlements in Early Modern England', *Economic History Review* 43, no. 1 (1990); Lloyd Bonfield, *Marriage Settlements, 1601–1740: The Adoption of the Strict Settlement* (Cambridge: Cambridge University Press, 1983).
44 Erickson, 'Common Law versus Common Practice'.
45 Susan Staves, *Married Women's Separate Property in England, 1660–1833* (Cambridge, MA, and London: Harvard University Press, 1990), 177.

jointures for wives. These were a legal agreement that regulated wives' maintenance after their husbands' passing. This was often in the form of a lump sum or an annuity.[46] Among the gentry and wealthy citizens provisions often lay in the mid-hundreds of pounds.[47] Marriage settlements became increasingly common during the eighteenth century.

Still, Philip Eliot's letter suggests that he thought these legal instruments insufficient. He emphasized his sister's future dependence on her husband's good will and the dangers this bore:

> so then if he dyes & leaves her childless her estate or jointure is absolutely out of her power, it going to such whom her husband has thought proper to give after his death by will, & by this means she is deprived of second marriage in case her inclinations lead thereto & at the same time liable to be ill used by her Husband, who probably has more ill humours than good, in order to procure the whole possession into his own hands ... Every penny she wants application must be made to ye husband for if she dyes childless her husband increases his fortune, but on the other hand if he dyes first she has only the income of her jointure ye principal he bequeathes away as he sees meet by will, so that she is doomed to a single life, having nothing for a second adventure in case her inclination leads thereto.[48]

For women who were themselves just wealthy enough not to have to work, it might have been preferable to remain single than to marry someone from the same or a lower income group. That the social status that came with marriage alone was not necessarily valued higher than maintaining control over one's assets is indicated by Philip Eliot's letter to his father. He wrote about his sister:

> It's true in one light, she may be called a wife, but as the case now stands is no other than an upper servant, for I will make it appear that she has need of all her understanding to support herself & formerly with any common decency, & when done noe more power of the improvements which by her care she has gained then they have, all she saves is her husbands, if trade do not succeed the fault lays at the door of his wife.[49]

Concern over the loss of women's independence after marriage went beyond purely financial worries. Eighteenth-century feminists argued that 'women, as rational and accountable beings, are free agents as well as men', and that married women therefore should be treated as equals by their husbands.[50]

---

46 Erickson, 'Common Law versus Common Practice'.
47 Staves, *Married Women's Separate Property*, 96.
48 John Eliot, Letter Book, Honoured Father, London, 8/vii/1749.
49 Ibid.
50 Langford, *Polite and Commercial People*, 112.

Quaker women may have been more sceptical than most, as some authors have argued that the Quaker ideal of marriage saw wives and husbands as equal partners, who supported each other.[51] At least some upper middling London Friends shared this expectation of equality. This is evidenced in a debate Betty Fothergill and her cousins had with her uncle Dr John Fothergill. In her diary she reported how he

> drew us forth into a dispute upon the prerogative of husbands and wives. He insisted upon blind obedience of the latter to the former and we as strenuously opposed him. After he had diverted us a little he placed the affair upon a proper footing that there should be no obligation on one side more then another but a mutual endeavour to promote each other's happiness. We all concurred in this sentiment and the affair was amicable settled.[52]

In practice, however, Friends were still actors within an intensely patriarchal society, their lives influenced by values of male command and female submission. Even for Quaker women, marriage usually meant obeying their husbands, and thus a pronounced loss of personal liberty.[53] It is not surprising, then, that polite women of this period were 'highly sceptical of the value of marriage for young women'.[54] Women's writing both in England and the colonies conveys the sense that marriage was considered a hazardous enterprise, and that 'the risk of marriage was not commensurate with its rewards'.[55] Novels, poems, private commonplace books, newspapers and literary magazines of the period convey the great concern people had over the 'potentially tyrannical nature of marriage'.[56] Often these writers came to the conclusion that in order to maintain her freedom and protect herself, a woman's only choice really was to remain single. This public discourse created the possibility of respectable, rather than pitiable, singleness for polite women.[57] Betty Fothergill's diary also reflects these concerns of eighteenth-century feminists. On 21 December 1769 she wrote:

> this day I shall remember for taking the first Solemn step towards matrimonial preparations. I may well sigh at the name ... these men! How came I to be entangled with one of them – tho really and impartially my better judgement pleas for a single life. Yet I cannot help proceeding from one step to another

---

51 Pullin, *Female Friends*, 90.
52 Fothergill, Diary, 48.
53 Wulf, *Not All Wives*, 43, 55.
54 Laura E. Thomason, *The Matrimonial Trap: Eighteenth-Century Women Writers Redefine Marriage* (Lewisburg, PA: Bucknell University Press, 2013), 16.
55 Thomason, *The Matrimonial Trap*, 4.
56 Wulf, *Not All Wives*, 22.
57 Ibid., 28.

for when any of my former objections occur … this AC [her fiancé] by one means or another persuades me to think different so this I suppose is the case with other poor women who are cajoled by degrees to lose their liberty and then they have nothing to do but quietly submit … but my reflections come too late they ought to have arisen before the table linen, etc etc was bought.[58]

For Quaker women, not marrying may have been an even more viable option than for women of other faiths. Historians agree that Quakerism afforded women a degree of independence unusual in this period, as well as authority within both faith and family.[59] The Society of Friends supported female agency and independence through its government structure. Women actively shaped the Quaker 'church' through their work in the women's meetings. These existed parallel to men's meetings on every level of the Society of Friends' formal organization, from local committees administering poor relief to women's Yearly Meetings, at the top of church government. What is more, women were numerous and influential among the early leaders of the movement. They preached publicly and travelled far and wide, without male companions, in order to spread Truth. Rebecca Larson's study of colonial women ministers travelling across the Atlantic world shows that about a third of them never married. Among those who did marry, many did so later in life, in their forties or fifties, thus foregoing having children. Female ministers' autobiographies state clearly that they postponed marriage in order to maintain their independence and travel for the cause of Truth.[60] This suggests that women did not turn to the ministry as an alternative after having failed to find a husband. They chose to remain single. Quakerism created space for single women to live independent lives, to travel and preach, a respectable role outside the household and family, which allowed an exquisite degree of liberty. Interestingly, the percentage of women among English travelling ministers increased over the course of the eighteenth century, from 23 per cent of known cases in 1700 to 51 per cent in 1779.[61] As discussed in chapter one, Friends' marriage patterns from the mid-eighteenth century onwards displayed high female celibacy rates. Quaker women obtained an even greater share in the community's public life at exactly the same time that more and more of them were to remain single.

The authority Quakerism afforded women outside the household was empowering and supported the possibility of planning a life outside traditional family structures.[62] Together with the contemporary discourse empha-

---

58 Fothergill, Diary, 36.
59 Wulf, Not All Wives, 8.
60 Amy M. Froide, 'The Religious Lives of Singlewomen in the Anglo-Atlantic World: Quaker Missionaries, Protestant Nuns, and Covert Catholics', Women, Religion, and the Atlantic World (1600–1800) 12 (2009), 62, 64.
61 Pullin, Female Friends, 13.
62 Ibid., 94.

sizing the downsides of marriage, while highlighting the merits of singleness, Quakerism's attitude towards women may have made remaining single a viable alternative to marrying and starting a family. The disadvantages marital law held for women made it an unattractive prospect. Rather than a lack of men robbing female Friends of opportunities to marry, a rational weighing of the advantages of marriage against its risks may have led Quaker women to *choose* to remain single.

Endogamy

In light of the centrality of keeping marriage within the Society of Friends to the theory of Quaker marriage, the records of London Friends offer us a rare chance to see how contemporaries felt about the doctrine of martial endogamy and the risks involved in breaking it. 'Marriage out' appears in two of the sources. First, Jenkins wrote in 1786:

> I am informed by a letter from my kinsman Jn. Fry Junr. that he was married to Elizabeth Head of Philadelphia the latter end of the 9th month last. Most of his Friends are sorry that they were married out of the Society & that she is 10 years older than him; however, all accounts … allow, that she is very sensible & accomplished, & has a moderate fortune.[63]

In this entry the fact that the bride was not a Friend is listed as a negative point – as is Jenkins' standard concern about the age difference between partners. However, the tone of his account suggests that the former was not necessarily a major impediment to a marriage. Rather, it was one factor weighed against others, such as the person's character and income. Marriage 'out' was regrettable, not disastrous. From Jenkins' entry it appears that contemporary Quakers approved or at least sympathized with Fry Jr.'s choice to 'marry out'.

The degree of tolerance towards such a choice may have depended on commentators' piousness. The second example comes in the letters of the deeply religious Philip Eliot, who had a very different take on marriage outside the Society. When his father arranged a marriage for Philip's sister to the non-Quaker Edward Lambert, the gloves came off. Philip accused his father of arrogance as apparently 'none in the Society could be thought worthy to be thy son in law'. Philip Eliot warned that this marriage would lay 'fresh foundations of unhappiness both as to herself & Friends'. He went on to attack his father as materialistic and cynical about religion:

---

63 Jenkins, Diary, 12/xi/1786.

In the first place the principal point wch appears so strong in my view is with regard to ye difference of religion, which I find has not that weight wth thee as I could wish. Neither has it ever appeared that thou was once (not) sanguine in ye promoting such alliance always judging the people thou professed religion with not sincere, having other motives in view than honesty, & therefore al such was slighted & even not allowed the common civilities that was necessary in such cases, greatness & grandeur being the principal thing in view. Nothing less than nobility or men of large estates when Earthly homage was to be paid was looked at.[64]

Still, it is important to note that among the various arguments Philip Eliot put forth, possible disciplinary repercussions from the Society of Friends did not figure.

These sources illustrate that eighteenth-century Friends entered marriages for various reasons, including both love and financial interests. Quaker marriages brought many of the same risks of economic dependency and uncertain relationships that afflicted all English marriages in this period. The surviving records indicate that Friends preferred marriage within the community. However, membership in the Society was not a decisive factor for choosing a partner. What is more, there is no evidence that the writers took the possibility of sanctions from the monthly meetings into consideration when choosing a spouse or commenting on the out-marriages of others. This is particularly important as all the sources stem from the later eighteenth century, when disownments for out-marriages already occurred much more frequently. This lack of concern over sanctions for breaking the rule of endogamy reflects the findings from the merchant correspondence regarding sanctions for debts. It indicates that even if sanctions took place, they were not perceived to be a very strong penalty, let alone a sufficient deterrent to stop people from making certain choices.

The scale of Quaker marriage discipline

The trend of London meetings' sanctions for marriage delinquencies follows the same patterns outlined in previous chapters. As illustrated by figure 10, London meetings dramatically increased their sanctions for marriage delinquencies after 1750. The period from c. 1670 to 1749 saw only fifty-one sanctions for marriage delinquencies. The period from 1750 to 1799 in contrast witnessed 316 such cases, despite the fall in the size of the Quaker population in this period.

The total of 367 sanctions includes 305 testimonies of denial, and sixty-two self-condemnations. Meetings did not disown any offenders who submitted

---

64 Eliot, Letter Book, Honoured Father, London, 8/vii/1749.

self-condemnations. The main causes of sanctions related to marriage were 'marriage by a priest' and marriage to a non-Quaker. Frequently, these offences are listed together with others, such as drinking to excess or abandoning one's family. As table 9 shows, during the eighteenth century the primary type of delinquency leading to sanctions changed dramatically. In the period prior to 1750, 'marriage by a priest' constituted the primary cause for sanctions. After 1750, sanctions for 'marriage by a priest' grew. Far more important, however, became 'marriage to a non-Quaker'.

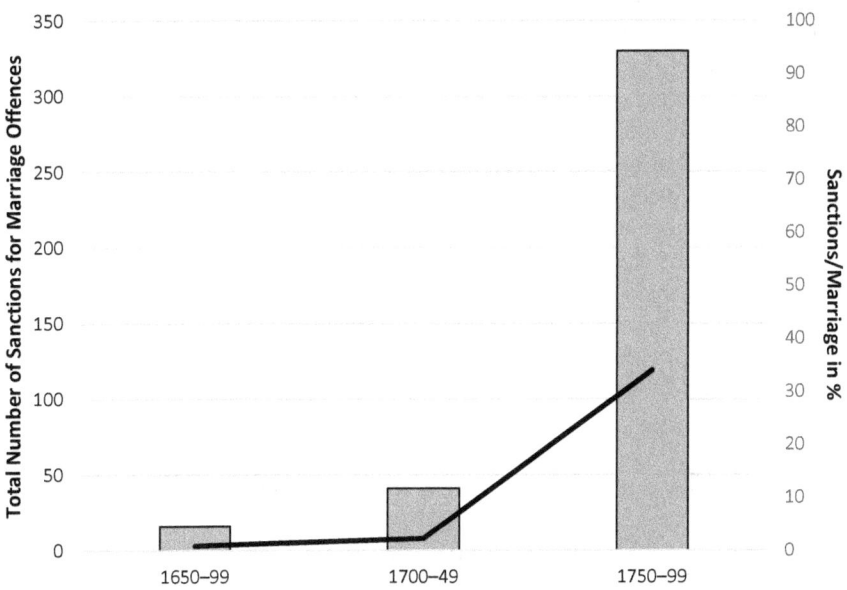

Figure 10. Sanctions for Marriage Offences by London Monthly Meetings
Source: see text.

Table 9. Causes for Marriage Sanctions

Period	Marriage to a non-Quaker % (N)	Marriage by a priest % (N)	Total
<1750	11 (6)	89 (48)	(54)
1750–1800	73 (230)	27 (84)	(314)
Total	(236)	(133)	(368)

Sources: London monthly meeting records. Here included are only the cases of these two particular offences, in order to compare them to each other.

What did these terms mean in practice? While we can assume that all marriages to non-Quakers were conducted before a priest, not all marriages by a priest were necessarily to a non-Quaker. Richard Vann, in a study of disownments for marriages in the English counties of Buckinghamshire, Norfolk and Norwich 1654–1740, interpreted marriage by a priest as marriage 'between two Quakers with a clergyman officiating'. He found this was more common than marrying a non-Quaker.[65] The expression 'marriage by priest' in this period could refer to three different scenarios: first, a regular marriage in a parish church, second, marriage by licence, and third, a clandestine marriage, which was very common among Anglicans in this period.

The motivations behind marriages that breached the discipline could vary. Some Friends may have chosen to be married by a priest rather than in a Quaker meeting house because they preferred the greater privacy licensed or clandestine marriages would afford. It is also possible that in the earlier period, Friends were concerned about the validity of their marriages and therefore chose to marry before a priest. Finally, a couple in which both partners were Quakers may have chosen to marry 'by a priest' if their choice of partner was unlikely to be accepted by the monthly meeting. This might happen if the parents of either party withheld their consent, or if the union violated one of the Society's rules against kin marriage. Marriages among kin were traditionally prohibited in most of Europe. Friends implemented the same rules about kin marriages as the surrounding society.[66]

The comprehensiveness of marriage sanctions

The reformation brought increased attention to Friends' marriage choices. London meetings' records include sanctions for Friends' *repeated* offences for irregular marriage. The period between 1750 and 1786 includes seventeen such cases. None of their names are found among earlier self-condemnations. Among these offenders, at least four registered children from their previous marriages with their meetings. This strongly indicates that in these cases, the monthly meetings were aware of the individuals' marital situation, i.e. that they had married outside the Society. What is more, half of these delinquent parents had children born after 1750, at a time when the meetings' enforcement of the discipline had begun to tighten.

---

65 Vann, *Social Development*, 187. He estimated that these counties contained about 5 per cent of the total Quaker population of England at the time.
66 Edwina Newman, 'Quakers and the Family', in *The Oxford Handbook of Quaker Studies*, ed. Dandelion and Angell, 437. See also Lloyd, *Social History*, 58, 59.

Table 10. Quaker Apprentice Marriages

Birth cohort	Apprentices Total	Apprentices marrying Quakers (n)	Apprentices marrying Quakers (%)
1650–1699	72	7	9.7
1700–1749	97	11	11.3
1750–1799	92	31	33.7
All	218	49	18.6

Source: See text. Note that this table allocates apprentices to each half century based on their birth year, not the year they were married. Thus, an apprentice included in the table in 1749 will have married in the 1760s at the earliest.

We can further explore the consistency with which marital endogamy was practised, and the meetings' responses to out-marriages, through the marriages of Quaker apprentices. Apprenticeships were among the most important forms of occupational training in early modern England. London was a particularly important centre of this type of training, with about 6.5 per cent of teenage boys from across the country becoming indentured there every year.[67] If the Society's commitment to marital endogamy was constant, we would anticipate the frequency with which Quaker apprentices married Quaker women to also be constant over time. A comparison of Quaker birth, and London stamp duty records yielded 264 Quaker apprentices.[68] Forty-nine of these 264 apprentices, that is 18.6 per cent, appear in English or Welsh Quaker marriage records. The remaining 218, that is 82.6 per cent, did not appear in Quaker marriage records, either in the London and Middlesex area or elsewhere in England and Wales.[69]

Table 10 shows how the frequency with which Quaker apprentices appear in Quaker marriage records changed over time. Apprentices drawn from later birth cohorts were much more likely to marry fellow Quakers than those born in earlier cohorts. The percentage of Quaker apprentices marrying fellow Friends increased significantly from 1750 onwards, rising from just over one in ten in 1700–49, to one in three after 1750. The small number of Quaker apprentices

---

[67] Patrick Wallis, 'Apprenticeship and Training in Premodern England', *Journal of Economic History* 68, no. 3 (2008).
[68] I thank Chris Minns for identifying these apprentices for me by linking Quaker birth records with his and Patrick Wallis's database from stamp duty records. For details on the database see Chris Minns and Patrick Wallis, 'Why Did (Pre-)Industrial Firms Train? Premiums and Apprenticeship Contracts in Eighteenth-Century England', LSE Economic History Working Paper No.155/11 (2011).
[69] Quaker records outside London and Middlesex were consulted via ancestry.com.

appearing in Quaker marriage records in the seventeenth century may be due to limited record survival. The difference between the 1700–49 and 1750–99 cohort is, however, large enough to suggest that there is indeed a trend towards greater persistence within the religion in the later eighteenth century. This corresponds to the development of the London meetings' membership, which dropped from the late seventeenth century until about 1720, and then stabilized.

The Quaker marriage records may not be 100 per cent complete, but they are very good data by the standards of the time. It is therefore likely that the vast majority of the 218 Quaker apprentices who did not subsequently appear in Quaker marriage records did in fact not get married in Quaker meetings. Some may have died young: Leonard Schwarz estimated that due to the urban disease environment about 10 per cent of London apprentices died during their term.[70] Others may have been married by a priest without being caught. Still others may have remained unmarried or emigrated. Richard Vann and David Eversley estimated that in the period 1700–49 at least 1.2 per cent of the urban male Quaker population remained unmarried, and 2.7 per cent for the period 1750–99.[71] Bearing all this in mind, however, it is likely that only a minority of the apprentices married Quaker women, but that their number increased after 1750. Significantly, none of the apprentices appear in the London monthly meetings' sanctioning records, further underlining their lack of full coverage of Quaker marriage defaults. This suggests that the strength of the expectation that Friends would marry within the community grew in the second half of the eighteenth century, in line with the enforcement of other aspects of the Society's discipline, and that before 1750 institutional policing of marriage was weak.

It is possible that some of the apprentices captured in the sample in the pre-1750 period were only loosely associated with the Society by the time they started or finished their apprenticeships. The degree to which the Quaker discipline was enforced by the meetings may have depended on how closely involved the apprentice was with the Society. Families who registered the births of their children with meetings might easily have drifted away from the community in later years and their children may no longer been part of the community.

We can determine whether this was the case by looking particularly for Quaker apprentices who trained with Quaker masters. As serving an apprenticeship involved living in one's master's household, we can assume that Quaker apprentices who trained with Quaker masters were more closely involved with the community and thus more strongly inculcated with the Quaker norm of marital endogamy. They were also unlikely to come from families who had abandoned the faith. If we find that apprentices who trained with Quaker

---

70 Leonard Schwarz, 'London Apprentices in the Seventeenth Century: Some Problems', *Local Population Studies* 38 (1987).
71 Vann and Eversley, *Friends*, 108.

Table 11. Quaker Apprentices training with Quaker Masters

	Quaker Apprentices (n)	Marrying a Quaker (n)	Marrying a Quaker (%)
Quaker master	78	15	19.2
Non-Quaker master	186	34	18.3

Source: see text.

masters were more likely to be found marrying Quaker women, then we might conclude that the norm of marital endogamy was strong within the community, and that the small share of these apprentices who appear in Quaker marriage records in the pre-1750 period is due to the misidentification of former Quakers as active Quakers in the sample. If, on the other hand, we find that Quaker apprentices training with Quaker masters did not preferably marry Quaker women, this indicates that the norm of marital endogamy was not very strong and offers some reassurance about our sample.

The Quaker marriage records include the names of seventy-eight of the Quaker apprentices' masters. In other words, 29.5 per cent of our Quaker apprentices served with Quaker masters. The share of Quaker apprentices who trained with non-Quaker masters was not significantly different after 1750 than before 1750.[72] As shown in table 11, the share of Quaker apprentices marrying within the Society is very close in both groups. It appears that serving an apprenticeship in a Quaker household had no impact on the likelihood of marrying a Quaker woman.

Whether young Friends trained with a Quaker master or a non-Friend had no impact on their choice of marriage partners. Moreover, the non-disownment of apprentices marrying out before 1750 was not seemingly caused by them having drifted away from the community at an early age. This further supports the argument that Quaker meetings did not comprehensively enforce marital endogamy, either before or after 1750. However, the increase of sanctions shows that the meetings did become more sensitive to breaches of the discipline after 1750.

London Quaker meetings increasingly sanctioned marriage offences. This was in fact the largest category of delinquencies. No similar research exists for Philadelphia. As mentioned above, the nature of the sources makes it difficult to undertake such a study. Jack Marietta included marriage delinquencies in his study of the development of discipline among Pennsylvania Quaker meetings.

---

72   Share of Quaker apprentices training with non-Quakers: 1700–49: 30.1 per cent; 1750–99: 28.3 per cent.

Unfortunately, he does not provide total numbers of marriage offences, nor the percentage by which these increased. Increase however they did. The growth of sanctions for marrying out began slowly in the 1710s, and took a dramatic turn upwards from around 1750. Compared to other types of offences, he found that 'Marriage delinquency was growing two and one-half times faster than delinquency as a whole.' His findings therefore suggest that the pattern of sanctions for marriage offences in the Quaker city mirrored that of Friends' meetings in London.[73]

As with other areas of the discipline, the Society of Friends became much more sensitive to ensuring marital endogamy within the community in the second half of the eighteenth century. Sanctions for marriage to non-Quakers expanded by an exceptional degree. The evidence from the sanctioning records, and in particular the study of Quaker apprentice marriages, however, shows that it was not so much that London Friends slackened in their attitude towards the discipline, but the meetings which became stricter in their enforcement.

---

73 Marietta, *Reformation*, 51.

10

War and Political Crisis

From the 1750s onwards, Quaker monthly meetings in London and Philadelphia increased their sanctions dramatically. This increase was not caused by a decline in Friends' conduct. Instead, the reform spirit that took hold of the Society during the eighteenth century led the meetings to apply stricter standards to Friends' behaviour. The meetings increasingly policed their congregations. This constituted a profound institutional change. The epistles of the London Yearly Meeting, the Philadelphia Yearly Meeting's Book of Discipline, and finally the monthly meetings' records specify that the meetings' goal in administering sanctions was to protect the Society of Friends' reputation. The dramatic increase in sanctions from the mid-eighteenth century onwards therefore implies not only a spiritual change, but an increased concern over Friends' collective reputation. In order to understand the growth of sanctions after 1750, we therefore need to ask: what triggered the Society's concern over its reputation in the 1750s? In order to answer this question, we have to take into account the political context within which mid-eighteenth-century Friends acted.

The Quaker Party

The origins of the Society's reputational worries of the mid-eighteenth century lie in Pennsylvania. Since about 1700, Friends in the colony had become outnumbered by followers of other religions. They continued, however, to dominate economic and political life, as a large number of Philadelphia merchants belonged to the Society, and Friends held important political offices.[1] During the first half of the eighteenth century, Pennsylvania Friends were politically divided. This changed with the founding of the Quaker Party. This political party united Quaker interests in Pennsylvania, and also gained the support of many non-Quakers. The party won the 1740 assembly elections in a landslide. Their opponent, the Proprietary Party, representing the interests of

---

1 Tolles, *Meeting House*, 12, 64; Bauman, *Reputation*, 1, 2. Doerflinger, *A Vigorous Spirit of Enterprise*.

the proprietor and his allies gained not a single seat.² Pennsylvania Friends now enjoyed a new position of power, not merely in the colony as of itself, but also vis-à-vis the proprietor. William Penn's son, Thomas Penn, was no longer a member of the Society of Friends, and unlike his father's, his interests in Pennsylvania were purely economic. The Quaker Party's strength challenged his control over the province, and caused continuous conflict between him and the Pennsylvania Assembly, the colony's main legislative body. In particular, they competed over the right to issue currency and the authority to levy taxes. In this period, the British North American colonies struggled with a lack of cash, which impeded their economic development. The colonial governments wanted to issue their own currencies. This desire ran counter to the English government's policy of the time, which was aimed at exerting greater control over the colonies than had been the case previously. Hence, neither colonial proprietors nor the government at Whitehall were willing to concede the right to print their own money. The situation was thus, that Pennsylvania's legislative branch, the Quaker-dominated Assembly, sought greater independence in its political and economic decisions. The colony's executive branch, the proprietor, as well as the Board of Trade back in London, wanted greater control.

As it happened, the consolidation of Quaker control over the Assembly coincided both with the beginning of a long period of armed conflict and violence in Pennsylvania, and nascent efforts to reform Quaker doctrines, including pacifism within the Society. This coincidence of developments in the political and religious spheres is important, as it would shape Pennsylvania Friends' political fortunes as well as those of the Society of Friends as a whole. Let us therefore take a quick look at state of Quaker pacifism at the time.

Quaker pacifism in Pennsylvania

As discussed in chapter two, Quaker pacifism emerged in the aftermath of the Fifth Monarchy Men's uprising in 1660. This rebellion was followed by intensified oppression and persecution of dissenters. Leading Quakers sought to alleviate the burden of the suffering Friends. George Fox issued forceful testimonies regarding Friends' pacifist principles. This marked the beginning of the overall acceptance of the peace doctrine within the Society of Friends. Following this doctrine, Friends would not personally take up arms. This did not mean that they refused to participate in military operations entirely. For instance, unarmed Friends stood watch against French and Spanish troops in Barbados, which was specifically approved by the London Six Weeks Meeting

---

2 Marietta, *Reformation*, 134.

and George Fox himself.³ What is more, Friends had no qualms about levying taxes for the support of military operations; both London and Philadelphia Yearly Meetings had directed them to do so in the 1690s. The logic behind this apparent contradiction was that Friends also embraced another doctrine closely related to their pacifism: the duty to obey the worldly government, aka 'Rendering unto Caesar the things that are Caesar's'. During the seventeenth and the first half of the eighteenth century, Philadelphia Yearly Meeting took the stance that Friends themselves might not take up weapons and fight. They did not, however, oppose the government doing so. In fact, they expected the government to protect its subjects, including Friends. For the situation in Pennsylvania this meant that it was the Assembly's duty to support the colonial and imperial governments through levying taxes, if requested to do so. At the same time, it was no business of the Assembly to tell the government how to use these funds. Following this logic, the Pennsylvania Assembly from the 1690s to the 1740s repeatedly voted money 'for the king's use' or 'the queen's use', well aware that these funds would be used for military purposes.

This approach began to cause problems from 1739 onwards. For the first time in decades, fighting directly threatened Pennsylvania colonists. At the same time, reformers within the Society of Friends were beginning to highlight what they perceived to be a decline in Quaker conduct, and called on Friends to 'return' to a purer form of their faith. Quaker missionaries were active in the public realm in Philadelphia, speaking in meetings and also addressing the Assembly directly. They promoted a stricter interpretation of pacifist ideas than had theretofore been usual for the Society of Friends. The reformers of the mid-eighteenth century argued that Quaker assemblymen would not be able to defend the colony while also adhering to what they thought was the proper Quaker attitude towards violence. In the context of these developments, Pennsylvania Friends began to discuss and adjust their understanding of pacifism.

The War of Jenkins' Ear

While Friends were discussing the state of their Society, the first of three political conflicts that would shape their destiny unfolded. The War of Jenkins' Ear saw two major European powers, Spain and Britain, face each other. This war's battles took place primarily on American soil. While fighting lasted from 1739 to 1748, it was largely finished by 1742. Pennsylvania did not become a battleground in this conflict. However, its deputy governor, George Thomas,

---

3 Hermann Wellenreuther, 'The Political Dilemma of the Quakers in Pennsylvania, 1681–1748', *Pennsylvania Magazine of History and Biography* 94, no. 2 (1970), 141.

suggested the Pennsylvania Assembly support the war raging in nearby colonies by creating a provincial militia, assisting in the recruitment of soldiers for the regular British army, and preparing the naval defence of the colony and its shipping against privateering. The Assembly refused. This triggered the first of several attempts to remove the Quakers from colonial government. The governor made a complaint to the Board of Trade in London. He argued that Quaker power in Pennsylvania endangered the security of the Empire – and demanded that Friends be removed from all political offices. His effort received support through a petition, signed by 265 non-Quaker Philadelphia merchants and businessmen. Picking up on Friends' debates surrounding the meaning and reform of Quaker principles, they argued that their pacifism made Friends unable to defend Pennsylvania, and therefore unfit to serve in government. Proprietor Thomas Penn took the petition to the board, and the Penns lobbied on its behalf.

Since the religious persecution of Friends during the seventeenth century, the Society had maintained an institution dedicated entirely to defending Friends' interests during conflict with worldly authorities. The London Meeting for Sufferings in this situation, as in previous instances, fulfilled its designated purpose of defending Friends against religious persecution. It lobbied on behalf of the Pennsylvania Quakers at Whitehall. Its efforts were successful. Despite the claims the petitioners made, the Privy Council Committee on Plantation Affairs in May 1743 decided that the situation in Pennsylvania 'did not constitute a grave danger to the lives and property of Englishmen'.[4] Therefore, it did not justify the Crown's interference with the electoral process in Pennsylvania and remove Quaker assemblymen.

This was not the end of the story, however. The tension between the Assembly and the Proprietary camp over who held the upper hand in Pennsylvania politics simmered on. In 1754 the Seven Years' War erupted. In this situation, the conflict between the Assembly and the proprietor came to a head.

The Seven Years' War

The Seven Years' War involved several European powers, who battled each other around the globe. In North America, fighting took place between French and English colonies. Both sets of colonists also had Native American allies. Hence, in the United States, this part of the war is known as the French and Indian War. The mounting pressure of the war on Pennsylvania, including the threat presented by French troops and Native American warriors, conflicted

---

4   Marietta, *Reformation*, 133, 134.

with an increasing sensitivity about violence among reform-oriented Pennsylvanian Friends.

The Pennsylvania Assembly decided to use the imminent threat of attacks on the colony as an opportunity to try to wrest control over spending from the proprietor. It refused to allocate money to defence, unless its demand to the right to print currency was accepted. In response, Thomas Penn had his governor veto all the Assembly's money bills from 1751 to 1754.[5] For both sides the conflict was an ideological one about who had the right to decide financial matters: the proprietor or the elected representatives of the people. The two branches of colonial government were locked in a stalemate. Then war arrived in the colony.

The opposition, led by the proprietor and his allies, recognized the situation as a new opportunity to remove Quakers from government in Pennsylvania. Pursuing the same strategy as in the War of Jenkins' Ear, they aimed to bring the Quaker Party into disrepute with the government in London. London, they hoped, would then interfere in Pennsylvania and remove the Quaker Party from the Assembly. To achieve their aim, they again petitioned the Crown. This time, they argued that Friends used pacifism merely as an excuse not to contribute to the defence of the colony. The true motivation for their reluctance, they argued, was the Society's schemes for maintaining political power and defending their commercial interests. They also published a number of pamphlets, which aimed to stir up public opinion in England against the Pennsylvania Quakers. The most important among these came from the pen of William Smith, Anglican cleric and Provost of the College of Philadelphia. In his *Brief State of the Province of Pennsylvania* (1755), he argued that Friends were 'quite intoxicated' with power almost to the point of treason: 'they seem even to claim a kind of Independency of their mother country, despising the order of the Crown, and refusing to contribute their Quota, either to the general defence of America, or that of their own particular Province'.[6] Friends were 'an obstinate and perverse people'[7], who 'under the mask of extraordinary sanctity and conscience, lord it over their fellow-subjects'.[8] They had become 'forgetful of the public Good, [and] they seem wholly to have employed themselves in grasping after Power'.[9] Indeed, he accused Friends of 'turning *Religion* into a political *scheme of power*'.[10] This pamphlet attacked not merely the Quaker assemblymen, but all Friends, falsely arguing that their pacifism made them unable, or unwilling, to defend the province and the colonists against the Indians. At first this pamphlet

---

5   Ibid., 138, 139.
6   Marietta, *Reformation*, 145.
7   William Smith, *A Brief State of the Province of Pennsylvania* (1755), 24.
8   Ibid., 44.
9   Ibid., 16.
10 Ibid., 11, emphasis in original.

received little attention, too far-fetched did its accusations seem. Then, however, the war took a turn for the worse.

In July 1755, British General Braddock and his army suffered a humiliating defeat at the hands of Native American and French troops in Pennsylvania. They had attacked the French fort Duquesne, located at today's Pittsburgh, about 300 miles inland from Philadelphia. Their aim was to drive the French out of the Ohio River territories. The battle was catastrophic, costing many soldiers, including the general himself, their lives.

Upon learning of Braddock's defeat, the Assembly quickly passed a bill to raise £50,000 for defence. However, in the bill they included an unprecedented tax on the proprietor's lands. This was a novelty. The Assembly thought that the threat to the colony in the light of Braddock's defeat would pressure Penn to sign it. He refused.

In the autumn of 1755, Delaware and Shawnee warriors began a series of attacks on colonial settlements in western Pennsylvania. The Pennsylvanian frontier collapsed, sending colonists fleeing towards the capital. Philadelphians were terrified. This tense situation sparked a political scuffle in which the Assembly and the Proprietor each tried to dodge blame for the casualties. Upon learning of the attack, the Assembly quickly passed a new defence bill, this time for £60,000. Again, however, it included the tax on the proprietor's lands. And once more, Penn had it vetoed. In order to shift the blame onto the Assembly, he volunteered £5,000 of his own money to defend the province, hoping thereby to shift blame for the border casualties onto the Assembly. Afraid that his strategy would work, the Assembly thereupon dropped the tax on Penn's lands and passed the bill without it. Far from being the end of the matter, however, this concession prompted criticism from another direction.

Some Pennsylvania Friends were not happy with the bill. They protested against it, publicly declaring that they would refuse to pay the tax. Philadelphia Yearly Meeting debated the bill during its gathering that year. As we learned above, Friends traditionally did not object to the Assembly raising money for 'the king's use', even knowing it would be employed for military purposes. This situation, however, was different. Rather than raising funds and signing them over to the governor, the Assembly had appointed a committee which was to decide how the funds would be used. Including several Friends, this committee would distribute the money and channel it directly into the war effort. Further influenced by the reform efforts within the Society, Philadelphia Yearly Meeting decided the assemblymen were crossing a line. They explained their concerns in a publication titled *An Epistle of Tender Love and Caution*. Later, a copy of this would make its way to court, further supporting the proprietary camp's efforts to undermine the Quaker Assembly.

All in all, the proprietary party's efforts were successful. As the Indian attacks continued, the Pennsylvania public began to blame the Assembly. To appease them, the Assembly, with the support of its Quaker members, passed an act for a volunteer militia, the first in Pennsylvania's history.[11] What was more, in April 1756, some assemblymen, including Quakers, asked the governor to declare war upon the Delawares and offer bounties for their scalps.[12] In the spring of 1756 the colony offered to pay $130 for the scalp of every male Indian aged over twelve, and $50 for each Indian woman's scalp. Many Friends were shocked by this decision. The historiography has made much of Friends' supposedly harmonious relationship with their Indian neighbours. In reality, this was difficult from the beginning, and deteriorated further as European colonization increased.[13] Still, the scalp bill was a new low point. For many Friends, having Quaker politicians support such a violent move was unacceptable. In response, some Quaker assemblymen resigned from the House; others who did not were swiftly disowned by their monthly meetings.

A number of Pennsylvania Friends decided to proactively work towards peace with the Indians. They founded the 'Friendly Association for Regaining and Preserving Peace with the Indians by Pacifistic Measures'. Its membership was entirely made up of Quakers, predominantly wealthy city Friends who favoured the reform movement. Under the leadership of prominent Philadelphia merchant Israel Pemberton, the Association worked towards improving the colony's relationship with its native American neighbours. These Friends held the view that the Indians' war was justified, in that it constituted a response to the colonists robbing them of their land. They defended this position, publicly siding with the Indian opponents, rather than their fellow colonists.[14] What was more, they raised £5,000 out of Friends' private capital to invest in their work with the Indians.[15] This peaceable effort would later provide further ammunition for Friends' enemies.

The military disaster surrounding Braddock's defeat spiked London's interest in what was going on in Pennsylvania. They started paying attention to the proprietary camp's letters and petitions, which painted the situation in the colony in the darkest colours. The colonists, they argued, were helpless and desperate, as the Quaker-led Assembly was unwilling to defend them. The protests of some Pennsylvania Friends, who refused to pay the tax the Assembly had levied after the Indian attacks had started, played into the

---

11 Marietta, *Reformation*, 150–55.
12 Matthew C. Ward, 'The "Peaceable Kingdom" Destroyed: The Seven Years' War and the Transformation of the Pennsylvania Backcountry', *Pennsylvania History: A Journal of Mid-Atlantic Studies* 74, no. 3 (2007), 267.
13 Carey, *Peace*, 14.
14 Marietta, *Reformation*, 188.
15 Theodore Thayer, 'The Friendly Association', *Pennsylvania Magazine of History and Biography* 67, no. 4 (1943); Michael Goode, 'A Failed Peace: The Friendly Association and the Pennsylvania Backcountry during the Seven Years' War', *Pennsylvania Magazine of History and Biography* 136, no. 4 (2012).

proprietor's hands. What is more, they obtained a copy of Philadelphia Yearly Meeting's *Epistle of Tender Love and Caution*, which argued that Quaker pacifism forbade paying the tax. William Smith had it printed and circulated in London. The king was not amused.[16]

The proprietor's campaign was further aided by the fact that prominent London Friends who did not share in the reformers' new, stricter interpretation of the Peace Testimony held substantial commercial interests in the colonies. In fact, Jacob Price found that it was in the context of the Seven Years' War that most Quaker merchant fortunes were built.[17] David Barclay, merchant and banker, procured a thousand muskets for Penn.[18] Robert Plumsted, a large-scale colonial merchant, carried on a great trade in gunpowder with New England. The Friend with the greatest financial interests in the war was probably John Hanbury, member of the Meeting for Sufferings. He served as paymaster and commissary to the British forces. Together with his brother Capel, also a member of the Meeting, he shared an interest in the defence of the Ohio River Valley due to their tobacco business there. The Hanburys were the principal Englishmen among the founders of the Ohio Company to conquer and obtain the fur trade of the area. John Hanbury was crucial to the operation of the company: he was its financial agent, solicitor and, most importantly, powerful lobbyist who conducted company business with the Board of Trade, the Privy Councillors, Thomas Penn and others.[19] In fact, a 1756 pamphlet claimed that

> This Man, being at the Head of a Sect which has constantly supported the M—r in all his strenuous Endeavours for Power, and designs upon his Country, was attended to with greater Deference, and had more Weight than the Remonstrances of Two Missions of faithful American Subjects, who were still totally neglected: So much can the Interest of one Man, who heads a factious Sect in favour of a M—r prevail beyond the public Good of the Subjects of this Kingdom, and the Honour of its Sovereign.

It accused John Hanbury,

> this very person, whose passive Principles of Christian Patience prevent him from bearing Arms in Defence of this Land, which was granted him, had yet the unrelenting conscience to obtain many hundreds of his fellow-subjects to oppose their lives, and fall as sacrifice in repossessing his Property. Such are the Proceedings of this sect of anti-constitutional and pernicious Beings.[20]

---

16 Marietta, *Reformation*, 159.
17 Price, 'Business Families', 384.
18 Marietta, *Reformation*, 162.
19 Ibid., 143.
20 John Shebbeare, *A Letter to the People of England* (1756), Letter I, 20.

The author went on to argue that 'the money which it has and will cost the Nation, and the lives which it has lavished in the Service of a non-resisting Quaker, were altogether useless and unnecessary'. In fact, he explained, John Hanbury was personally responsible for the British defeat at Fort Duquesne. 'The disgraceful Deafeat of our Army, the disreputation of our General, the Destruction of our subjects, the expense of the expedition, and dishonour of the nation,' he claimed, 'might have been prevented.'[21]

As if all this were not enough, the proprietary cause gained further support when in February, George II called for a national day of religious fasting. Some London Friends, for religious reasons, would not participate and opened their shops. A mob attacked them, and their conduct further fuelled growing anti-Quaker sentiment in the capital.[22]

The proprietary propaganda, reporting that Pennsylvania stood defenceless against French and Indian aggression, with Quaker assemblymen refusing to contribute financially to its defence, while their English brethren profited from the War, conspired to make Friends the perfect scapegoat for General Braddock's defeat. The Privy Council responded by discussing means of ridding Pennsylvania of its Quaker politicians. In the winter of 1755–56, it considered the suggestions made in the 'Brief State' that a test oath be established in Pennsylvania. As Friends would not swear, this would serve to exclude them from the Assembly.[23] This in turn triggered the official involvement of the Meeting for Sufferings in London.

In charge of defending Friends against religious persecution, the Meeting for Sufferings tried to solve the conflict between the Quaker assemblymen and the Penns. The Meeting managed to broker a deal with the government: Pennsylvania Quakers would withdraw from colonial government for the duration of the war. In return, Friends would not be banned from holding political office in the colony.[24] Once the war was over, and defence spending no longer required, Friends could return to the Assembly. The meeting dispatched emissaries to Pennsylvania to enforce its decision among Philadelphia Friends. But even before they arrived, large numbers of Friends left the Assembly. Not being able to agree with various aspects of its policies, they resigned their seats. In the elections of October 1756, the Quaker Party again won a majority. However, only few Friends remained among its delegates. Quakers no longer constituted a majority in the Pennsylvania Assembly.[25]

21 Ibid., Letter I, 21.
22 Marietta, *Reformation*, 159.
23 Bauman, *Reputation*, 22; Jack D. Marietta, 'Conscience, the Quaker Community, and the French and Indian War', *Pennsylvania Magazine of History and Biography* 95, no. 1 (1971), 8.
24 Marietta, *Reformation*, 161.
25 Marietta, 'Conscience', 8.

The Paxton Pamphlet War

The Seven Years' War was immediately followed by Pontiac's War, lasting from 1763 to 1766. This was an uprising of native Americans against the ever-expanding European colonization of their land. The concluding act in the power struggle between the proprietary camp and the Assembly, it caused further severe damage to the Society of Friends' reputation.

Pontiac's uprising brought new violence between Indians of different nations with European colonists. Within this context fell a series of events which proved to have a lasting impact on the Society of Friends, the ongoing reformation, and the development of Quaker discipline. In December 1763, a mob of white colonists formed in Paxton, Lancaster County, and brutally murdered a group of Conestoga Indians at a nearby settlement. A few days later, a second group of men stormed the Lancaster jail, and murdered fourteen Conestoga Indians who had stayed there for their protection. They justified their actions through false claims that the victims had participated in atrocities against Europeans. They had in fact lived for years peacefully among the white colonists in the area. In February 1764, 250 men, who now called themselves 'the Paxton Boys', marched towards Philadelphia, in order to murder further Conestogas who had sought refuge there.[26] In Philadelphia, the militia was mobilized to defend the city – and the Conestoga – against the marchers. To Philadelphians' surprise, and of great importance to the future of the Society of Friends, several Quaker men spontaneously took up arms and joined the militia. There was to be no violent clash between the militiamen and the Paxtonians, however. A delegation from the Assembly, led by none other than Benjamin Franklin, intercepted the marchers at Germantown, near Philadelphia. The delegates listened to the Paxtonians' complaints and promised to take them under consideration. Then everyone went home.[27]

Initially, the European public in Pennsylvania was horrified at the events and condemned the Paxton Boys' massacres severely. However, the public soon changed its assessment of the situation and its protagonists. The proprietary camp took the Paxton march as an opportunity for a third attempt to gain political control over the Assembly. This time, they employed a new strategy: rather than try to influence political decisions in London, they hoped to sway public opinion in Pennsylvania.

At this point, Friends constituted only a minority among the Assemblymen. However, the Quaker Party still held all the seats. It continued on the same political course as before. William Smith and his fellow agitators took to the

---

26 John Smolenski, 'Embodied Politics: The Paxton Uprising and the Gendering of Civic Culture in Colonial Pennsylvania', *Early American Studies: An Interdisciplinary Journal* 14, no. 2 (2016), 377–78.

27 Bauman, *Reputation*, 110–11.

printing presses, aiming to incite hatred against the Assembly. Their strategy was to exploit religious differences in Pennsylvania. Friends had long been outnumbered by other protestants in the colony. They were now a minority, albeit a wealthy one that held a lot of political power. The proprietary campaigners released a tide of pamphlets which slandered the Quakers as enemies of the people. The people, in this case, were the colonists in the western counties, which included the Paxton Boys. The population in these counties was mostly German and Scotch-Irish, and predominantly non-Quaker. The Scots Irish were Presbyterians, a religion which at this point had become the largest in the colony. The proprietary writers portrayed the conflict as a religious one: The eastern, urban Quakers controlled the Assembly, and oppressed the western, rural, Presbyterians. The pamphlets also adopted the arguments from the anti-Quaker campaign of the Seven Years' War.[28] They argued that the pacifist Quaker Assembly neglected the Europeans at the frontier and refused to protect them from Indian aggression.[29] In their endeavour to wrest greater political power from the proprietor, according to the Paxtonians, Friends were willing to go over the dead bodies of their fellow colonists. In the next election, the campaigners hoped, the persecuted non-Quaker population would vote the Quaker Party out of the Assembly.

The Quakers and their supporters responded to the Paxtonian pamphlets with publications of their own. In these they defended both Friends and the Assembly. Over the following months, Pennsylvania saw an 'astonishing amount of pamphlet literature, unprecedented in quantity and variety'.[30] Sixty-four pamphlets and ten political cartoons appeared.[31] This was the greatest number of pamphlets published about any local issue in Pennsylvania's history, including the 1755–56 crisis over Quaker reluctance to participate in the French and Indian War. Their sales were huge as a great part of Pennsylvania's inhabitants followed the debate.[32]

A media war
The Paxtonian pamphleteers' argumentation was based on falsehoods and misrepresentation. It was also not entirely consistent in the claims it made based on these falsehoods. The gist of it was the following: the Quakers were interested only in money and power. They wanted to make a profit at any cost. They maintained a monopoly on the fur trade with the Indians. From this

---

28 Peter Rhoads Silver, *Our Savage Neighbors: How Indian War Transformed Early America* (New York: W. W. Norton, 2008), 202.
29 Silver, *Our Savage Neighbors*, Ch. 7.
30 Alison Olson, 'The Pamphlet War over the Paxton Boys', *Pennsylvania Magazine of History and Biography* 123, no. 1/2 (1999), 31.
31 'Introduction', digitalpaxton.org.
32 Olson, 'Pamphlet War', 31, 33.

trade they profited immensely, and would therefore do anything to defend it.[33] As one pamphlet rhymed:

> Pray, worthy FRIENDS! Observe the Text,
> Get money first, and Virtue next.
> Nought makes our Carolina Curs
> To bark and lie, but Skins and Furs.[34]

In order not to have to share the benefits of this trade with non-Quakers, the pamphlets argued, Friends wanted to hold on to political power in the colony. They did so by denying other Europeans in Pennsylvania seats in the Assembly, and thereby all political representation. Thus, the Quakers made slaves of their fellow Europeans.[35] But that was not all. When Indians attacked the frontier settlers, the Quakers refused to help.[36] On the contrary: during the war, they supposedly allied themselves with the Indian enemy. In order to weaken the colonists at the frontier and thereby meet the threat these posed to Friends' hold over political power, they enticed the Indians to attack the settlers and 'plunder, tomahawk and burn them'.[37] The Indians, so the pamphlets reported, savagely tortured the frontiers people, drenching the frontier in 'streams of innocent blood'.[38] The pamphlets emphasized their point by vividly describing the horrible sufferings of the frontier settlers. As one author told it:

> Many Children were either spitted alive & roasted or covered under the Ashes of a large Fire, before their helpless Parents Eyes. The Hearts of some taken out & eaten reeking hot, while they were yet beating between their Teeth and others, where Time & Opportunity would admit of it were skinned, boiled & eaten.[39]

The proprietary pamphlets represented the massacres at Lancaster as Europeans' response to this cruelty. It was self-defence. The Paxton Boys' march on Philadelphia, they argued, constituted a desperate attempt by the frontiersmen to be heard by the Philadelphian elites, who had been neglecting

---

33 Marietta, *Reformation*, 191; also John R. Dunbar, 'THE QUAKER Unmask'd; OR, PLAIN TRUTH: Humbly address'd to the Consideration of all the FREEMEN of PENNSYLVANIA', in *The Paxton Papers* (The Hague: Martinus Nijhoff, 1957), 211.
34 Dunbar, 'The Cloven-Foot Discovered', in *The Paxton Papers*, 85. Emphasis in original.
35 Dunbar, 'The Plain Dealer: Or, Remarks on Quaker Politicks in Pennsylvania. Numb. III. to be Continued. By WD Author of No. I', in *The Paxton Papers*, 384.
36 Dunbar, 'Plain Dealer III', in *The Paxton Papers*, 378.
37 Ibid., 376; see also Dunbar, 'Plain Dealer I', in *The Paxton Papers*, 349.
38 Dunbar, 'Plain Dealer I', in *The Paxton Papers*, 343.
39 Dunbar, 'The Apology of the Paxton Volunteers', in *The Paxton Papers*, 185; see also Dunbar, 'Plain Dealer I', in *The Paxton Papers*, 343.

their calls for help. But instead of yielding to their fellow colonists' pleas, the Quakers increased their support for the enemy. The pamphleteers targeted the Friendly Association.[40] After all, as was well known, 'the Quakers' had raised £5,000 out of their private fortunes to support the Indians – in their endeavour to murder the frontier settlers and destroy their homes:

> GO on good Christians, never spare
> To give your Indians Clothes to wear;
> Send 'em good Beef, and pork, and Bread,
> Guns, Power, Flings and store of Lead,
> To Shoot your Neighbours through the head.[41]

One reason for Friends' supposed preference for the Indians over their fellow Europeans was their commercial interest in the fur trade, which brought them huge profits, and which they would not share with others. Yet another reason for the Quakers' preference of Indians was perhaps even more despicable. Rumour had it that at a conference with the Delaware in 1762, Israel Pemberton had had sex with an Indian woman. Pemberton was the most prominent leader of the Friendly Association. He was also a vocal pacifist, assemblyman, and wealthy Philadelphia merchant. Once the pamphlets began exploiting the rumour, Israel Pemberton became 'a sort of negative celebrity, a figure of public hatred' and a repeated target for personal attacks in further pamphlets. Other prominent Friends were targeted as well. Alongside Israel Pemberton, Abel James, merchant and clerk of the Friendly Association, and James Fox, assembly speaker, barracks master and Indian commissioner, appeared in cartoons embracing Indian women. The alleged sexual encounters of the Friendly Association's leaders with Indian women made the 'whole of Friends' relationship with the Indians appear morally "contaminated"'. Further cartoons depicted the same Friends handing out tomahawks to groups of Indians, with the instruction to 'Exercise those on the Scots Irish & Dutch'.[42]

This demonstrates a further important point: Quaker pacifism is fake. One pamphlet under the revealing title 'The Quaker Unmask'd' let a character explain this as follows:

> It is true, we profess to have an Aversion to War: But this, with most of us, is from Policy rather than Principle. Nay we secretly rejoice when we hear of whole settlements murdered and destroyed.[43]

---

40 Marietta, *Reformation*, 191.
41 Dunbar, 'Cloven-Foot', in *The Paxton Papers*, 85.
42 Silver, *Our Savave Neighbors*, 208–10.
43 Dunbar, 'Unmask'd', in *The Paxton Papers*, 212.

The clear message of these pamphlets and cartoons was that Friends only relied on their pacifist doctrine when it came to spending money for the safety of non-Quaker fellow colonists, whom they did not care about. But if they saw their own interest threatened, all pacifist scruples were quickly forgotten. Clear evidence of this was provided by the fact that when the Paxton Boys marched on Philadelphia, Friends quickly armed themselves to confront them.[44] On that occasion, we finally saw 'the Quaker unmask'd, with his Gun upon his Shoulder ... eagerly desiring the Combat, and thirsting for the Blood of those his Opponents'.[45]

As Friends did not care about the fate of their fellow Europeans in western Pennsylvania, they refused to support British troops during the Seven Years' War. When the king's soldiers were in dire need of help fighting the French, the Quaker Assembly refused to raise money for military support.[46] This made the Quakers' disregard for the frontiers people's suffering more than morally condemnable: it was treason. True, when the pressure became too great, the Assembly did eventually raise funds for defence. However, they did not put this to proper use, but squandered 'half a million pound[s]' by

> taking every public measure which might tend to enrich themselves, reduce the rest of this province to slavery, poverty and misery, and sacrifice the wretched lives of the frontier inhabitants, by refusing them any seasonable or effectual protection, and by aiding and encouraging their enemies.[47]

According to the Paxtonians, Friends had wasted public funds, and misused them to enrich themselves. Quakers could not be trusted with money. What was more, this misuse of defence funds meant that the Quakers were really responsible for British defeats and losses during the Seven Years' War. It also made them fully responsible for the suffering of the frontier settlers.[48] In fact, Quakers perversely enjoyed the 'bleeding' and 'suffering of their fellow-subjects'.[49]

---

44 Olson, 'Pamphlet War', 50; Bauman, *Reputation*, 110; Philip Gleason, 'Trouble in the Colonial Melting Pot', *Journal of American Ethnic History* 20, no. 1 (2000), 8; Silver, *Our Savage Neighbors*, 207.
45 Dunbar, 'Unmask'd', in *The Paxton Papers*, 211, 212.
46 Dunbar, 'A BATTLE! A BATTLE! A Battle of Squirt, Where no Man is kill'd And no Man is hurt! To the TUNE of three blue BEANS, in a blue BLADDER; RATTLE BLADDER, RATTLE!', in *The Paxton Papers*, 175.
47 Dunbar, 'Plain Dealer III', in *The Paxton Papers*, 370.
48 Dunbar, 'Apology', in *The Paxton Papers*, 189, 190.
49 Petition, submitted by Justice of the Peace William Moore, actually authored by William Smith, cited in Silver, *Our Savage Neighbors*, 201.

In short, the Quakers were greedy and bloodthirsty. As 'Wolves, in Lambs Disguise', they were hypocritical in their pacifism.[50] When it came to protecting their commercial interests, Friends, 'the bloodiest people in our land', forgot all their supposed convictions and rushed to arms.[51] Thus, Friends 'lately prov'd their very Religion to be a political Engine, to which they themselves pay no conscientious regard, but as it suits their crafty purposes'.[52] They exploited the commercial and political opportunities of war, and made a profit at the expense of their fellow colonists. Suffering under the 'Quaker Yoke', white Pennsylvanians of other faiths were butchered or kidnapped by Indians.

Luckily, the Paxtonian pamphlets had a remedy in store. The way to throw off the 'Quaker-yoke' and finally obtain protection from Indian aggression was to reapportion the Assembly seats. This would allow for more representation of rural, non-Quaker colonists. If implemented, such a restructuring of the electoral set-up would have shifted power within the Assembly away from the Quaker Party with its eastern, urban electorate, and into the hands of the Proprietary Party.[53]

Friends and their allies responded to these allegations with pamphlets of their own. They tried to convince the reading public that the bloodshed on the border was the fault of the proprietor, as he would not let his land be taxed to pay for defence. They argued he should be removed.[54] Furthermore, members of the Quaker Party, under the leadership of Benjamin Franklin, devised a radical plan to disempower the proprietors: they would appeal to Westminster for a royal charter that would replace Thomas Penn with a royal governor.[55] Their efforts, however, were futile. The public assumed that the proprietor was actually in a weak position vis-à-vis the Quaker-led Assembly, and it was the powerful Assembly that had consistently refused to vote adequate appropriations for frontier defence.[56] In the autumn of 1764, Pennsylvania voters were once more called to the polls. Historically, participation in elections in Pennsylvania had been low, always hovering around 10 per cent of eligible voters. In 1764, this number almost quadrupled, as participation shot up to about 40 per cent.[57] The results made the public's sympathies clear: It was the

---

50   Dunbar, 'THE ADDRESS OF THE People call'd Quakers, in the Province of PENNSYLVANIA, to JOHN PENN, Esquire, Lieutenant-Governor of the said Province, &c.', in *The Paxton Papers*, 181.
51   'Brief View', cited in Silver, *Our Savage Neighbors*, 198.
52   Dunbar, 'Unmask'd', in *The Paxton Papers*, 213.
53   Silver, *Our Savage Neighbors*, 199.
54   Olson, 'Pamphlet War', 34.
55   Marietta, *Reformation*, 194. The campaign continued, unsuccessfully, until 1768.
56   Olson, 'Pamphlet War', 44.
57   Silver, *Our Savage Neighbors*, 222.

'greatest defeat the Quaker party ever suffered at the polls'.[58] The colonists believed the proprietary propaganda, and Friends were discredited.

Conclusion

The series of armed conflicts that took place in Pennsylvania in the middle of the eighteenth century had a great impact on the Society of Friends. They coincided with a power struggle between the colony's proprietor, Thomas Penn, and his allies on the one side, and the Pennsylvania Assembly, dominated by Friends and the Quaker Party, on the other. Both sides aimed to extend their political control over the colony. Both exploited the threat of war and violence to wrest concessions from their opponent. The conflict came to a head over the raising and allocation of funds for defence.

The power struggle between the Assembly and the proprietor coincided with nascent reform efforts within the Society of Friends. Internally, the Society saw a movement of some Friends to reform the Quaker community, to return it to a purer, original state. This state was fictional. However, the reformers believed in it, or at least thought it would help their cause. In order to achieve this purer state, the reformers promoted stricter interpretations of values that had existed in the Society before, but were not central doctrines. One of these was pacifism.

The proprietary camp repeatedly launched defamation campaigns in order to discredit the Quaker Party with both the imperial government in London and the electorate in Pennsylvania. They equated the Quaker Party with the Society of Friends as a whole. They falsely argued that Friends refused to defend the colony, and that they justified this through their pacifism. In truth, according to the proprietary line of argument, Friends used their pacifism as a mere pretext which allowed them to pursue their own commercial and political interests. Quakers put money and personal power over the interests of Britain and her subjects in Pennsylvania, causing great human suffering. The campaign was successful. The public in Pennsylvania and London, as well as the metropolitan government, became convinced that Friends were bloodthirsty hypocrites who lusted after money and power. The strategy worked because Friends in this period did not act in concert. Friends were not of one mind in regards to their pacifist doctrine. Interpretations of it varied. The reformers promoted a strict version of pacifism, emphasizing that Friends could not support war, at least not directly. These Friends refused to pay taxes levied to support defence measures, and preached their convictions to the Assembly and the public. Simultaneously, some Friends in the Assembly politically supported defence measures. Some Quaker merchants invested in war-related business ventures and profited from

58 Marietta, *Reformation*, 198.

them financially. The different interpretations and policies regarding pacifism within the Society made it possible for their antagonists to make Friends' behaviour appear inconsistent. The proprietary camp exploited this apparent contradiction, offering it as evidence of Quaker hypocrisy. It helped them make Friends appear selfish, cruel and dishonest. Friends used their religious doctrines selectively, in order to further their own political and financial interests. They allied themselves with the Indian enemy and instigated the murder of their fellow Europeans. The proprietor's efforts were probably aided further by the fact that in the aftermath of the Seven Years' War, Pennsylvania was going through a severe economic crisis. Friends at this point constituted a religious minority in the colony, albeit one that was wealthy and had a disproportionate amount of political influence. This made them a convenient scapegoat for political turmoil and economic hardship. The responsibility for the bloodshed at the frontier, the British losses at Fort Duquesne and the Seven Years' War itself was laid at the feet of the Society of Friends. After three wars and decades of political strife, Friends' reputation lay in tatters. Quakerism had become equated with dishonesty, avarice and violence.

11

Reformation and Reputation

The seventeenth- and eighteenth-century Society of Friends was a transatlantic community. Friends from Europe and America corresponded, travelled, worshipped and traded together. Consequently, major events affecting Quaker meetings in one geographical region also impacted meetings in another. Political and religious developments on both sides of the Atlantic Ocean influenced and shaped each other. The series of wars that threatened Pennsylvania during the 1750s and 1760s constituted such events. They met with nascent reform efforts within the Society to create challenges to the Quakers' political hegemony in Pennsylvania. These challenges in turn influenced Quakerism's ideological developments and fuelled its reformation. In the course of these conflicts, the War of Jenkins' Ear, the Seven Years' War and the Paxton Pamphlet War during Pontiac's Uprising, the Society of Friends suffered grave reputational damage. The public in England and Pennsylvania began to perceive Quakers as greedy and hungry for power. A morally corrupted sect, Friends were thought to place their own political and financial interests before the welfare of their fellow colonists and the Empire.

Reputation was of crucial importance in the pre-modern world. It determined a person's standing in their community, both socially and economically. With little currency in circulation, economic transactions, from purchasing bread at the local baker's to intercontinental trade, were based on credit.[1] Credit was only available to those whose reputation suggested that they would honour the commercial contracts they engaged in, and pay their debts. One's name needed to be associated with honesty, diligence and reliability. It must not ever be linked to wastefulness, tainted with the slightest whiff of dishonesty. The understanding was that misconduct in one area of one's life suggested the possibility of unreliability and misconduct in other areas of life as well. Any form of moral failure was damaging, not only those aspects immediately related to the conduct of business. Hence the rumours of merchant Israel Pemberton's extramarital sexual relations with a Delaware woman reflected badly on him as a businessman. If a person's reputation was tarnished, this could mean that others would refuse to deal with them, spelling economic and social catastrophe.

---

1 Smolenski, *Friends and Strangers*, 131.

As a consequence, people went to great lengths to defend their good name. In both Europe and North America, litigation because of slander and defamation was common. Often such suits were a response to having been charged 'with fraudulent or deceptive business practices' that suggested 'a lack of trustworthiness'.[2] In colonial Pennsylvania, accusations of commercial malfeasance were among the three most common causes of slander accusations.[3] This highlights the importance colonists attributed to reputation.

Nobody was more dependent on their reputation than the middling sorts. In Britain and her colonies, middling people emerged as an economically, socially and politically influential group from the late seventeenth century. The road to social mobility in the Anglosphere commonly went through commerce. Trade was the way to move upwards. Friends were part of this movement, gaining respectability and wealth by participating in the Atlantic trade. In this period, public offices were staffed with wealthy individuals who had the education and means to undertake tasks, sometimes without being remunerated for their labour. In line with contemporary customs, the Society of Friends' governing structure, the yearly meetings, the Meeting for Sufferings and the monthly meetings were largely staffed with merchants. These were keenly aware of the importance of reputation. When the Pennsylvania Wars and the proprietary defamation campaign tarnished the Society of Friends' reputation, they knew that individual Quakers would suffer. Merchant-officers like Israel Pemberton and John Hanbury, whom pamphlets targeted individually, would have experienced the consequences first hand. How could they respond to this crisis? Action had to be taken.

As discussed in chapter two, the Society had successfully managed a reputational crisis in the past. When public attacks on Friends increased during the 1650s, Friends responded through a concerted public relations campaign. They published over a thousand pamphlets defending Friends and their beliefs and lobbied England's political leaders. Their efforts were successful. Friends achieved toleration and eventually legal equality.

In the wake of the Pennsylvania scandals, it again became necessary to guard Friends' collective reputation. In order to protect their political and commercial interests as well as their personal safety, Quaker meetings again printed pamphlets and lobbied for their interests with those in power. In addition, this time, monthly meetings employed a tool readily available to them: testimonies of denial. As discussed in chapter five, the Society assigned the power to ostracize members to the monthly meetings in 1719. It specifically instructed them to disown those Friends whose behaviour 'shall give or occasion public

---

2   Mary Beth Norton, 'Gender and Defamation in Seventeenth-Century Maryland', *William and Mary Quarterly* 44 (1987), 14.
3   Smolenski, *Friends and Strangers*, 131.

scandal'.⁴ When the Society's reputation suffered unprecedented harm from the 1750s onwards, monthly meetings fulfilled their responsibility and began to disown ever greater numbers of Friends. By publicly distancing themselves from individuals associated with anti-social behaviour, Friends hoped to clear the Society's name and disassociate themselves from scandal. Thus commenced what one historian has termed 'the greatest suicide of a church in history'.⁵

The offences for which meetings disowned Friends shed light on the norms against which their behaviour was measured. They reflect values of the eighteenth-century middling sorts. Their values were 'heavily marked by the experience of commerce and emphasised virtues associated with self-improvement through hard work'. They advocated soberness, prudence, frugality and diligence, the same values that the commercial advice literature, sermons and Quaker Yearly Meeting epistles promoted.⁶ Eighteenth-century middling parents encouraged their children to safeguard their credit and avoid extravagant spending. Contemporaries frequently warned of the 'dangers of bad company and aimless leisure pursuits'.⁷ Correspondingly, testimonies of denial condemned Friends for 'keeping evil company', 'gambling' or the 'unnecessary frequenting of ale houses': in essence, behaviours that constituted threats to financial security.⁸ Sources from this period reflect the fear of losing the precarious security and comfort middling people had only recently obtained. Thus, the meetings' testimonies aimed at demonstrating the Quakers' commitment to middle-class values. Disowning members for breaking these norms signalled to outsiders that Friends, as a whole, were decent people. The growth in testimonies of denial after 1750 is evidence of an increased need to do so.

To be clear: the Quaker reformation was not merely a public relations exercise. The Society embarked on its reform course before the Pennsylvania scandals hit. It is impossible to pinpoint exactly what caused it to set out on this path. Part of the reason will have lain in the contemporary religious climate. Those familiar with eighteenth-century religious history will notice the coincidence of the Quaker reformation with the First Great Awakening and the rise of various new religious movements, such as Methodism. The reformation may

4   Philadelphia MM, Book of Discipline, 39–41.
5   Rowntree, *Quakerism*, 156.
6   Hunt, 'Middling Sort', 1, chapter 2; Peter Earle, *The Making of the English Middle Class: Business, Society and Family Life in London, 1660–1730* (London: Methuen, 1989), 11–13.
7   Hunt, 'Middling Sort', 747; see also chapters 2, 4.
8   Examples for 'evil company': ToD Stanfield Parkinson 1795, ToD Josiah Stamper Jr. 1740, ToD Samuel Simkin 1750, all in Ratcliff MM, Testimonies. For 'unnecessary frequenting of ale houses' see ToD Jeremiah Roberts 1764, ToD John Weaver 1763, both Peel MM, Sufferings; and ToD Joseph Draper 1766 in Ratcliff MM, Testimonies. For gambling see ToD John Fell 1756, Peel MM, Sufferings; ToD Joseph Pearce 1760, ToD William Knowles 1762, both in Horsleydown MM, Disorderly Walkers.

therefore have been an effort to define the Society's identity in contrast to the changing religious environment. This included both an intensification of older doctrine and new ideas. Thereby, the Society also delineated the boundaries of its membership from other religious groups, which may help explain why the main cause of disownment in both Philadelphia and London was exogamous marriage. Moreover, the records include many disownments for 'absence from meetings.' Not attending meetings for worship would hardly have caused public scandal. Rather, these testimonies suggest that the Society eliminated the hybrid borderlands of association with various denominations. Defining who was a member meant defining who might be associated with Friends and whose behaviour therefore needed to be monitored, lest they cause scandal.

From the 1740s onwards, the Society of Friends increasingly reviewed its values. The conflicts over political interests in Pennsylvania served to accelerate this development. When the efforts of reform-oriented Friends met with the power struggles between the Assembly and the proprietor during the War of Jenkins' Ear, then the Seven Years' War, and finally the Paxton Pamphlet War, the Society became entangled in conflicts that threatened its name, and thereby Friends' political and economic interests. The pressure of reputational damage that followed the Pennsylvania scandals moved certain ideas into focus. These are reflected in the primary causes for disownments in Philadelphia and London, respectively. In the financial centre that was London, public debates on debt and credit conspired with the attacks on individual Quaker businessmen to make monthly meetings focus on delinquencies related to honesty and the payment of debts. In Philadelphia, the threat of armed conflict and accusations of Quaker duplicity regarding the colony's defence focused meetings' attentions on offences related to pacifism.[9]

Both concerns, financial honesty and pacifism, are related to a third issue that took a prominent place among Philadelphia disownments: slavery. Abolitionist activism had a long history among Quakers. It only became official policy of the Society of Friends, in that it considered delinquencies related to slavery serious enough to merit disownment, in 1758. That year, Philadelphia Yearly Meeting forbade Friends to buy and sell enslaved Africans. The move was certainly a success for those Friends who – like the abolitionist pioneers Benjamin and Sarah Lay, and later leaders John Woolman and Anthony Benezet – had out of sincere humanitarian concern long campaigned against slavery. Making the trafficking of enslaved Africans a disownable offence, however, also made sense in the context of protecting the Society's reputation. For one, by the 1760s, the slave trade had become widely unpopular in Pennsylvania. Scotch-Irish Presbyterians and Lutheran Germans, the two largest ethnicities in the colony

9   Marietta, *Reformation*, 6.

at the time, shared Friends' views on slavery.[10] These two communities had also been key opponents of the Quakers during the pamphlet war. Disowning members for involvement in the slave trade was therefore a promising form of virtue signalling. What is more, researchers have long established that Quaker concern about slavery grew out of three roots. The first was the golden rule, i.e. not to do to others what you would not want them to do to you. The other two roots directly relate to Friends' reputational problems in the 1750s and 1760s. Quaker abolitionists argued against slavery on the grounds of pacifism. Obviously, holding human beings in a state of slavery only works if one is prepared to use severe violence to keep them there.[11] Moreover, contemporaries believed that slaves procured in Africa were prisoners of war. Ergo, purchasing slaves supported warfare. As pacifism moved to the forefront of Quaker concern during the 1750s, these arguments against slavery also gained weight. The third reason Friends opposed slavery was that they regarded it as a form of conspicuous consumption. Like wearing obviously expensive clothes or jewellery, owning slaves was a way of showing off one's wealth. Contemporaries also thought that owning slaves made people lazy.[12] Like disowning members for offences related to honesty in business and bankruptcy – squandering other people's money – disowning slave traders and later slave owners served to demonstrate that Friends valued honesty and hard work. Slavery stood for the opposite of what Friends wanted to be associated with, and was therefore detrimental to their reputation. Thus, through the intertwined political and religious developments of the mid-eighteenth century, honesty in business and pacifism emerged as central elements of Quakerism's identity.

As we saw in chapter four, Quaker business ethics were not distinct. Chapters seven and eight demonstrated that Quaker meetings rarely sanctioned delinquencies. They began doing so more frequently from the 1750s onwards. Even then, however, did they not sanction delinquencies relating to honesty in business comprehensively. As chapter nine showed, the same is true for meetings' policing of marital endogamy. The meetings' purpose was not to monitor their congregations closely and capture all breaches of the discipline. Rather, their sanctions were aimed at protecting the Society's reputation. Meetings targeted those Friends whose behaviour – be it in respect to business, marriage or other areas of their lives – posed a potential threat to the Society of Friends' reputation.

If Quaker business ethics were not distinct, and the meetings did not enforce contracts sufficiently to make Friends exceptionally honest, where does the Quaker reputation for honesty in business come from? There is in fact little if any evidence for such a reputation during the seventeenth and eighteenth centuries. During the nineteenth century, however, the situation appears to

10 Soderlund, *Slavery*, 157–58.
11 Carey, *Peace*, 30, 31, 35; Soderlund, *Slavery*, 18.
12 Soderlund, *Slavery*, 18.

change. In 1877, the Quaker Oats company was founded. The company's label design depicts a man in classic Quaker garb, with a broad-brimmed hat. Significantly, the company was never owned by Friends. Completely unrelated to the Society themselves, the founders chose to advertise their product as 'Quaker' because they thought it would evoke trust in consumers. Most recently, in the aftermath of the 2008 financial crisis, Barclay's Bank issued public statements in which they referred to their 'Quaker roots'. They were hoping that linking themselves to Quakerism would help salvage their reputation, which had suffered as a consequence of their role in creating a global economic crisis.

The existence of a Quaker reputation for honesty setting in a few decades after meetings began to publicly condemn malpractice in business suggests that the Society's efforts to repair its reputation in the aftermath of the Pennsylvania scandals were successful. In advertising its support of the middling sort's values through testimonies of denial, it constructed a new identity. By focusing on the ideals of honesty, peace and humanitarianism, it redefined what it means to be a Friend.

Appendix I

Queries of the London Yearly Meeting

Are meetings for worship and discipline kept up, and do friends attend them duly, and at the time appointed; and do they avoid all unbecoming behaviour therein?

Is there among you any growth in the truth; and hath any convincement appeared since last year?

Are friends preserved in love towards each other; if differences arise, is due care taken speedily to end them; and are friends careful to avoid and discourage tale-bearing and detraction?

Do friends endeavour by example and precept to train up their children, servants, and those under their care, in a religious life and conversation, consistent with our Christian profession, in the frequent reading of the Holy Scriptures, and in plainness of speech, behaviour, and apparel?

Are friends just in their dealings, and punctual in fulfilling their engagements; and are they annually advised carefully to inspect the state of their affairs once in the year?

Are friends careful to avoid all vain sports and places of diversion, gaming, all unnecessary frequenting of taverns and other public-houses, excess in drinking, and other intemperance?

Do friends bear a faithful and Christian testimony against receiving and paying tithes, priests' demands, and those called church-rates?

Are friends faithful in our testimony against bearing arms, and being in any manner concerned in the militia, in privateers, letters of marque, or armed vessels, or dealing in prize-goods?

APPENDIX I

Are friends clear of defrauding the king of his customs, duties, and excise, and of using or dealing in goods suspected to be run?

Are the necessities of the poor among you properly inspected and relieved; and is good care taken of the education of their offspring?

Have any meetings been settled, discontinued, or united since last year?

Are there any friends prisoners for our testimonies; and if any one hath died a prisoner, or been discharged, since last year, when and how?

Is early care taken to admonish such as appear inclinable to marry in a manner contrary to the rules of our society; and to deal with such as persist in refusing to take counsel?

Have you two or more faithful friends, appointed by the monthly meeting, as overseers in each particular meeting; are the rules respecting removals duly observed; and is due care taken, when any thing appears amiss, that the rules of our discipline be timely and impartially put in practice?

Do you keep a record of the prosecutions and sufferings of your members; is due care taken to register all marriages, births, and burials; are the titles of your meeting-houses, burial-grounds, &c. duly preserved and recorded; and are all legacies and donations properly secured and recorded, and duly applied?[1]

---

1 London Yearly Meeting, *Extracts from the Minutes and Advices of the Yearly Meeting of Friends Held in London from its First Institution* (1802), 143–44.

Appendix II

Philadelphia Meetings' Self-Condemnations

Year	SC other	SC business	SC total
1685	0	0	0
1690	1	0	1
1700	0	0	0
1705	2	0	1
1710	1	0	1
1715	2	0	2
1720	0	0	0
1725	1	0	1
1730	1	0	1
1735	1	0	1
1740	2	1	3
1745	6	0	6
1750	8	0	8
1755	10	1	11
1760	21	1	22
1765	18	0	18
1770	10	1	11
1775	10	0	6
1780	11	0	11
1785	14	0	14
1790	6	2	8
1795	9	0	9
1800	6	1	7

Bibliography

Primary Sources

Manuscripts

Birmingham City Library, Birmingham
Papers relating to the financial affairs of Farmer & Galton, 1754–70.
Letters from James Farmer, 1748–60.
Letter Book of Samuel Galton, 1755–57.

Haverford Quaker Collections, Haverford, PA
Monthly Meeting of the Northern Liberties, Meeting Minutes.
Monthly Meeting of the Southern District, Meeting Minutes.
Philadelphia Yearly Meeting, Book of Discipline, 1719.
Philadelphia Monthly Meeting, Certificates of removal received.
Philadelphia Monthly Meeting, Minutes.

Historical Society of Pennsylvania, Philadelphia
Claypoole, James. Letter Book, 1681-84.

Library of the Religious Society of Friends, London
Devonshire House Monthly Meeting, Testimonies of Denial.
Devonshire House Monthly Meeting, Minutes.
Devonshire House Monthly Meeting, Certificates of Public Friends.
Devonshire House Monthly Meeting, Certificates of removal, issued.
Fothergill, Betty. Diary, 1769–70.
Horsleydown Monthly Meeting, Book of Disorderly Walkers, 2 vols, 1728–83, 1784–1805.
Horleydown Monthly Meeting, Minutes.
Jenkins, James. Diary, 1763–1830.
London Quarterly Meeting, Minutes.
London Six Weeks Meeting, Minutes.
Norwich Monthly Meeting (1776–1800), Typescript
Peel Monthly Meeting, Minutes.

Peel Monthly Meeting, Book of Sufferings 1753–73 (Condemnations and Sanctions 1676–1773).
Ratcliff Monthly Meeting, Minutes.
Ratcliff Monthly Meeting, Testimonies of Denial, 1697–1797.
Westminster Monthly Meeting, Minutes.

London Metropolitan Archives, London
Briggins, Peter. Diary.
Eliot, John. Letter to Sister Mariabella, 1763.
Eliot, John. Letter Book.
Lime Street Independent Meeting House, 1692–1764.

The National Archives, London
Bankruptcy Commission Docket Books.
Fleet Prison Committment Books.

National Library of Scotland, Edinburgh
Ormston, Charles (of Kelso). Letter Book.

Pennsylvania State Archives, Harrisburg, PA
'Bankruptcy File, 1785–1790'. In *RG 027 Pennsylvania's Revolutionary Governments, 1775–1790*.
Insolvent Debtors' Petitions, 1781–1815.

Philadelphia City Archives, PA
Court of Common Pleas. 'Index of Insolvency Petitions and Bonds: 1790–1868.

Online Material
Digitalpaxton.org.
'The Statutes at Large of Pennsylvania', edited by the Province and Commonwealth of Pennsylvania, www.palrb.us/stlarge.

Published Primary Sources

A friend to peace and good order. *The Rights of Caesar: A Sermon. In which the Scripture-Doctrine of Magistracy Is Opened Up and Enforced*. Edinburgh, 1795.
Abernethy, John. *Sermons on Various Subjects*, 294–324, 1751.
Barclay, Robert the Elder, and William Works with prefaces etc by William Penn. *Truth Triumphant through the Spiritual Warfare, Christian Labours and Writings Of ... R. Barclay [Collected Works. With a Preface by William Penn]*. London: Thomas Northcott, 1692.

Berriman, William. 'Sermon XIV: The Guilt and Danger of Making Haste to be Rich'. In *Christian Doctrines and Duties Explained and Recommended: Forty Sermons, Preached in the Parish Churches of St Andrew Undershaft, and Allhallows the Great: And Divers of Them, in Eton College Chapel, and Other Places*, 275–92. London, 1751.

Bradford, Samuel. *The Honest and Dishonest Ways of Getting Wealth. A Sermon Preach'd in the Parish Church of St.Mary Le Bow, on Sunday, November 20th, 1720*. London, 1720.

Brent, Charles. *Money Essay'd; or, the True Value of it Tryed. In a Sermon Preach'd before the Worshipful Society of Merchants, in the City of Bristol*. London, 1728.

Calamy, Edmund. *A Sermon at the Merchants' Lecture in Salters' Hall, on December 7th 1708, Upon Occasion of the Many Late Bankrupts*. London, 1709.

Clarke, Samuel. *One Hundred and Seventy Three Sermons, on Several Subjects*. Dublin, 1751.

Defoe, Daniel. *The Complete English Tradesman: Directing Him in the Several Parts and Progressions of Trade, from His First Entering Upon Business, to His Leaving Off ... Calculated for the Use of All Our Inland Tradesmen, as Well in the City as Country*. London: C. Rivington, 1738.

Delany, Patrick. *Twenty Sermons on Social Duties, and Their Opposite Vices*. London, 1747.

Dunbar, John R. *The Paxton Papers*. The Hague: Martinus Nijhoff, 1957.

Enfield, William. *Sermons for the Use of Families*. London, 1772.

Fiddes, Richard. *Fifty-Two Practical Discourses Preached on Several Subjects*. London, 1720.

Fleetwood, William. *Two Sermons, the One before the King ... the Other Preach'd in the City, on the Justice of Paying Debts*. London, 1718.

Foster, James. *Sermons*. London, 1744.

Fox, George. *The Line of Righteousness and Justice Stretched Forth over All Merchants*. London, 1661.

Fox, George. *A Warning to All the Merchants of London, and Such That Buy and Sell*. 1658.

Friends, Society of. *Collection of Epistles from the Yearly Meeting of Friends in London*. New York: Samuel Wood & Sons, 1821.

Gilbert, John. *A Sermon on the Sin of Stealing Custom, and the Duty of Paying Tribute*. Plymouth, 1699.

Gisborne, Thomas the Elder. *An Enquiry into the Duties of Men in the Higher and Middle Classes of Society in Great Britain*. London, 1797.

Glass, D. *Inhabitants of London within the Walls, 1695*. London: London Record Society, 1966.

Hacket, Laurence. *A Sermon Preached at St Bennet-Finct [sic] Church*. London, 1707.

Keith, George, and Protestant Episcopal Historical Society. *Collections of the Protestant Episcopal Historical Society for the Year 1851*. 1851.
Lamont, David. *Sermons on the Most Prevalent Vices*. London, 1780.
London Yearly Meeting. *Extracts from the Minutes and Advices of the Yearly Meeting of Friends Held in London from Its First Institution*. 1802.
Mandeville, Bernard. *The Fable of the Bees, Etc.* London: T. Ostell, 1806.
Milbourne, Luke. *Debtor and Creditor Made Easy: Or, the Judgement of the Unmerciful Demonstrated in a Sermon*. London, 1709.
Mun, Thomas. *England's Treasure by Forraign Trade, Or: The Balance of our Forraign Trades Is the Rule of our Treasure*. London, 1664.
N. H. *The Compleat Tradesman, or, the Exact Dealer's Daily Companion*. London, 1684.
Penn, William. *Fruits of a Father's Love: Being the Advice of William Penn to His Children*. London, 1726. First published 1669.
Penn, William. *No Cross, No Crown*. London, 1669.
Rigge, Ambrose. *A Brief and Serious Warning to Such Who Are Concerned in Commerce and Trading*. London, 1678.
Rowntree, John Stephenson. *Quakerism, Past and Present: Being an Inquiry into the Causes of its Decline in Great Britain and Ireland*. London, 1859.
Scott, William. *A Sermon on Bankruptcy, Stopping Payment, Debts, Preached at Various Churches in the City. Previously Published As: The Justice of Paying Debts. A Sermon Preach'd in the City, London 1718*. London, 1773.
Shebbeare, John. *A Letter to the People of England*. 1756.
Sheridan, William. *Practical Discourses Upon the Most Important Subjects*. London, 1720.
Smith, William. *A Brief State of the Province of Pennsylvania*. 1755.
Stebbing, Henry. *Sermons on Practical Christianity*. London, 1759.
Steele, Richard. *The Religious Tradesman, or, Plain and Serious Hints of Advice for the Tradesman's Prudent and Pious Conduct, from His Entrance into Business, to His Leaving It Off*. London, 1747.
Stubbs, J., G. Fox and R. Hubberthorn. *A Declaration from the Harmless & Innocent People of God, Called: Quakers against All Plotters and Fighters in the World. For the Removing Of the Ground of Jealousie and Suspition from Both Magistrates and People in the Kingdome, Concerinig Wars and Fightings. And Also Something in Answer to That Clause of the King's Late Proclamation, Which Mentions the Quakers, to Clear Them from the Plot and Fighting, Which Therein Is Mentioned, and for the Clearing Their Innocency. This Declaration Was Given Unto the King, Upon the 21st Day of the 11th Month, 1660*. J. Bringhust, 1684.
Unwin, William. *The Sinfulness of Buying Run Goods, Attempted to Be Shewn*. London, 1773.
Wheatland, Thomas. *Twenty-Six Practical Sermons on Various Subjects*. London, 1739.
Wilson, Thomas. *Sermons*. London, 1785.

Secondary Sources

Abend, Gabriel. *The Moral Background: An Inquiry into the History of Business Ethics*. Princeton, NJ: Princeton University Press, 2014.

Aghassian, Michel, and Keram Kenovian. 'The Armenian Merchant Network: Overall Autonomy and Local Integration'. In *Merchants, Companies and Trade. Europe and Asia in the Early Modern Era*, edited by Sushio Chaudhury and Michel Morineau, Cambridge: Cambridge University Press, 1999.

Angell, Stephen W. 'God, Christ, and the Light'. In *The Oxford Handbook of Quaker Studies*, edited by Stephen W. Angell and Pink Dandelion, 158–71. Oxford: Oxford University Press, 2013.

Ayto, John, and Judith Siefring. *From the Horse's Mouth: Oxford Dictionary of English Idioms*. Oxford: Oxford University Press, 2009.

Bacon, Margaret Hope. 'Quaker Women in Overseas Ministry'. *Quaker History* 77, no. 2 (1988): 93–109.

Bauman, Richard. *For the Reputation of Truth: Politics, Religion, and Conflict among the Pennsylvania Quakers, 1750–1800*. Baltimore and London: Johns Hopkins University Press, 1971.

Beck, William, T. Frederick Ball / Simon Dixon and Peter Daniels. *The London Friends' Meetings: Showing the Rise of the Society of Friends in London; Its Progress, and the Development of Its Discipline; with Accounts of the Various Meeting-Houses and Burial-Grounds, Their History and General Associations*. London: Pronoun Press, 2009.

Becker, Sasha, and Ludger Woessman. 'Was Weber Wrong? A Human Capital Theory of Protestant Economic History'. *Quarterly Journal of Economics* 124, no. 2 (2009): 531–96.

Beier, A. L. 'Engine of Manufacture; the Trades of London'. In *London, 1500–1700: The Making of the Metropolis*, edited by A. L. Beier and Roger Finlay. London: Longman, 1986.

Berg, Maxine. 'Women's Property and the Industrial Revolution'. *Journal of Interdisciplinary History* 34, no. 2 (1993): 233–50.

Berg, Maxine, and Elizabeth Eger (eds). *Luxury in the Eighteenth Century: Debates, Desires, and Delectable Goods*. Basingstoke: Palgrave Macmillan, 2003.

Berry, Christopher. *The Idea of Luxury: A Conceptual and Historical Investigation*. Cambridge: Cambridge University Press, 1994.

Bonfield, Lloyd. *Marriage Settlements, 1601–1740: The Adoption of the Strict Settlement*. Cambridge: Cambridge University Press, 1983.

Bosher, J. F. 'Huguenot Merchants and the Protestant International in the Seventeenth Century'. *The William and Mary Quarterly* 50, no. 1 (1995).

Botticini, Maristella, and Aloysius Siow. 'Are There Increasing Returns in Marriage Markets?'. Boston University Department of Economics, Working Papers WP 2006-050 (2006).

Bouchon, Genevieve. 'Trade in the Indian Ocean at the Dawn of the Sixteenth Century.' In *Merchants, Companies and Trade. Europe and Asia in the Early Modern Era*, edited by Sushil Chaudhury and Michel Morineau, Cambridge: Cambridge University Press, 1999.

Boulton, Jeremy. 'Clandestine Marriages in London: An Examination of a Neglected Urban Variable'. *Urban History* 20, no. 2 (1993): 191–210.

———. 'London Widowhood Revisited: The Decline of Female Remarriage in the Seventeenth and Early Eighteenth Centuries'. *Continuity and Change* 5, no. 3 (1990): 323–55.

Bouton, Terry. 'Moneyless in Pennsylvania: Privatisation and the Depression of the 1780s'. In *The Economy of Early America: Historical Perspectives and New Directions*, edited by Cathy Maston, 218–35. University Park: Pennsylvania State University Press, 2006.

Braithwaite, William Charles. *The Beginnings of Quakerism*. 2dn edn, rev. by Henry J. Cadbury. Cambridge: Cambridge University Press, 1955.

Braithwaite, William Charles, and Henry J. Cadbury. *The Second Period of Quakerism*. York: William Sessions in association with the Joseph Rowntree Charitable Trust, 1961.

Brodsky-Eliott, Vivienne. 'Single Women and the London Marriage Market: Age, Status and Mobility, 1598–1619'. In *Marriage and Society: Studies in the Social History of Marriage*, edited by R. B. Outhwaite, 81–101. New York: St Martin's Press, 1982.

Bronner, Edwin B. 'Philadelphia County Court of Quarter Sessions and Common Pleas, 1695. *American Journal of Legal History* 1, no. 1 (1957): 79–95.

Brown, Richard. *Society and Economy in Modern Britain 1700–1850*. London: Routledge, 1990.

Brown, Roger Lee. 'The Rise and Fall of the Fleet Marriages'. In *Marriage and Society: Studies in the Social History of Marriage*, edited by R. B. Outwaite. New York: St Martin's Press, 1981.

Butler, Jon. '"Gospel Order Improved": The Keithian Schism and the Exercise of Quaker Ministerial Authority in Pennsylvania'. *William and Mary Quarterly* 31, no. 3 (1974): 431–52.

Carey, Brycchan. *From Peace to Freedom: Quaker Rhetoric and the Birth of American Antislavery, 1657–1761*. New Haven, CT: Yale University Press, 2012.

Carlos, Ann, and Jessica Lamping. 'Conformity and the Certificate of Discharge: Bankruptcy in Eighteenth-Century England'. Economic History Association Working Papers, 2010.

Carlos, Ann M., Edward Kosack and Luis Castro Penarrieta. 'Bankruptcy, Discharge, and the Emergence of Debtor Rights in Eighteenth-Century England'. *Enterprise & Society* (2018): 1–32.

Carlos, Ann, and Larry Neal. 'The Micro-Foundations of the Early London Capital Market: Bank of England Shareholders During and after the South Sea Bubble, 1720–25'. *Economic History Review* 59, no. 3 (2006): 498–538.

Carroll, Kenneth L. 'A Look at the "Quaker Revival of 1756"'. *Quaker History* 65, no. 2 (1976): 63–80.

Casson, Mark. 'Entrepreneurship and Business Culture'. In *Entrepreneurship, Networks, and Modern Business*, edited by Jonathan Brown and Mary B. Rose, 30–54. Manchester: Manchester University Press, 1993.

Cazden, Elizabeth. 'Quakers, Slavery, Anti-Slavery, and Race'. In *The Oxford Handbook of Quaker Studies*, edited by Stephen W. Angell and Pink Dandelion. Oxford: Oxford University Press, 2013.

Cole, W. A. 'The Quakers and Politics, 1652–1660'. PhD thesis, University of Cambridge, 1956.

Conklin, Carli. 'A Variety of State-Level Procedures, Practices, and Policies: Arbitration in Early America'. *Journal of Dispute Resolution* 55 (2016).

Cooper, J. P. 'Patterns of Inheritance and Settlement by Great Landowners from the Fifteenth to the Eighteenth Centuries'. In *Family and Inheritance: Rural Society in Western Europe, 1200–1800*, edited by Jack Goody, Joan Thirsk and E. P. Thompson, 192–327. Cambridge: Cambridge University Press, 1979.

Crabtree, Sarah. *Holy Nation: The Transatlantic Quaker Ministry in an Age of Revolution*. Chicago: University of Chicago Press, 2015.

Dale Spencer, Carole. 'Quakers in Theological Context'. In *The Oxford Handbook of Quaker Studies*, edited by Stephen W. Angell and Pink Dandelion, 141–57. Oxford: Oxford University Press, 2013.

Dandelion, Pink, and Peter Collins. *The Quaker Condition: The Sociology of a Liberal Religion*. Newcastle: Cambridge Scholars, 2008.

Daniels, Jason. 'Protest and Participation: Reconsidering the Quaker Slave Trade in Early Eighteenth-Century Philadelphia'. *Pennsylvania History* 85, no. 2 (2018): 239–65.

Davidoff, Leonore, and Catherine Hall. *Family Fortunes: Men and Women of the English Middle Class 1780–1850*. London: Hutchinson, 1987.

Davies, Adrian. *The Quakers in English Society, 1655–1725*. Oxford: Clarendon Press, 2000.

Davies, Kathleen. 'Continuity and Change in Literary Advice on Marriage'. In *Marriage and Society: Studies in the Social History of Marriage*, edited by R. B. Outhwaite, 58–80. New York: St Martin's Press, 1981.

De Krey, Gary Stuart. *A Fractured Society: The Politics of London in the First Age of Party 1688–1715*. Oxford: Clarendon Press, 1985.

———. 'Trade, Religion, and Politics in London in the Reign of William III'. Doctoral thesis, 1979.

Dixon, Rosemary. 'Sermons in Print 1660–1700'. In *The Oxford Handbook of the Early Modern Sermon*, edited by Peter McCullough, Hugh Adlington and Emma Rhatigan, 460–79. Oxford: Oxford University Press, 2011.
Dixon, Simon. 'The Life and Times of Peter Briggins'. *Quaker Studies* 10, no. 2 (2006).
———. 'Quaker Communities in London, 1667–c .1714'. Doctoral thesis, University of London, 2006.
Doan, Petra L., and Elizabeth P. Kamphausen. 'Quakers and Sexuality'. In *The Oxford Handbook of Quaker Studies*, edited by Stephen W. Angell and Pink Dandelion, 445–47. Oxford: Oxford University Press, 2013.
Doerflinger, Thomas M. *A Vigorous Spirit of Enterprise: Merchants and Economic Development in Revolutionary Philadelphia*. Chapel Hill: University of North Carolina Press, 1986.
Dudley, Leonard, and Ulrich Blum. 'Religion and Economic Growth: Was Weber Right?'. *Journal of Evolutionary Economics* 11, no. 2 (2003): 207–30.
Duffy, Ian P. H. *Bankruptcy and Insolvency in London during the Industrial Revolution*. New York and London: Garland, 1985.
Dyer, Jeffrey H., and Wujin Chu. 'The Role of Trustworthiness in Reducing Transaction Costs and Improving Performance: Empirical Evidence from the United States, Japan, and Korea'. *Organization Science* 14, no. 1 (2003): 57–68.
Earle, Peter. *The Making of the English Middle Class: Business, Society and Family Life in London, 1660–1730*. London: Methuen, 1989.
East, Robert Abraham. *Business Enterprise in the American Revolutionary Era*. New York: AMS Press, 1969.
Egnal, Marc. *New World Economies: The Growth of the Thirteen Colonies and Early Canada*. New York and Oxford: Oxford University Press, 1998.
Emden, Paul Herman. *Quakers in Commerce: A Record of Business Achievement*. London: Sampson Low & Co., 1940.
Erickson, Amy Louise. 'Common Law versus Common Practice: The Use of Marriage Settlements in Early Modern England'. *Economic History Review* 43, no. 1 (1990): 21–39.
Field, Jacob F. *Clandestine Weddings at the Fleet Prison, c. 1710–1750: Who Married There?*, 2017.
Fincham, Andrew. 'Faith in Numbers: Re-Quantifying the English Quaker Population During the Long Eighteenth Century'. *Religions* 10, no. 2 (2019): 83.
Finn, Margot C. *The Character of Credit: Personal Debt in English Culture, 1740–1914*. Cambridge and New York: Cambridge University Press, 2003.
Fischer, Paul. 'Bankruptcy in Early Modern German Territories'. In *The History of Bankruptcy: Economic, Social and Cultural Implications in Early Modern Europe*, edited by Max Thomas Safley. New York: Routledge, 2013.

Francis, Keith A. 'Sermons: Themes and Developments'. In *The Oxford Handbook of the British Sermon*, 31–46. Oxford: Oxford University Press, 2012.

Froide, Amy M. 'The Religious Lives of Singlewomen in the Anglo-Atlantic World: Quaker Missionaries, Protestant Nuns, and Covert Catholics'. *Women, Religion, and the Atlantic World (1600–1800)* 12 (2009): 60.

Frost, J. William. 'The Affirmation Controversy and Religious Liberty'. In *The World of William Penn*, edited by Richard S. Dunn and Mary Maples Dunn, 303–22. Philadelphia: University of Pennsylvania Press, 1986.

Frost, Jerry William. *A Perfect Freedom: Religious Liberty in Pennsylvania*. Cambridge: Cambridge University Press, 1990.

Gauci, Perry. *Emporium of the World: The Merchants of London, 1660–1800*. London: Hambledon Continuum, 2007.

———. *The Politics of Trade: The Overseas Merchant in State and Society, 1660–1720*. Oxford: Oxford University Press, 2001.

Geiter, Mary K. 'Notes and Documents: London Merchants and the Launching of Pennsylvania'. *Pennsylvania Magazine of History and Biography* 121, no. 1/2 (1997): 101–22.

Gelderblom, Oscar, and Regina Grafe. 'The Rise, Persistence and Decline of Merchant Guilds: Re-Thinking the Comparative Study of Commercial Institutions in Pre-Modern Europe', *Journal of Interdisciplinary History* XL, no. 4 (2010): 477–511.

Gelderblom, Oscar. *Cities of Commerce: The Institutional Foundations of International Trade in the Low Countries, 1250–1650*. Princeton: Princeton University Press, 2013.

Gerbner, Katharine. 'Antislavery in Print: The Germantown Protest, the "Exhortation", and the Seventeenth-Century Quaker Debate on Slavery'. *Early American Studies* (2011): 552–75.

Gibson, William. 'The British Sermon 1689–1901: Quantities, Performance, and Culture'. In *The Oxford Handbook of the British Sermon, 1689–1901*, edited by Keith C. Francis and William Gibson. Oxford: Oxford University Press, 2012.

Glaisyer, Natasha. *The Culture of Commerce in England, 1660–1720*. London: Royal Historical Society, 2006.

Gleason, Philip. 'Trouble in the Colonial Melting Pot'. *Journal of American Ethnic History* 20, no. 1 (2000): 3–17.

Goldberg, Jessica. *Trade and Institutions in the Medieval Mediterranean: The Geniza Merchants and Their Business World*. Cambridge; New York: Cambridge University Press, 2012.

Goode, Michael. 'A Failed Peace: The Friendly Association and the Pennsylvania Backcountry During the Seven Years' War'. *Pennsylvania Magazine of History and Biography* 136, no. 4 (2012): 472–74.

Gräfe, Regina. 'On the Spatial Nature of Institutions and the Institutional Nature of Personal Networks in the Spanish Atlantic'. *Culture and History Digital Journal* 3, no. 1 (2014).

Grassby, Richard. *Kinship and Capitalism: Marriage, Family, and Business in the English Speaking World, 1580–1720*. Cambridge: Woodrow Wilson Center Press and Cambridge University Press, 2001.

Greif, Avner, Paul Milgrom, and Barry Weingast. 'Coordination, Commitment and Enforcement: The Case of the Merchant Guild'. *The Journal of Political Economy* 102, no. 4 (1994): 745–76.

Greif, Avner. *Institutions and the Path to the Modern Economy. Lessons from Medieval Trade, Political Economy of Institutions and Decisions*. Cambridge; New York: Cambridge University Press, 2006.

Grubb, Isabel. *Quakerism and Industry before 1800*. London: Williams and Norgate, 1930.

Guinnane, Timothy. 'Trust: A Concept Too Many'. *Jahrbuch fur Wirtschaftsgeschichte* 1 (2005): 77–92.

Gyani, Gabor. 'Middle-Class Kinship in Nineteenth-Century Hungary'. In *Kinship in Europe: Approaches to Long-Term Developments (1300–1900)*, edited by David Warren Sabean and Simon Teuscher, 284–300. New York: Berghahn Books, 2007.

Haagen, Paul. 'Eighteenth-Century English Society and the Debt Law'. In *Social Control and the State*, edited by Stanley Cohen and Andrew Scull, 222–47. Oxford: Palgrave Macmillan, 1983.

Haggerty, Sheryllynne. *'Merely for Money'?: Business Culture in the British Atlantic, 1750–1815*. Liverpool: Liverpool University Press, 2012.

Hall, David J. 'What Should Eighteenth Century Quakers Have Read?'. *Journal of the Friends Historical Society* 62, no. 2 (2018).

Hamilton, Gillian, and Aloysius Siow. 'Class, Gender and Marriage'. *Review of Economic Dynamics* 10, no. 4 (2007): 549–75.

Hamm, Thomas. '"Chipping at the Landmarks of our Fathers": The Decline of the Testimony against Hireling Ministry in the Nineteenth Century'. *Quaker Studies* 13, no. 2 (2009): 136–59.

Hancock, David. 'The Trouble with Networks: Managing the Scots' Early Modern Madeira Trade'. *The Business History Review* 79, no. 3 (2005): 467–91.

———. 'A Revolution in Trade: Wine Distribution and the Development of the Infrastructure of the Atlantic Market Economy, 1703–1807'. In *The Early Modern Atlantic Economy*, edited by John McCusker and Kenneth Morgan. Cambridge: Cambridge University Press, 2000.

Hannah, Leslie. 'The Moral Economy of Business: An Historical Perspective on Ethics and Efficiency'. In *Civil Histories: Essays in Honour of Sir Keith Thomas*, edited by Peter Burke, Brian Harrison and Paul Slack. Oxford: Oxford University Press, 2000.

Hirschman, Albert O. *The Passions and the Interests: Political Arguments for Capitalism before Its Triumph*. Princeton, NJ: Princeton University Press, 1977.

Hoppit, Julian. 'Attitudes to Credit in Britain, 1680–1790'. *Historical Journal* 32, no. 2 (1990).

———. *Risk and Failure in English Business 1700–1800*. Cambridge: Cambridge University Press, 1987.

Horle, Craig W. *The Quakers and the English Legal System, 1660–1688*. Philadelphia: University of Pennsylvania Press, 1988.

Houlbrooke, Ralph A. *The English Family, 1450–1700*. London: Longman, 1984.

Hufton, Olwen H. *The Prospect before Her: A History of Women in Western Europe. Vol.1, 1500–1800*. London: HarperCollins, 1995.

Hundert, Gershom D. 'The Role of the Jews in Commerce in Early Modern Poland-Lithuania'. In *Merchant Networks in the Early Modern World: 1450–1800*, edited by Sanjay Subrahmanyam. Aldershot: Ashgate Variorum, 1996.

Hunt, Margaret. 'The Middling Sort: Commerce, Gender, and the Family in England, 1680–1780'. Berkeley: University of California Press, 1996.

Hurwich, Judith J. 'Marriage Strategy among the German Nobility, 1400–1699'. *Journal of Interdisciplinary History* 29, no. 2 (1998): 169–95.

———. 'The Social Origins of the Early Quakers'. *Past & Present* 48 (1961).

Ingram, Martin. 'Spousal Litigation in the English Ecclesiastical Courts, c. 1350–1640'. In *Marriage and Society: Studies in the Social History of Marriage*, edited by R. B. Outhwaite, 35–57. New York: St Martin's Press, 1981.

Jarnagin, Laura. *A Confluence of Transatlantic Networks: Elites, Capitalism, and Confederate Migration to Brazil*. Tuscaloosa, Al.: University of Alabama Press, 2008.

Jensen, Arthur Louis. *The Maritime Commerce of Colonial Philadelphia*. Madison: State Historical Society of Wisconsin, for the Department of History, University of Wisconsin, 1963.

Jha, Saumitra. 'Trade, Institutions and Ethnic Tolerance: Evidence from South Asia'. *American Political Science Review* 107, no. 4 (2013): 806–32.

Jones, Rufus M. *The Later Periods of Quakerism*. Macmillan, 1921.

Juterszenka, S. 'Meeting Friends and Doing Business: Quaker Missionary and Commercial Activities in Europe, 1655–1720'. In *German Historical Institute London, Bulletin, Supplement No. 2: Cosmopolitan Networks in Commerce and Society, 1660–1914*, edited by Andreas Gestrich and Margit Schulte-Beerbuehl. London: German Historical Institute, 2011.

Kadens, Emily. 'The Last Bankrupt Hanged: Balancing Incentives in the Development of Bankruptcy Law'. *Duke Law Journal* 59, no. 7 (2010).

Kirby, Ethyn Williams. 'The Quakers' Efforts to Secure Civil and Religious Liberty, 1660–96'. *Journal of Modern History* 7, no. 4 (1935): 401–21.

Kirby, Maurice. 'Quakerism, Entrepreneurship and the Family Firm in North-East England, 1780–1860'. In *Entrepreneurship, Networks and Modern Buisness*, edited by Jonathan Brown and Mary B. Rose, 105–26. Manchester: Manchester University Press, 1993.

Klepp, Susan E. 'Fragmented Knowledge: Questions in Regional Demographic History'. *Proceedings of the American Philosophical Society* 133, no. 2 (1989): 223–33.

Landa, Janet Tai. *Trust, Ethnicity, and Identity: Beyond the New Institutional Economics of Ethnic Trading Networks, Contract Law, and Gift-Exchange*. Ann Arbor: University of Michigan Press, 1994.

Landes, Jordan. *London Quakers in the Trans-Atlantic World: The Creation of an Early Modern Community*. 2015.

———. 'The Role of London in the Creation of a Quaker Transatlantic Community in the Late Seventeenth and Eighteenth Centuries'. Doctoral thesis, University of London, 2011.

Langford, Paul. *A Polite and Commercial People: England 1727–1783*. Oxford: Oxford University Press, 1989, rev. edn 1998.

Laussat, A. *An Essay on Equity in Pennsylvania*. Lawbook Exchange, 1826/2002.

Lewis, Lawrence. 'The Courts of Pennsylvania in the Seventeenth Century'. *Pennsylvania Magazine of History and Biography* 5, no. 2 (1881): 141–90.

Liverant, Spencer R., and Walter H. Hitchler. 'A History of Equity in Pennsylvania'. *Dickinson Law Review* 37 (1933): 159–61.

Lloyd, Arnold. *Quaker Social History, 1669–1738*. London: Longman, 1948.

Lloyd, William H. 'The Courts of Pennsylvania in the Eighteenth Century Prior to the Revolution'. *University of Pennsylvania Law Review and American Law Register* 56, no. 1 (1908): 28–51.

Mann, Bruce H. *Republic of Debtors: Bankruptcy in the Age of American Independence*. Cambridge, MA, and London: Harvard University Press, 2002.

Marietta, Jack D. 'Conscience, the Quaker Community, and the French and Indian War'. *Pennsylvania Magazine of History and Biography* 95, no. 1 (1971): 3–27.

———. *The Reformation of American Quakerism, 1748–1783*. Philadelphia: University of Pennsylvania Press, 1984.

Marietta, Jack D., and G. S. Rowe. *Troubled Experiment: Crime and Justice in Pennsylvania, 1682–1800*. Philadelphia: University of Pennsylvania Press, 2006.

Matthew, H. C. G., and Brian Harrison. *Oxford Dictionary of National Biography*. New edn. Oxford: Oxford University Press, 2004.

McCusker, John J., and Russell R. Menard. *The Economy of British America, 1607–1789*. 2nd edn. Chapel Hill: University of North Carolina Press, 1986.

McEvily, Bill, Vincenzo Perrone and Akbar Zaheer. 'Trust as an Organizing Principle'. *Organization Science* 14, no. 1 (2003): 91–103.

Milgrom, Paul, Douglass North, and Barry Weingast. 'The Role of Institutions in the Revival of Trade: The Law Merchant, Private Judges and the Champagne Fairs'. *Economics and Politics* 2, no. 1 (1990): 1–23.

Miller, John. '"A Suffering People": English Quakers and their Neighbours, c. 1650–c. 1700'. *Past and Present* 188, no. 1 (2005): 71–103.

Milligan, Edward H. *Biographical Dictionary of British Quakers in Commerce and Industry 1775–1920*. York: Sessions Book Trust, 2007.

Minns, Chris, and Patrick Wallis. 'Why Did (Pre-)Industrial Firms Train? Premiums and Apprenticeship Contracts in Eighteenth Century England'. LSE Economic History Working Paper No. 155/11 (2011).

Moor, Barrington. *Moral Aspects of Economic Growth, and Other Essays*. Ithaca, NY: Cornell University Press, 1998.

Moore, Rosemary. 'Seventeenth-Century Context and Quaker Beginnings'. In *The Oxford Handbook of Quaker Studies*, edited by Pink Dandelion and Stephen W. Angell. Oxford: Oxford University Press, 2013.

Moore, Rosemary Anne. *The Light in Their Consciences: Early Quakers in Britain, 1646–1666*. University Park: Pennsylvania State University Press, 2000.

Morgan, Kenneth. *An American Quaker in the British Isles: The Travel Journals of Jabez Maud Fisher, 1775–1779*. London: Published for the British Academy by Oxford University Press, 1992.

———. *Slavery, Atlantic Trade and the British Economy, 1660–1800*. Cambridge: Cambridge University Press, 2000.

Muldrew, Craig. *The Economy of Obligation: The Culture of Credit and Social Relations in Early Modern England*. Basingstoke: Macmillan, 1998.

Murphy, Andrew R. 'Persecuting Quakers? Liberty and Toleration in Early Pennsylvania'. In *The First Prejudice: Religious Tolerance and Intolerance in Early America*, edited by C. Beneke and C. S. Grenda, 143–65. Philadelphia: University of Pennsylvania Press, 2011.

Murphy, Anne L. *The Origins of English Financial Markets: Investment and Speculation before the South Sea Bubble*. Cambridge: Cambridge University Press, 2009.

Nash, Gary B. 'The Early Merchants of Philadelphia: The Formation and Disintegration of a Founding Elite'. In *The World of William Penn*, edited by Richard S. Dunn and Mary Maples Dunn, 337–62. Philadelphia: University of Pennsylvania Press, 1986.

———. 'The Free Society of Traders and the Early Politics of Pennsylvania'. *Pennsylvania Magazine of History and Biography* 89, no. 2 (1965): 147–73.

———. *Quakers and Politics: Pennsylvania, 1681–1726*. New edn. Boston: Northeastern University Press, 1993.

———. 'Slaves and Slaveowners in Colonial Philadelphia'. *William and Mary Quarterly* (1973): 223–56.

Newman, Edwina. 'Quakers and the Family'. In *The Oxford Handbook of Quaker Studies*, edited by Pink Dandelion and Stephen W. Angell, 434–44. Oxford: Oxford University Press, 2013.

Newton, Gill. 'Clandestine Marriage in Early Modern London: When, Where and Why?'. *Continuity and Change 29, no. 2* (2014).

North, Douglass and Robert Thomas. *The Rise of the Western World: A New Economic History*. New York: Cambridge University Press, 1973.

Norton, Mary Beth. 'Gender and Defamation in Seventeenth-Century Maryland'. *William and Mary Quarterly* (1987): 4–39.

Offutt, William Jr. 'The Atlantic Rules: The Legalistic Turn in Colonial British America'. In *The Creation of the British Atlantic World: Anglo-America in the Trans-Atlantic World*, edited by Elizabeth Mancke and Carole Shammas, 160–81. Baltimore: Johns Hopkins University Press, 2005.

Offutt, William M. *Of 'Good Laws' and 'Good Men': Law and Society in the Delaware Valley, 1680–1710*. Urbana: University of Illinois Press, 1995.

Okazaki, Tetsuji. 'The Role of the Merchant Coalition in Pre-Modern Japanese Economic Development: An Historical Institutional Analysis'. CIRJE Discussion Paper F 284 (2004).

Olson, Alison. 'The Lobbying of London Quakers for Pennsylvania Friends'. *Pennsylvania Magazine of History and Biography* 117, no. 3 (1993): 131–52.

———. 'The Pamphlet War over the Paxton Boys'. *Pennsylvania Magazine of History and Biography* 123, no. 1/2 (1999): 31–55.

Palmer, Richard. 'Thomas Corbyn, Quaker Merchant'. *Medical History* 33 (1989): 371–76.

Pearson, Karl. *The Life, Letters and Labours of Francis Galton*. Cambridge, 1914.

Peters, Kate. 'The Dissemination of Quaker Pamphlets in the 1650s'. In *Not Dead Things*, 211–28. Leiden: Brill, 2013.

———. *Print Culture and the Early Quakers*. Cambridge and New York: Cambridge University Press, 2005.

Pressnell, L. S. *Country Banking in the Industrial Revolution*. Oxford: Clarendon Press, 1956.

Price, Jacob. *Capital and Credit in British Overseas Trade: The View from the Chesapeake, 1700–1776*. Cambridge, MA, and London: Harvard University Press, 1980.

———. 'The Great Quaker Business Families of Eighteenth Century London'. In *Overseas Trade and Traders: Essays on Some Commercial, Financial and Political Challenges Facing British Atlantic Merchants, 1660–1775*, edited by Jacob Price. Farnham: Ashgate, 1996.

———. 'What Did Merchants Do?'. *Journal of Economic History* 49, no. 2 (1989): 267–84.

——— (ed.). *Overseas Trade and Traders: Essays on Some Commercial, Financial, and Political Challenges Facing British Atlantic Merchants, 1660–1775*. Aldershot: Variorum, 1996.
Price, Jacob M., and G. E. Clemens Paul. 'A Revolution of Scale in Overseas Trade: British Firms in the Chesapeake Trade, 1675–1775'. *Journal of Economic History* 47, no. 1 (1987): 1–43.
Principe, Lawrence M., and William R. Newman. 'Some Problems with the History of Alchemy in Early Modern Europe'. In *Secrets of Nature: Astrology and Alchemy in Early Modern Europe*, edited by William R. Newman and Anthony Grafton, 285–434. Cambridge, MA: MIT Press, 2001.
Prior, Ann, and Maurice Kirby. 'The Society of Friends and the Family Firm, 1700–1830'. *Business History* 35, no. 4 (1993).
Pullin, Naomi. *Female Friends and the Making of Transatlantic Quakerism, 1650–1750*. Cambridge: Cambridge University Press, 2018.
Rabuzzi, Daniel. 'Eighteenth-Century Commercial Mentalities as Reflected and Projected in Business Handbooks'. *Eighteenth Century Studies* 29, no. 2 (1995–96): 169–89.
Raistrick, Arthur. *Quakers in Science and Industry: Being an Account of the Quaker Contributions to Science and Industry during the 17th and 18th Centuries*. London: Bannisdale Press, 1950.
Reay, Barry. 'Popular Hostility Towards Quakers in Mid-Seventeenth-Century England'. *Social History* 5, no. 3 (1980): 387–407.
———. *The Quakers and the English Revolution*. London: Temple Smith, 1985.
Rediker, Marcus. *The Fearless Benjamin Lay: The Quaker Dwarf Who Became the First Revolutionary Abolitionist*. Boston: Beacon Press, 2017.
Richards, W. A. 'The Birmingham Gun Manufactory of Farmer & Galton and the Slave Trade'. MA thesis, University of Birmingham, 1972.
Rigney, James. 'Sermons into Print'. In *The Oxford Handbook of the Early Modern Sermon*, edited by Hugh Adlington, Peter McCullough and Emma Rhatigan, 198–212. Oxford: Oxford University Press, 2011.
Rowntree, John Stephenson. *Quakerism, Past and Present: Being an Inquiry into the Causes of Its Decline in Great Britain and Ireland*. London, 1859.
Sabean, David Warren, Simon Teuscher and Jon Mathieu. *Kinship in Europe: Approaches to Long-Term Development (1300–1900)*. Oxford: Berghahn Books, 2007.
Sainsbury, John. 'John Wilkes, Debt, and Patriotism'. *Journal of British Studies* 34, no. 2 (1995).
Salmon, Marylynn. 'Notes and Documents: The Court Records of Philadelphia, Bucks, and Berks Counties in the Seventeenth and Eighteenth Centuries'. *Pennsylvania Magazine of History and Biography* 107, no. 2 (1983): 249–91.
Satia, Priya. *Empire of Guns: The Violent Making of the Industrial Revolution*. Stanford, CA: Stanford University Press, 2019.

Schwarz, Leonard. 'London Apprentices in the Seventeenth Century: Some Problems'. *Local Population Studies* 38 (1987): 18–22.
Sekora, John. *Luxury: The Concept in Western Thought, Eden to Smollett.* Baltimore and London: Johns Hopkins University Press, 1977.
Shepherd, James F., and Gary M. Walton. *Shipping, Maritime Trade, and the Economic Development of Colonial North America.* London: Cambridge University Press, 1972.
Silver, Peter Rhoads. *Our Savage Neighbors: How Indian War Transformed Early America.* New York: W. W. Norton, 2008.
Skidmore, Gil. *Strength in Weakness: Writings of Eighteenth-Century Quaker Women.* Walnut Creek, CA: Altamira Press, 2003.
Smith, Billy G. 'Death and Life in a Colonial Immigrant City: A Demographic Analysis of Philadelphia'. *Journal of Economic History* 37, no. 4 (1977): 863–89.
Smith, S. D., and T. R. Wheeley. '"Requisites of a Considerable Trade": The Letters of Robert Plumsted, Atlantic Merchant, 1752–58'. *English Historical Review* 124, no. 508 (2009): 545–70.
Smolenski, John. 'Embodied Politics: The Paxton Uprising and the Gendering of Civic Culture in Colonial Pennsylvania'. *Early American Studies: An Interdisciplinary Journal* 14, no. 2 (2016): 377–407.
———. *Friends and Strangers: The Making of a Creole Culture in Colonial Pennsylvania.* Philadelphia: University of Pennsylvania Press, 2011.
Soderlund, Jean R. *Quakers and Slavery: A Divided Spirit.* Princeton, NJ: Princeton University Press, 2014.
———. 'Women's Authority in Pennsylvania and New Jersey Quaker Meetings, 1680–1760'. *William and Mary Quarterly* (1987): 722–49.
Spaulding, John Gordon. *Pulpit Publications, 1660–1782.* New York: Ross Publishing, 1996.
Stagg, R. E. 'Friends' Queries and General Advices: A Survey of their Development in London Yearly Meeting, 1682–1860'. *Journal of the Friends Historical Society* 49 (1961): 209–48.
Staves, Susan. *Married Women's Separate Property in England, 1660–1833.* Cambridge, MA, and London: Harvard University Press, 1990.
Stevens, Sylvia. 'Travelling Ministry'. In *The Oxford Handbook of Quaker Studies*, edited by Pink Dandelion and Stephen W. Angell. Oxford: Oxford University Press, 2013.
Stevenson, Bill. 'The Social Integration of Post-Restoration Dissenters, 1660–1725'. In *The World of Rural Dissenters 1520–1725*, edited by Margaret Spufford. Cambridge: Cambridge University Press, 1995.
Stirk, Nigel. 'Arresting Ambiguity: The Shifting Geographies of a London Debtors' Sanctuary in the Eighteenth Century'. *Social History* 25, no. 3 (2000).

Stringham, Edward. 'The Extralegal Development of Securities Trading in Seventeenth-Century Amsterdam'. *The Quarterly Review of Economics and Finance* 43, no. 2 (2003): 321–44.

Stone, Lawrence, and Jeanne C. Fawcier Stone. *An Open Elite? England 1540–1880*. Oxford: Clarendon Press, 1984.

Tadmor, Naomi. 'Early Modern English Kinship in the Long Run: Reflections on Continuity and Change'. *Continuity and Change* 25, no. 1 (2010): 15–48.

Tai Landa, Janet. 'A theory of the ethnically homogeneous middleman group: an institutional alternative to contract law'. *The Journal of Legal Studies*, Vol. 10 (1981), 349–362.

Tawney, R. H. *Religion and the Rise of Capitalism: A Historical Study*. London: John Murray, 1926.

Taylor, James. 'The Impact of Pauper Settlement 1691–1834'. *Past & Present* 73 (1976).

Thayer, Theodore. 'The Friendly Association'. *Pennsylvania Magazine of History and Biography* 67, no. 4 (1943): 356–76.

Thomason, Laura E. *The Matrimonial Trap: Eighteenth-Century Women Writers Redefine Marriage*. Lewisburg, PA: Bucknell University Press, 2013.

Todd, Barbara. 'Demographic Determinism and Female Agency: The Remarrying Widow Reconsidered ... Again'. *Continuity and Change* 9, no. 3 (1994): 421–50.

Tolles, Frederick Barnes. *Meeting House and Counting House: The Quaker Merchants of Colonial Philadelphia, 1682–1763*. Chapel Hill: University of North Carolina Press, 1948.

Tolles, Fredrick. 'The Trans-Atlantic Quaker Community in the Seventeenth Century'. *Huntington Library Quarterly* 14, no. 3 (1951).

Trivellato, Francesca. *The Familiarity of Strangers: The Sephardic Diaspora, Livorno, and Cross-Cultural Trade in the Early Modern Period*. New Haven, Conn.; London: Yale University Press, 2009.

Vann, Richard T. *The Social Development of English Quakerism, 1655–1755*. Cambridge, MA: Harvard University Press, 1969.

Vann, Richard T., and David Eversley. *Friends in Life and Death: The British and Irish Quakers in the Demographic Transition, 1650–1900*. Cambridge: Cambridge University Press, 1992.

Wallis, Patrick. 'Apprenticeship and Training in Premodern England'. *Journal of Economic History* 68, no. 3 (2008): 832–61.

Walvin, James. *The Quakers: Money and Morals*. London: John Murray, 1997.

Ward, Madeleine. 'The Christian Quaker: George Keith and the Keithian Controversy'. *Brill Research Perspectives in Quaker Studies* 2, no. 1 (2019): 1–101.

Ward, Matthew C. 'The "Peaceable Kingdom" Destroyed: The Seven Years' War and the Transformation of the Pennsylvania Backcountry'. *Pennsylvania History: A Journal of Mid-Atlantic Studies* 74, no. 3 (2007): 247–79.

Wax, Darold D. 'Quaker Merchants and the Slave Trade in Colonial Pennsylvania'. *Pennsylvania Magazine of History and Biography* 86, no. 2 (1962): 143–59.

Weber, Max. *The Protestant Work Ethic and the Spirit of Capitalism*. New York: Charles Scribner's Sons, 1958.

Wellenreuther, Hermann. 'The Political Dilemma of the Quakers in Pennsylvania, 1681–1748'. *Pennsylvania Magazine of History and Biography* 94, no. 2 (1970): 135–72.

Wells, Robert V., and Michael Zuckerman. 'Quaker Marriage Patterns in a Colonial Perspective'. *William and Mary Quarterly* (1972): 415–42.

Welter, Friederike. 'All You Need Is Trust? A Critical Review of the Trust and Entrepreneurship Literature'. *International Small Business Journal* 30, no. 3 (2012): 193–212.

Wennerlind, Carl. *Casualties of Credit: The English Financial Revolution, 1620–1720*. Cambridge, MA, and London: Harvard University Press, 2011.

Williams, Eric Eustace. *Capitalism and Slavery*. 1944.

Wrigley, E. A. 'A Simple Model of London's Importance in Changing English Society and Economy 1650–1750'. *Past & Present* 37 (1967): 44–70.

Wulf, Karin A. *Not All Wives: Women of Colonial Philadelphia*. Ithaca, NY: Cornell University Press, 2000.

Zahedieh, Nuala. *The Capital and the Colonies: London and the Atlantic Economy, 1660–1700*. Cambridge: Cambridge University Press, 2010.

———. 'Making Mercantilism Work: London Merchants and the Atlantic Trade in the Seventeenth Century'. *Transactions of the Royal Historical Society, Sixth Series* 9 (1999).

Index

Aberdeen, Aberdeenshire 116
Abernethy, John 66
abolitionism 50–1, 175–6
accountants 56–7
advice manuals 56–8, 74
Affirmation Bill (1695) 29
African Company, Royal 48, 49–50, 115
Africans, enslaved 31–2, 40–3, 47, 48, 50, 51–2, 95, 119, 175–6
alchemy 105–7
America, United States of 125, 158
American Revolution (War of Independence) 19, 39, 42, 49, 94 n.50, 120, 121, 130
Anglicans 25, 26, 27, 42, 45, 58, 66, 67, 69, 72, 136–7, 138, 150, 159
Anne, queen of the United Kingdom 102
annual epistles 9, 28, 30, 59–60, 96
apothecaries 37, 49
apprentices 36, 59, 76, 78, 95, 110, 142, 153
  marriages of 151–2, 154
Arnold, Samuel 88
astrology 37
attachment, writs of 122

Bangs, John 108, 110
Bank of England 101–2
banking 6, 12, 14, 139, 162
bankruptcy 11, 12, 13, 21, 45, 48, 63–4, 67, 87, 91, 92, 101, 102–3, 104, 107–9, 110–16, 118, 122–3, 126–7, 129, 134, 176
banns 136–7
Baptists 26, 31
Barbados 26, 31, 40, 43, 49, 50, 51, 54, 112, 156
Barclay, David, of Cateaton 113, 114
Barclay, David (the Elder) 114
Barclay, David (the Younger) 114, 162

Barclay, John 114
Barclay, Robert 135
Barclay's Bank 139, 177
Barking, Essex 114
Bath, Somerset 90
Benezet, Anthony 51, 175
Bentley, John 92 n.48
Benwell, Thomas 111 n.50
Berriman, William 68
Bezer, John 132
Bible, Quaker use of 24, 44, 51, 61, 64, 66–7
Bilbao, Spain 4
Birmingham 48, 115, 116, 143
births, registration of 33, 78, 112 n.52, 152, 179
Bishop, Sarah 88 n.39, 99 n.17
Board of Trade 156, 158, 162
Boon, George 143
Boston, Massachusetts 30, 49
Braddock, Edward 160–1, 163
Bradford, John 66, 67
Bradford, William 50
Brent, Charles 73
Brewster, Susannah 82
Brientnall, Hannah 86 n.29
Briggins, Peter 36–7, 83
Briggs, Dorothy 89 n.40
Bristol 20, 26, 73, 113
Brookes, William 94
Broom, Elizabeth 88, 89 n.40
burials 33, 40, 78, 112, 179
business ethics, Quaker 5, 6–10, 20, 21, 55–75, 176

Calamy, Edmund 67, 73
Calvinism 55–6
Canons of the Church of England (1604) 27, 136, 137
capitalism 55

Carlisle, Cumbria 136
Carpenter, Samuel 42, 54
Carro (enslaved African) 51
Catholics 23, 26, 27, 136
celibacy 16, 17, 18, 19, 146
certificates 17, 29, 34, 76, 78, 79, 80, 103, 110, 114, 115, 117–18, 130–4, 136, 139
Chancery, Court of 37, 106, 112
Charles I, king of England 23
Charles II, king of England 27, 37, 101
China 57
chocolate 112
Civil War, English 23–4
Clapp, John 88 n.39, 99
Clark, Jane 109
Clark, William 104 n.17, 109
Clarke, Samuel 69
Claypoole, Edward 40
Claypoole, James 40, 54
Clerk, George 88 n.39, 99 n.17
Clifford, Thomas 49 n.99
clothiers 36
Coachman, Steven 84
Cocke, Obed 141
Cockfield, Zachariah 82
coffee 112
Company of Merchants of Great Britain 47
Conestoga (native American people) 164
confiscation 29, 36
Connecticut 49, 123
consanguinity *see* endogamy, marital
consumer revolution 32, 57
contracts 1, 3, 4, 7, 10, 12, 14, 63, 143, 172, 176
Conventicle Act (1664) 27, 36
Cooper, Elizabeth 89 n.40
Cooper, Thomas 132 n.47
Corbett, Thomas 136
Corbyn, Thomas 49
Cork, Ireland 47
Cornwall 47
cotton 57
courts 4, 31, 44, 45, 46, 135
coverture 19, 142, 143
Coysgarne, Joseph (the Elder) 113–14
Coysgarne, Joseph (the Younger) 113–14
Crawley, William 108
creolization 43
Cresson, John 125
Crew, John 130

Crofton, Richard 84
Cromwell, Oliver 23
Curaçao 53
currency 110, 156, 159, 172
customs and excise 64, 65, 66, 68, 71–2, 97, 179

Danzig 28
Darby, Pennsylvania 130
debtors, imprisonment of 103, 108, 122
debts, settlement of 5, 7, 10–12, 14, 20, 37, 45, 61–3, 66, 67, 68, 72, 78, 86, 88, 91, 94, 99, 101, 103, 104–5, 107, 108, 109–10, 111, 112, 115, 116, 117, 118, 121, 122–4, 125–6, 128, 129, 130–4, 142, 148, 172, 175
Defoe, Daniel 9, 67, 72, 74, 109
deism 96
Delany, Patrick 68, 72
Delaware 17, 37, 38, 41, 43, 81, 95
Delaware Indians *see* Lenni Lenape
denial, testimony of 77, 82, 85, 86–7, 88, 91, 93, 101, 104, 110, 124, 125, 128–9, 148, 173, 174, 177
Dickinson, Jonathan 40, 51–2
disciplinary proceedings 76, 77, 79, 85, 148 *see also* disownment
Discipline, Book of 81, 85, 96, 155
'Disorderly Walkers' 76, 81, 83, 84, 85, 87, 94, 99, 107, 108
disownment 10–12, 18, 22, 42, 44, 45, 50, 51, 77, 82–3, 84–6, 87–95, 104, 105, 107–12, 113 n.55, 114–15, 124, 125–30, 134, 148, 150, 153, 161, 173–6
divine right of kings 23
Draper, Joseph 174 n.8
Drinker, Henry 49
drunkenness 69, 80, 87, 92, 94, 96, 99, 105, 125, 128, 129, 149, 178
Dunn Creek, North Carolina 130
Duquesne, Fort (Pittsburgh) 160, 163, 171
Durston, Edmund 95
Dury, Dinah 82
Dutch Republic *see* Netherlands

East India Company 13, 57, 88, 89, 95, 101
Eccleston, John 114
ejections of ministers 27
Eliot, John 47, 90–1, 92
Eliot, John III 139

INDEX

Eliot, Philip   139, 140–1, 142, 144, 147–8
endogamy, marital   5, 14–15, 16, 20, 21, 22, 135–54, 176 *see also* marriage
Enfield, William   69
England, Church of *see* Anglicans
exogamy, marital *see also* marriage   18, 96, 175
Extracts, Book of   90, 96

fairs   3, 57
Farmer, James   48, 113, 114–16
Farmer, Priscilla   114 n.57
Farmer & Galton   48
Fell, John   174 n.8
Fell, Margaret   26
 feminism   144–5
Fifth Monarchists   26, 27, 156
Fincham, John   108
First Great Awakening   174
Fischer, Joshua   49
Fishbourn, William   82, 126–9
fishing   38
Fleetwood, William, bishop of Ely   67
flour   43, 119, 120, 125
Fothergill, Betty   37, 137, 138 n.17, 139–40, 145
Fothergill, John   137, 145
Fox, George   9, 21, 26, 28, 46, 59, 62, 65, 68, 135, 156, 157
Fox, James   167
fraud, Quaker attitudes to   61, 65–6, 69, 72, 94, 104–5, 107, 108, 109–10, 111, 126–9, 173
France   120, 121, 130
Franklin, Benjamin   164, 169
Free Society of Traders   37–8
French and Indian War   158–63, 165 *see also* Seven Years' War
Friendly Association   161, 167
Friends, Society of *see* Quakerism, origins of
frontiersmen   166–8
Fry, John   147
Fry, Zephaniah   141
furs   43, 54, 119, 166

Galton, Samuel   115
gambling   3, 87, 105, 111, 174, 178
Garrigues, Samuel   126, 127
George II, king of the United Kingdom   163
German Town Declaration (1688)   50

Germantown, Pennsylvania   164
Germany   23, 26, 42, 165, 175
Gilbert, John   68
Gleed, John   84
Glorious Revolution   45, 101
Goforth, Nathaniel   124
grain   54, 120
Greenleafe, Isaac   128
Griffitts, William   126, 127, 128–9
guilds   3, 58
gunmaking   48
Gurnell, Grizell   48

Hacket, Laurence   73
Hagen, Gilbert   84
Hamburg, Germany   53
Hanbury, Anna   49
Hanbury, Capel   114
Hanbury, John   49, 54, 114, 162–3, 173
Harvey, Joseph   130
Haylor, John   111
Head, Elizabeth   147
Henry VIII, king of England   102
Heydon, John   88
Hiscocks, Abigal   141
Hitchcock, John   88, 113
Hitchcock, Jonathan   88
Hoare, Samuel   47–8
Hobson, Jonathan   82, 107
Holmes, Benjamin   95
honesty, Quaker reputation for   5, 6, 8, 9, 10, 11, 20, 22, 46, 55, 90, 101–18, 123–4, 125–6, 148, 172, 175, 176, 177
Hoskins, James   105, 138
Hoskins, Josiah   82
Hough, Benjamin   132
House, Joseph   94
How, Richard   114
Howell, Abraham   126, 127
Hynd, Jane   87, 88 n.34

Illegitimacy   135, 136, 141
imprisonment   27, 28, 29, 45, 98, 103, 108, 121, 128
indentured servants   31, 38, 39, 41, 78, 95, 151
Independence, Declaration of   121
India   57
Industrial Revolution   1
insolvency   11, 12, 85, 101, 102, 103–4, 109, 110, 111, 112–14, 119, 121, 123, 125, 126, 132, 134

investment   15, 37, 49, 102
Ireland   16, 38, 42, 47, 48, 116, 117, 120, 130, 143, 165, 167, 175
Ireland, Church of *see* Anglicans
iron   26, 49, 116

Jack (enslaved African)   51
Jackson, James   83–4
Jamaica   26, 40, 50
James II, king of England   45
James, Abel   167
Jenkins, James   89–90, 92, 111, 139, 141, 142–3, 147
Jenkins' Ear, War of   157–8, 159, 172, 175
Jews   138
    Sephardic   4
joint stock companies   37, 101–2
Jones, Jacob   86 n.29
Jones, Owen   49 n.100
Joseph, Hannah   142

Kaye, William   110
Keith, George   44, 53
Kellet, Ann   117
Kelso, Roxburghshire   115–16
Kemp, Benjamin   92 n.48
Kendal Fund   25
Kerr, James   116
kinship, networks of   3, 5, 6, 13–16, 56
Knowles, William   174 n.8

Lamb, Elizabeth   139
Lambert, Edward   147
Lamont, David   66, 73
law, Quaker attitudes to   25
Lawrence, Samuel   82
Lay, Benjamin   50, 51, 175
Lay, Sarah   175
lay ministers, Quaker   25, 29, 44, 59, 62, 72, 96–7, 98, 116, 146
League of Augsburg, War of   45
Leeds, England   11, 12, 117
Leeward Islands   50
Lenni Lenape ('Delaware Indians')   38, 160, 161, 167, 172
Levant Company, English   13, 73
Lewis, Jonathan   125
licence, marriage by   136, 150
Lincoln, Lincolnshire   136
Lisbon, Portugal   48, 53, 115
    earthquake (1755)   48, 115

Lisle, Henry   94
livery companies   36, 135
Livorno, Italy   4
Lloyd, Charles   11 n.45
Locke, John   88, 125
London   1, 5, 20, 22, 27, 31–7, 38, 40, 44, 46, 47, 48, 49, 52, 54, 76, 77–82, 86–9, 90–1, 92–4, 95, 98, 99–100, 101–18, 119, 120, 125–6, 127, 129, 133, 134, 135, 137–8, 139, 145, 147, 148, 149, 150, 151, 152, 153, 154, 155, 156, 157, 158, 159, 161–2, 163, 164, 170, 175
    Bull & Mouth   32, 109, 113
    Christ's Hospital   69
    Clerkenwell (The Peel)   33, 60, 77, 78, 82, 83, 85, 87, 104, 105, 108, 111
    Devonshire House   32, 33, 60, 78, 87, 90, 99, 104, 108, 113, 114, 117
    Fleet Prison   112, 137
    Gracechurch Street   30 n.26, 32, 33, 76, 87 n.33, 88–9, 107, 110, 114
    Horsleydown, Southwark   18, 33, 60, 78, 82, 84, 86, 87, 99, 107, 111, 117, 130, 138
    Lime Street Independent Meeting House   79 n.5, 117 n.78
    Ratcliff   33, 60, 78, 82, 87, 105, 113, 117
    Savoy Meeting House   138
    Westminster   33, 78, 84, 87, 106, 108, 110, 117
London Six Weeks Meeting   78, 84, 86 n.30, 114, 156
London Yearly Meeting   8–10, 14, 21, 28, 29, 30, 45, 53, 60–1, 63–5, 71, 80, 85, 96–7, 178–9
lotteries *see* gambling
Louis XIV   101
Lovell, Joseph   111
Lovell, William   113, 114
lumber   43, 119, 126
Luther, Martin   23
Lutherans   175
luxury   57, 70–4

MacDonald, James   109
Maghrebis (merchants)   3, 4
Mandeville, Bernard   70
manufacturing   1, 30, 32, 34, 38, 42, 43, 48, 49, 102, 115, 119–20

INDEX

manumission 42
marriages 5, 34
   by priests 88, 99, 135, 136, 149–50, 152
   clandestine 136–8, 150
   clearness for 76
   database of 22, 34, 35, 112 n.52, 135
   legitimacy of Quaker 135–7
   Quaker patterns of 13–20
   of apprentices 151–4
   sanctions related to 149
   solemnisation of 25
   see also endogamy, marital; exogamy, marital
Marriage Act (1753) ('Hardwicke's Marriage Act') 138
Marriage Act (1836) 135
Massachusetts 123
Masters, William 86
Mathews, John 91
Mathews, William 90
Matlack, Timothy 124
Mayleigh, Thomas 37
Medici dynasty 4
meetings, Quaker
   Aberdeen 116
   Brighouse Meeting, Leeds 11, 117
   Bull & Mouth 32, 109, 113
   Clerkenwell (The Peel) 33, 60, 77, 78, 82, 83, 85, 87, 104, 105, 108, 111
   Devonshire House 32, 33, 60, 78, 87, 90, 99, 104, 108, 113, 114, 117
   Gracechurch Street 30 n.26, 32, 33, 76, 87 n.33, 88–9, 107, 110, 114
   Horsleydown, Southwark 18, 33, 60, 78, 82, 84, 86, 87, 99, 107, 111, 117, 130, 138
   London Six Weeks Meeting 78, 84, 86 n.30, 114, 156
   London Yearly Meeting 8–10, 14, 21, 28, 29, 30, 45, 53, 60–1, 63–5, 71, 80, 85, 96–7, 178–9
   Meeting for Sufferings 29, 31, 136, 158, 162, 163, 173
   monthly meetings ('meetings for business') 28, 41, 59, 65, 76, 86, 90, 94, 99–100, 101, 104–5, 107, 108, 109, 111, 112, 114, 117, 123–4, 125–6, 128, 129–30, 138, 173–4, 175, 176–7
   women's 76–7, 138, 146

Oustwick, Oxfordshire 91
Philadelphia Yearly Meeting 40, 41, 50, 60, 81, 85, 96, 97, 98, 155, 157, 160, 162, 175
quarterly meetings 28, 60, 78 97, 98
Ratcliff 33, 60, 78, 82, 87, 105, 113, 117
Savoy Meeting House 138
Second Day's Morning Meeting 29
Westminster 33, 78, 84, 87, 106, 108, 110, 117
yearly meetings 28, 29, 60, 73, 77, 78, 98, 173, 174
women's 146
Meng, John 126, 127
merchants 2, 3, 4, 5, 8, 10, 13, 14, 15, 21, 22, 31, 32, 33–5, 38, 39, 40, 42, 43, 46–54, 57–8, 65, 67, 73, 74, 89, 90, 95, 99, 102, 110–11, 112–16, 119–20, 123, 126–30, 134, 139, 148, 155, 158, 161, 162, 167, 170, 172, 173
Merrick, Thomas 86
metallurgy 15
Methodism 174
Middleton, Pennsylvania 132
'middling sort' 32, 35 n.17, 57, 111, 137, 139, 143, 145, 173, 174, 177
migration 18, 32, 38, 130
Milbourne, Luke 67
millennialism 24
Millers, Richard 83
mining 15, 38, 132
Montesquieu 56
monopolies 47, 102 n.3, 165
Mun, Thomas 73
Muslims 4

Nancarrow, John 132
Native Americans *see* Conestoga; Lenni Lenape; Shawnee
Navigation Acts 5
Nayler, James 26, 27
Nelms, Joseph 88 n.39, 99 n.17
Netherlands 26, 48, 101, 121, 167
New England 26, 43, 162
New Institutional Economists 2, 4
New Jersey 16, 17, 38, 54
New York 16, 30, 40, 43, 49, 123
New York Slave Revolt (1712) 40
Newark, New Jersey 132
Nichols, Elizabeth 104

Nichols, William   130
Nine Years' War   101
nonviolence   28, 38, 88, 94, 97, 156–7, 158, 159, 161, 162, 165, 167–9, 170–1, 175, 176 *see also* Peace Testimony, Quaker
Norris, Isaac   51, 52
Norton, William   116
Norwich, England   12, 20, 150
Nova Scotia   53
Nunington, Kent   117

oaths, swearing of   24, 29, 45, 69
Offutt, William   45
Ohio Company   162
Ohio River   160, 162
Ollive, Thomas   60
Ormston, Charles   115
Ormston, Joseph   38 n.24, 113, 115, 116
Oustwick, Oxfordshire   91
Owens, Robert   125 n.25

pacifism *see* nonviolence
Padley, John   84
pamphlets   9, 27, 44, 50, 59, 62, 71, 74, 159, 162, 164–70, 172, 173, 175–6
Parker, William   124
Parkinson, Stanfield   174 n.8
Parliamentarians   23, 24
Paxton, Pennsylvania   164
Paxton Boys   164–70
Peace Testimony, Quaker   28, 162 *see also* nonviolence
Pearce, Joseph   111 n.50, 174 n.8
peers   16
Pemberton, Israel   128, 161, 167, 172, 173
Penn, Thomas   156, 158, 159, 160, 162, 169, 170
Penn, William   9, 21, 26, 37–8, 42, 45–6, 59, 61, 64, 71, 72, 156
Pennsylvania   6, 9, 16, 22, 26, 37–46, 48, 49, 50, 51, 54, 76, 95, 96–7, 119–34, 135, 153, 155–71, 172, 173, 174, 175, 177
  legislative assembly   40, 45–6, 122, 126, 127, 129, 155–6, 157–61, 163–70, 175
  Welsh Tract   17
Philadelphia, Pennsylvania   10, 17, 20, 21, 22, 29, 30, 37–46, 48–54, 60, 76, 77, 79–82, 84, 85–6, 87–8, 92, 94–5, 96, 97, 98, 99, 118, 119–34, 135, 138, 147, 153, 155, 157, 158, 159, 160, 161, 162, 163, 164, 167, 175, 180
plantations   31, 32, 43, 47, 48, 95, 119, 158
Plumsted, Robert   48, 114 n.57, 162
Plymouth, Devon   68
Poll Tax (1692)   34, 46
Pontiac's War   164, 172
poor relief   76, 77, 78, 79, 80, 84, 97, 117 n.78, 122, 146
Powell, Rachel   141
Powell, Thomas   141
preaching   25, 29, 59, 83, 84, 97, 146, 170 *see also* sermons
predestination   56
prenuptial contracts   143
Presbyterians   66, 67, 165, 175
privateering   94, 97, 158, 178
probate   143
property, rights of   1, 2, 4, 8, 19, 138, 142
Proprietary Party (political party)   155, 158, 160, 161, 163, 164–6, 169–71, 173
Puritanism   56
Purslow, Norris   36
Pusey, Joshua   126, 127, 129

Quaker Act (1662)   27
Quaker Oats Company   177
Quaker Party (political party)   155–6
quaking   25

Radnor, Pennsylvania   130
Rand, George   111 n.50
rape   87
Reformation, Protestant   23
reformation, Quaker   96–100, 150, 164, 172, 174
Removal, Certificates of   78, 79, 80, 114, 115, 117–18, 130–3, 179
Renton, Hannah   82
reputation, multilateral   3
Rhine Valley   26
Rhode Island   49, 123
Richardson, Francis   106–7
Richardson, James   111
Rickman, Benjamin   111
Ridgeway, Allen   126, 129
Rigge, Ambrose   59, 62, 72, 74
Roberts, George   105–7
Roberts, Jeremiah   174 n.8
Roper, William   104 n.17
Rowntree, John Stephenson   98

scalping 161
Schoemaker, Jacob 128
schools 57, 77, 141
Scotland 38, 117, 130
Scotland, Church of 66
Scott, William 74
Seekers (sect) 31
Self-Condemnation 82, 86–7, 88, 94, 95, 104, 109, 128, 130, 148–9, 150, 180
Seller, William 116 n.75
sermons 21, 26, 58–59, 67–9, 71, 73, 74, 122, 174 *see also* preaching
Settlement Acts (Poor Law) *see* poor relief
Seven Years' War 41, 42, 48, 49, 52, 54, 95, 120–1, 123, 158–63, 164, 165, 168, 171, 172, 175 *see also* French and Indian War
shares 101, 102
Shawnee (native American people) 160
Sheridan, William, bishop of Kilmore and Ardagh 67
ships, surveyors of 111
Shophoards, Hannah 84
silk 57, 116
Simkin, Samuel 174 n.8
skins 43, 119
slave trade 32, 38–42, 43, 47, 48, 49–52, 95, 116, 176 *see also* Africans, enslaved
slaves *see* Africans, enslaved
Smith, William 82, 107
Smith, William, Provost of the College of Philadelphia 159, 162, 163
Snowden, Leonard 85
Somerton, William 140–1
Soundy, Thomas 91
South Sea Bubble 67, 102, 116, 125
South Sea Company 49, 101
Spriggins, Rebecca 89 n.40
Stall, John 132
stamp duty 151
Stamper, Josiah 174 n.8
Staple, John 83
state, role of 2, 3, 8, 28, 54, 64, 68, 71, 76, 101
Stebbing, Henry 67
Steele, Richard 74
Steen, Thomas 84
Stephens, Joshua 104
Stewart, Dugald 56
Stringelo, John 83
Strutt, Joseph 112, 113

sugar 31, 32, 47
Summerfield, Thomas 86 n.28
Swarthmoor, Cumbria 26, 31
Sweden 38
Switzerland 15
Sykes, William 126, 127

tailors 111
taxes 34, 46, 52, 61, 64, 66, 68–9, 72, 137, 156–7, 160, 161–2, 169, 170
Taylor, Joseph 79 n.5, 82
tea 32, 57, 139
Testimony of Denial 77, 78 n.4, 82, 85, 86–7, 88, 91, 93, 101, 104, 110, 124, 125, 128, 129, 148, 173, 174, 177
textiles 15
Thackall, John 110
Thirty Years War 23
Thomas, Elizabeth 130
Thorne, Ralph 86 n.28
Tillotson, Nathan 92 n.48, 105
tithes 25, 72, 89, 104, 186
Titley, Benjamin 107, 108 n.29
tobacco 32, 36, 43, 47, 49, 114, 119, 162
Toleration Act (1689) 29
Townsend, John 141
trade, expansion of 1–4, 30
treason, accusations of 45, 159, 168
trust, concept of 7, 11, 53, 55, 177

underwriting (insurance) 47, 54
Unwin, William 69

Wakefield, Thomas 89
Walker, Miles 117
Wallis, John 119
Wapping, London 60
watchmakers 111
Weaver, John 174 n.8
Weber, Max 63–4
West Indies (Caribbean) *see also* Barbados; Jamaica; Leeward Islands 28, 32, 47, 48, 49, 50, 52, 53, 54, 95, 119, 120
Weston, Daniel 60
whaling 38, 54
Widdowfield, Peter 124
Widow, W. 83
widows 62, 107, 136, 142, 143
William III, king of England 101
Williams, Hercules 85, 86 n.26
Williamson, Robert 86 n.28

Wilson, Thomas 69
Wister, Daniel 49 n.100
witchcraft 27
wool trade 4
Woolman, John 51
workhouses 77, 105

Wright, Thomas 82–3

xenophobia 27

York, England 12

PEOPLE, MARKETS, GOODS: ECONOMIES AND SOCIETIES IN HISTORY

ISSN: 2051-7467

PREVIOUS TITLES

1. *Landlords and Tenants in Britain, 1440–1660:*
Tawney's Agrarian Problem *Revisited*
edited by Jane Whittle, 2013

2. *Child Workers and Industrial Health in Britain, 1780–1850*
Peter Kirby, 2013

3. *Publishing Business in Eighteenth-Century England*
James Raven, 2014

4. *The First Century of Welfare:*
Poverty and Poor Relief in Lancashire, 1620–1730
Jonathan Healey, 2014

5. *Population, Welfare and Economic Change in Britain 1290–1834*
edited by Chris Briggs, Peter Kitson and S. J. Thompson, 2014

6. *Crises in Economic and Social History: A Comparative Perspective*
edited by A. T. Brown, Andy Burn and Rob Doherty, 2015

7. *Slavery Hinterland: Transatlantic Slavery and*
Continental Europe, 1680–1850
edited by Felix Brahm and Eve Rosenhaft, 2016

8. *Almshouses in Early Modern England: Charitable Housing in the Mixed*
Economy of Welfare, 1550–1725
Angela Nicholls, 2017

9. *People, Places and Business Cultures:*
Essays in Honour of Francesca Carnevali
edited by Paolo Di Martino, Andrew Popp and Peter Scott, 2017

10. *Cameralism in Practice: State Administration*
and Economy in Early Modern Europe
edited by Marten Seppel and Keith Tribe, 2017

11. *Servants in Rural Europe, 1400–1900*
edited by Jane Whittle, 2017

12. *The Age of Machinery:
Engineering the Industrial Revolution, 1770–1850*
Gillian Cookson, 2018

13. *Shoplifting in Eighteenth-Century England*
Shelley Tickell, 2018

14. *Money and Markets: Essays in Honour of Martin Daunton*
edited by Julian Hoppit, Duncan Needham and Adrian Leonard, 2019

15. *Women and the Land, 1500–1900*
edited by Amanda L. Capern, Briony McDonagh and Jennifer Aston, 2019

16. *Globalized Peripheries: Central Europe and
the Atlantic World, 1680–1860*
edited by Jutta Wimmler and Klaus Weber, 2020

17. *Financing Cotton: British Industrial Growth and Decline, 1780–2000*
Steven Toms, 2020

www.ingramcontent.com/pod-product-compliance
Lightning Source LLC
Chambersburg PA
CBHW070804230426
43665CB00017B/2486